HAMPSHIRE
A PICTORIAL JOURNEY

STEVE VIDLER
TEXT BY DIANA LEPPARD

Published by Heartwood Publishing
Bath, United Kingdom
www.heartwoodpublishing.co.uk

Photography by Steve Vidler

Text by Diana Leppard

Book design by Ian Gordon, Artstyle

Photographs and text copyright
Steve Vidler © 2022
Except pp.220-221 copyright Jinny Goodman

Map copyright Anna Thompson © 2022

All rights reserved. This book is sold subject to the condition that it shall not, by way of trade or otherwise, be lent, resold, hired out or otherwise circulated without Steve Vidler's prior written consent in any form of binding or cover other than that in which it is published and without a similar condition including this condition being imposed on the subsequent purchaser. No part of this publication may be reproduced, stored in a retrieval system or transmitted in any form or by any means, electronic and mechanical, photocopying, recording or otherwise without prior permission of Steve Vidler.

British Library Cataloguing in Publication Data

A catalogue record for this book is available from the British Library.

ISBN 978 1 914515 29 3

Printed and bound in India by
Replika Press Pvt Ltd

HAMPSHIRE
A PICTORIAL JOURNEY

HEART OF THE COUNTY A Circuit from Winchester — 16

NATURE UNTETHERED The New Forest — 114

MAGNIFICENT MARITIME Southampton and Portsmouth — 152

SAIL ACROSS THE SOLENT The Isle of Wight — 204

HAMPSHIRE
AND THE ISLE OF WIGHT

HEART OF THE COUNTY

As a county, Hampshire has pretty much everything. One of the most affluent in Britain, it is a popular place to live and also has a fascinating history, with many heritage attractions that are enjoyed by visitors from around the world.

On England's South Coast, bordered by Dorset to the west and West Sussex to the east, Hampshire covers just over 3700 square kilometres. This makes it the ninth largest of England's forty-eight ceremonial counties by area, although with around 1.85 million people, it is sixth on the list by population.

Alongside its bustling cities, beautiful coastline and ancient woodlands, Hampshire is also known for farming and agricultural produce. Many of the towns have regular farmers' markets and locally grown crops are exported across Britain and beyond. There are currently nineteen pubs and restaurants in the county that have achieved the Michelin Plate icon for the quality of their food, including The Black Rat in Winchester, which achieved a Michelin star within two years of opening as a quirky restaurant and held the accolade for more than a decade. They source ingredients from local suppliers and have their own forager who seeks out the freshest and most seasonal produce.

The county is famous for its watercress, which has been grown commercially since the 19th century. Historically thought to enhance brain power, the plant was also praised by philosopher and statesman, Francis Bacon who claimed that it could restore bloom to the cheeks of 'old-young ladies'. Four hundred years later, it's a suggestion in need of an update but maybe watercress can restore bloom for us all – who knows? It certainly tastes good.

Vineyards also flourish in the favourable climate. The chalky soils are similar to those found in the Champagne region of France and Hambledon Vineyard's Non-Vintage Classic Cuvée caused a stir when it beat famous French names in a blind tasting. Hambledon is England's oldest commercial vineyard of the modern era and covers over 200 acres. It was established in 1952 and produces a range of award-winning sparkling wines.

Home to both the New Forest National Park and the western section of the South Downs National Park, Hampshire is a mecca for walkers with around 3,000 miles of footpaths, bridleways and byways. For the more adventurous walker, there are thirteen long distance trails, including the Test Way and sections of the Clarendon Way and the South Downs Way. Fans of Jane Austen can enjoy the Jane Austen Trail that leads from Alton High Street to her home in Chawton, and a circular walk that starts in Chawton village.

Our journey around the heart of the county begins in Winchester, the ancient capital of England, which has proved a source of inspiration for artists and writers over the centuries. One of J M W Turner's sketchbooks in the Tate Collection has watercolours of the Cathedral and City Mill, and best-selling novelist Tracy Chevalier's recent book, A Single Thread, is set in 1930s Winchester.

Winchester Cathedral has a history that stretches back more than 900 years, although there is evidence of earlier religious buildings on the site. Founded in 1079, the buildings were extended and altered over the following five centuries resulting in a mixture of styles that demonstrates each major phase of English church architecture over that period.

Known more formally as the Cathedral Church of the Holy Trinity, Saint Peter, Saint Paul and Saint Swithun, it is one of the largest cathedrals in Britain and the seat of the Bishop of Winchester. The nave is a masterpiece of Perpendicular Gothic and is the longest in Europe. The choir is located under the tower and some of the stalls and misericords date from the 14th century *(above)*. The ornate screen separating the choir from the nave was designed by George Gilbert Scott in the 1870s.

The most prominent landmark in the city, the cathedral can be viewed from the surrounding hills *(top right)* and is a popular tourist attraction, as well as an important place of worship. *Also p.16*

Dating from the mid-15th century, the Great Screen *(left 3rd from top)* is one of many fine features within Winchester Cathedral. The original stone figures that adorned the screen were destroyed in the 1550s, but a major restoration project followed in the Victoria era and new statues were created. There are more than fifty in all, including one of Queen Victoria. Notable names were involved in the work, the crucifix being made under the direction of George Frederick Bodley who was a founder of Watts & Co.

Within the cathedral are seven beautiful chantry chapels. These were added between the 14th and 16th centuries as places where masses were said for the bishops who had them built, including William Wayneflete *(left 2nd from top)* who was Bishop of Winchester between 1447 and 1486.

A more recent addition is Sound II by Antony Gormley, which has stood in the cathedral's crypt since the late 1980s *(right)*. This statue of a life-sized man who is looking down at water cupped in his hands was created from a cast of the artist's body. In wet weather the crypt is flooded, with the statue reflected in the water.

The cathedral also has temporary installations and displays, including *Held in a Burst of Colour (left bottom)* by Reverend Gill Sakakini, which added a new dimension to the magnificent nave in the summer of 2020.

Buried in the north aisle of the cathedral is one of the world's best-loved authors, Jane Austen, who died in 1817 at the age of 41 *(left top)*.

Of the icons found in Winchester Cathedral, some of the most prominent are a series of nine by Sergei Fyodorov. They were commissioned in the 1990s and hold an important position in the retrochoir. At the left-hand end of the row is St Birinus *(left)*, with St Swithun at the far right *(above)*.

Below: Statue of Joan of Arc. A piece of stone from the tower in Rouen where she was held during trial is said to be inside the base.

Beside Winchester Cathedral is the picturesque Cathedral Close, which has many buildings of historic interest. The main entrance to the Close is through the 15th century Prior's Gate *(below left & right)*, with its impressive wisteria that provides a floral display in late spring.

A short stroll along Dome Alley leads to Kingsgate, which is one of the two medieval gates to the city that still survive. The small church of St Swithun-upon-Kingsgate sits above the gate and located under the arch is the unique Kingsgate Books and Prints shop *(far left)*, which was established in 1991.

With a majestic frontage on The Broadway in Winchester, the design of the Guildhall (far left) was decided by competition. There were forty-six applications, and the winners were Jeffrey and Skiller, who were architects from Hastings. Gothic in style, the original build was finished in 1873, with the statues on the front reflecting Winchester's history, both real and legendary. An electrical fire in the late 1960s caused considerable damage and significant changes were made during renovations just over a decade later. As well as providing office space for the local council, the building is the city's largest multi-use event space.

At the eastern entrance of The Broadway sits the statue of Alfred the Great (left). It was designed by Hamo Thornycroft and unveiled in 1901 as part of the celebrations marking the millenary of the death of Alfred. The main statue is a single bronze casting, although the sword is a separate piece.

Winchester's High Street *(above right)* has many notable buildings and features, while offering all the amenities of a modern-day city. Now a bank, number 49 was the old Guildhall and a statue of Queen Anne *(above left)* and an impressive clock *(above 3rd from left)* adorn its façade. Nearby stands the Buttercross or City Cross *(above 2nd from left)*, which dates from the 15th century although it was restored in the 1865 by George Gilbert Scott. It is decorated with the statues of twelve religious and historical figures of various ages.

Below: Cricket in Winchester.

The Great Hall, which sits on Castle Avenue to the west of Winchester Cathedral, is a very fine example of a medieval aisled hall. It was added to the Norman structure of Winchester Castle by Henry III in the 1220s and is now the only significant part of the castle still standing. The most famous exhibit in the hall is an Arthurian Round Table *(right)* that hangs majestically on the end wall. Originally made in the late 13th century, it was repainted for Henry VIII, and it is said that portrait of King Arthur bears a resemblance to him. The names of Arthur's knights are painted around the table's edge.

Below: Stained glass windows in the Great Hall.

Winchester's Military Museum Quarter is home to six regimental museums based around Peninsula Barracks, a historic site near to the Great Hall. Although they all have a military theme, each museum is run independently and so visitors can enjoy one at a time or spend a whole day immersed in the fascinating history that they reveal.

Left: The Gurkha Museum. *Above (clockwise from top left):* The Gurkha Museum. HorsePower, the Regimental Museum of The King's Royal Hussars (Corporal of the 10th Hussars at the Khyber Pass). The Rifles Museum (Private of the 60th Royal American Regiment). The Rifles Museum (*3rd Battalion, The Rifles on Patrol with Afghan National Army Forces in Helmand Province* by Marcus Hodge). The Gurkha Museum (Pathan Warrior on the North-West Frontier). The Royal Green Jackets Museum (*The Rout of the French Imperial Guard at Waterloo, 18 June 1815* by Jason Askew).

Founded in the 12th century by Henry of Blois, the Hospital of St Cross is a Grade I listed building by the River Itchen in Winchester and is believed to be one of England's oldest charitable institutions. It originally supported thirteen frail men, although a further one hundred came to get food at the gates each day. The Norman church *(left & above left)*, which has walls that are over one metre thick, is all that remains of the original hospital.

The Order of Noble Poverty was founded in the 15th century by Cardinal Henry Beaufort, who added the Almshouse *(above top)* to the existing hospital. The buildings have changed very little since this time. Twenty-five retired gentlemen, the Brothers, live in the Almshouse today.

The site is open to visitors at various times throughout the year and also hosts weddings and other events. Popular with film and television companies, the Hospital of St Cross and Almshouse of Noble Poverty was used as a location in the BBC drama, Wolf Hall starring Mark Rylance and Claire Foy.

Above right: Brethren's Hall.

The second surviving medieval gateway in Winchester is Westgate (*above & right*), which stands at the western end of the High Street. Now a museum, visitors can discover the history of the building and there are good views of the city from its roof.

It was a debtor's prison for nearly 200 years and some of the 16th and 17th century detainees have left their mark as graffiti on the walls. Exhibits include an important group of pre-imperial weights and measures and a fine Tudor ceiling painting made for Winchester College.

The imposing ruins of Wolvesey Castle sit to the east of Winchester Cathedral. Once the main residence of the Bishops of Winchester, the remains of this 12th century palace are now under the care of English Heritage. Also known as the Old Bishop's Palace, it was an important building. The wedding banquet of Queen Mary and Philip II of Spain was held here in 1554 and the palace remained in use until the 1680s, when a replacement was built on an adjoining site.

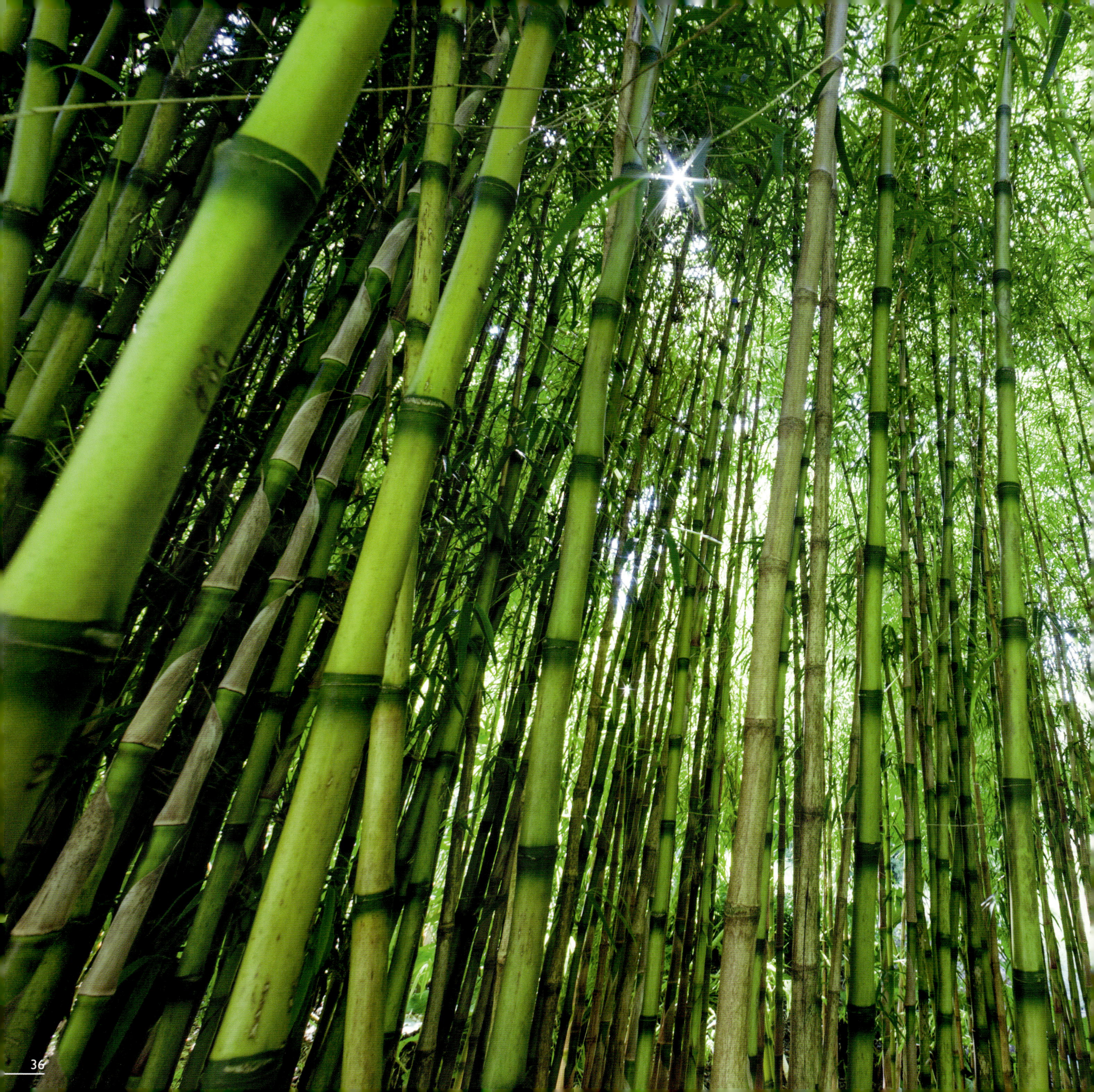

South-west of Winchester is the village of Ampfield, home to the Sir Harold Hillier Gardens. This arboretum covers 180 acres and has more than 42,000 trees and shrubs. The gardens were established by Sir Harold in 1953 and are now cared for by Hampshire County Council. The seasonal displays ensure that returning visitors can enjoy a changing spectrum of colour. Guided tours are available, and you may be fortunate to meet head arborist, Jon Hammerton *(above)* who shares his expert knowledge when he's not in action ensuring that the trees under his care stay healthy.

Left: Bamboo Grove

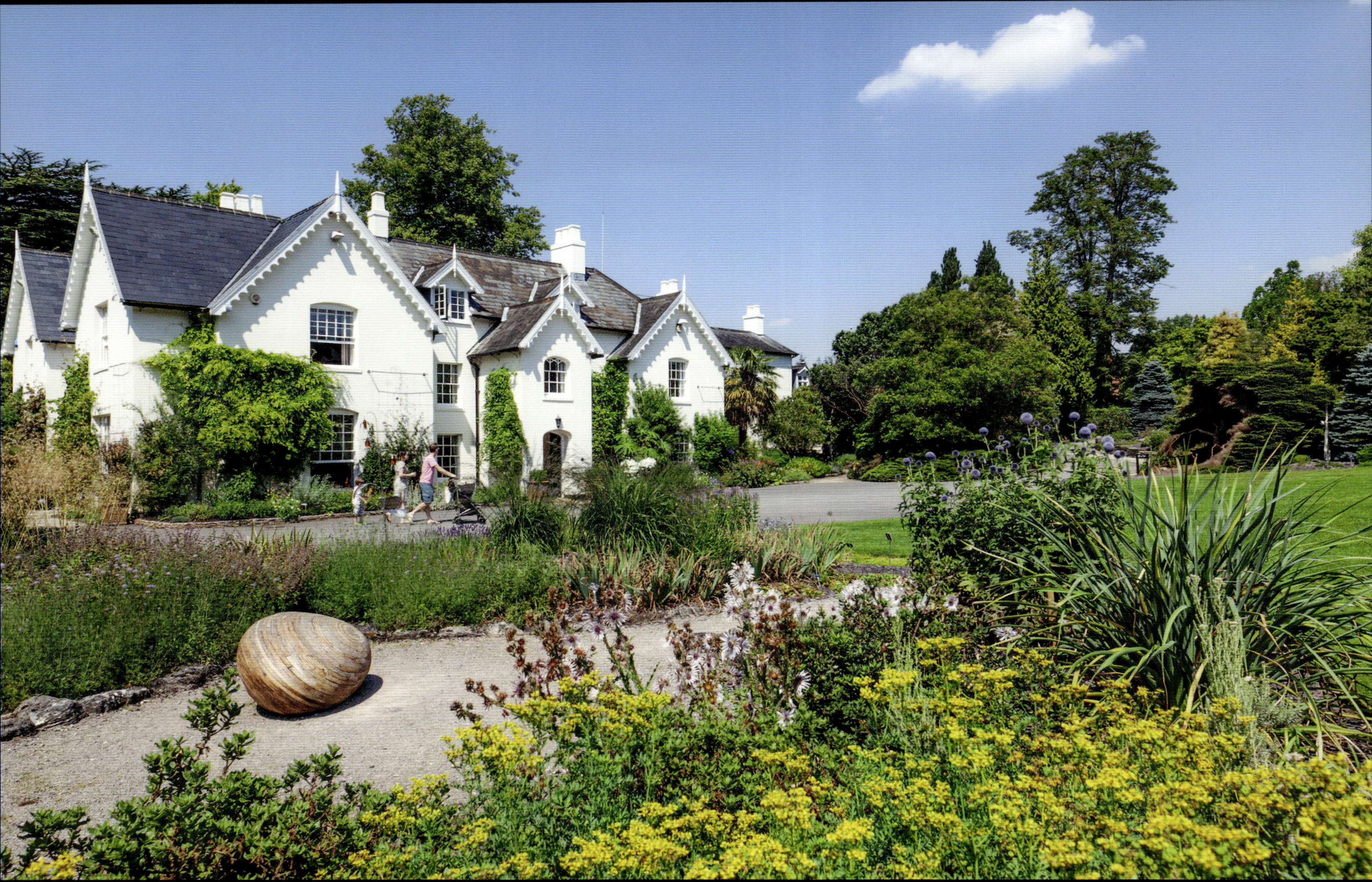
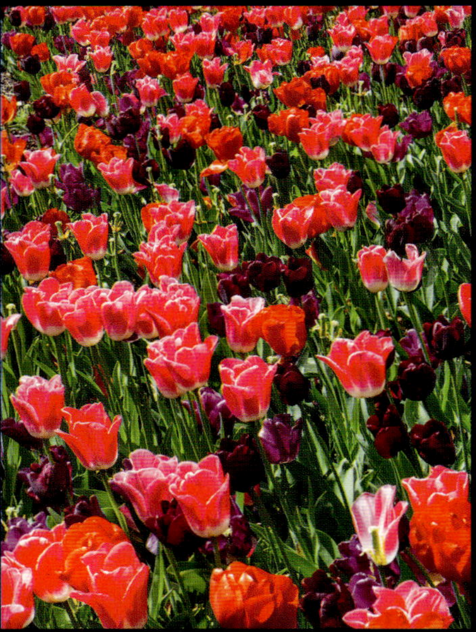
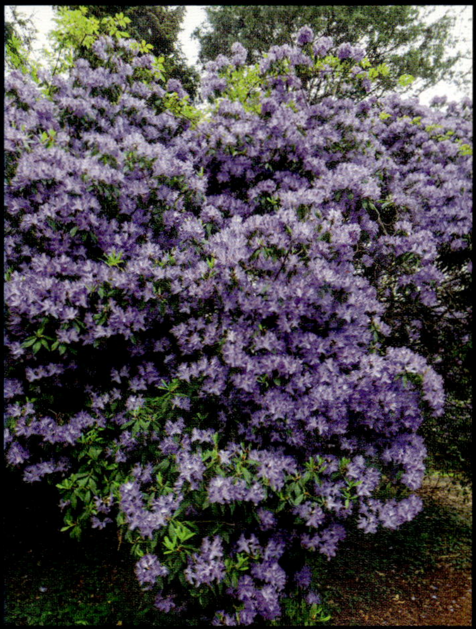
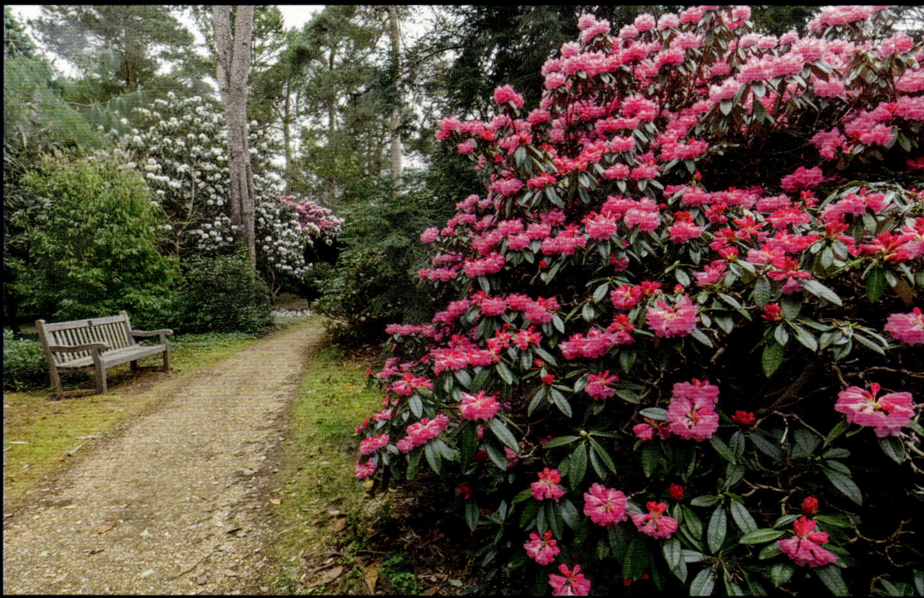

When Sir Harold Hillier moved into Jermyn House *(p.38 top)* it was surrounded by fields, but he was an expert plantsman and gathered trees and shrubs from places as far away as New Zealand, Korea and Mexico. The oaks, magnolia, camellia and rhododendron that can be seen today are particularly fine.

The gardens also have the most comprehensive collection of Champion Trees in Britain, with more than 600 that are exceptional examples of their species either in terms of size, age or rarity.

Located in the grounds of the Sir Harold Hillier Gardens is the Hillier Garden Centre Braishfield, which provides plenty to tempt the horticultural enthusiast with its colourful displays.

Established for over forty years, it offers some interesting plant varieties that reflect those growing in the gardens.

41

42

Four miles from Ampfield, is the historic market town of Romsey, home to Romsey Abbey *(left)*, which is the largest parish church in Hampshire. A Benedictine nunnery throughout the Middle Ages, the abbey was known as a place of learning for the children of noblemen and prospered until the Black Death, when the population of both the nunnery and the local town was ravaged. Although much reduced in size, the community continued until the Dissolution of the Monasteries in the 16th century. Romsey Abbey is now a busy parish church at the heart of the community.

Above top: The Nave.
Above middle: John St Barbe memorial.
Above: Temporary display.

There are many fascinating features in Romsey Abbey for visitors to discover. The area under the tower between the nave and choir is the crossing *(above)*, with its fine Norman arches. It was originally possible to see right up to the abbey roof before a chamber was built for the bell ringers in the 17th century. This obscured the tops of the arches but was later raised so that their simple elegance was once again revealed.

South of the crossing, in the Chapel of St Nicholas is the grave of Earl Mountbatten of Burma *(far right)*. His body was unusually placed north-to-south, so that he faces the sea. The Earl lived locally at Broadlands and also held the title of Baron Romsey.

Right: west end of Romsey Abbey.

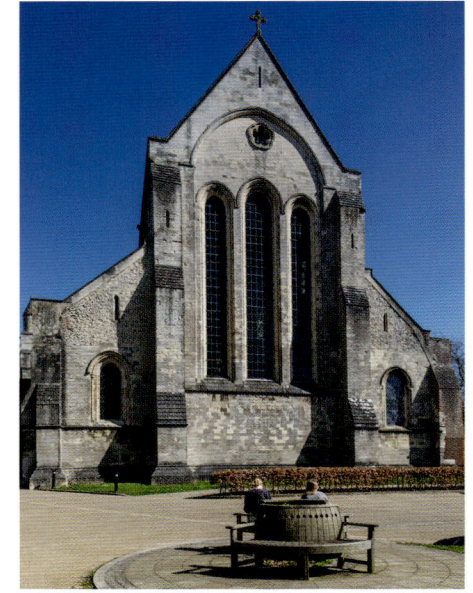

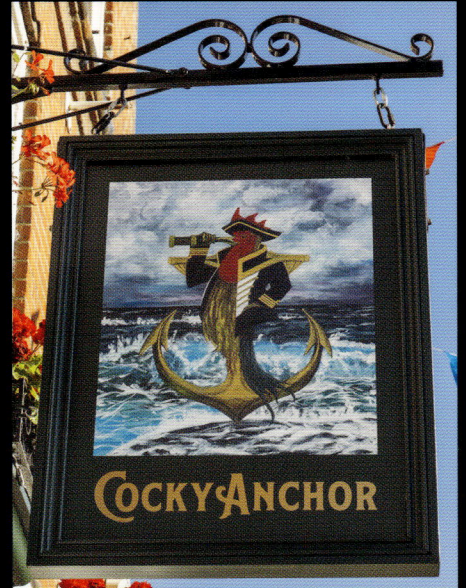

With a population of around twenty thousand, the town of Romsey sits just over three miles from the eastern edge of the New Forest National Park. A street market is held in Cornmarket and Market Place three days a week *(above)* under the watchful eye of the statue of Lord Palmerston *(far left)*, which has stood in Market Place for more than 160 years. Lord Palmerston was twice Prime Minister of Britain in the mid-19th century and was a notable resident of Romsey, being born and brought up at Broadlands.

Left: Cocky Anchor micropub.

Our journey around the heart of Hampshire heads to the north and reaches Mottisfont *(right & above top right)*, a historic abbey that is now managed by the National Trust. An Augustinian Priory was founded here in 1201 but, following the Dissolution of the Monasteries, the estate was gifted to Lord Sandys who was Lord Chamberlain to Henry VIII. Sandys transformed the priory into a grand residence. Later refurbishments in the Georgian period resulted in the house and grounds recognisable today.

The interior is displayed in the neo-classical style introduced by Maud Russell and her family when they moved here in 1930s. Maud created a relaxing weekend retreat where she entertained writers and artists. The trompe l'oeil murals *(above top left)* in the saloon were painted for her by Rex Whistler.

Above middle left: White Bedroom. *Above left & right:* Dining Room. *Above middle:* Morning Room.

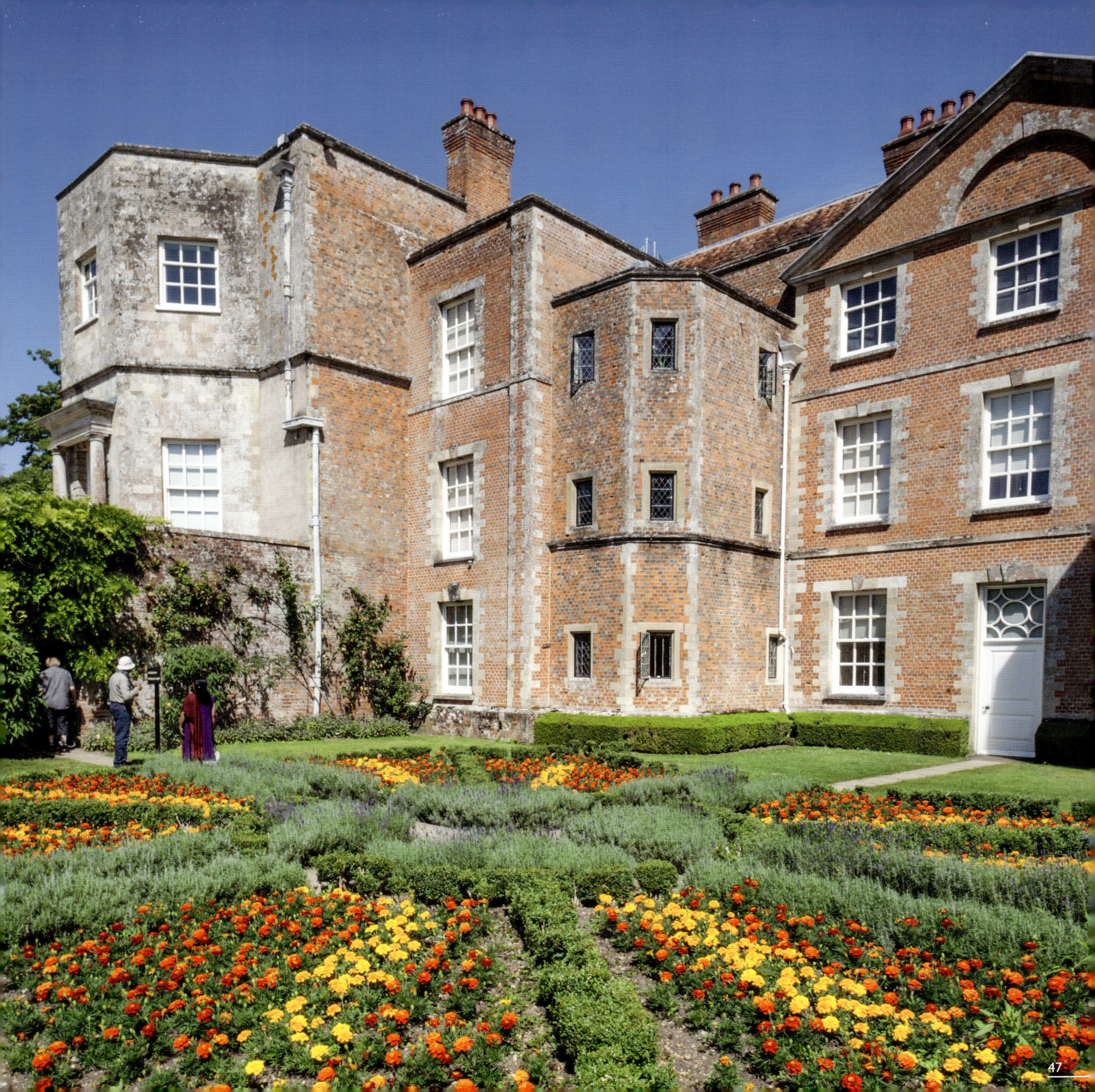

Although Maud Russell made Mottisfont into an elegant home, she was fascinated by the history of the house and worked with this, rather than trying to replace it. She commissioned a number of artists to add enhancements, both inside and out. Boris Anrep created a mosaic angel *(right)*, which can be seen outside, in a niche under the steps by the morning room. It was installed just after the Second World War and, following the death of her husband, Maud began a new relationship with the artist that lasted until his death. It is now thought that the angel is actually Maud, although she wasn't initially aware of this herself.

Continuing north, the road leads to the village of King's Somborne, with the thatched Crown Inn at its centre.

The Parish Church of St Peter and St Paul has some interesting stained glass *(right)*, including the Sopwith Memorial Window designed by John Hayward *(far right)*. Sir Thomas Sopwith was a pioneer of aviation and was 101 years old when he died. He lived locally at Compton Manor and is buried in the churchyard at nearby Little Somborne.

P.48 top left: Gardens at Mottisfont.

P.48 below left: St Andrews Church in Mottisfont village.

DENHAM
BROUGHTON CRAFTS
ORVIS
ORVIS

THE LOCAL FISHING & SHOOTING SHOP ~ COUNTRY CLOTHING
FLY FISHING TACKLE
ROBJENT'S
ROBJENT'S
THE LOCAL FLY FISHING & SHOOTING SHOP

Clos du Marquis
French Restaurant

ROBJENT'S
THE LOCAL
FLY FISHING &
SHOOTING SHOP

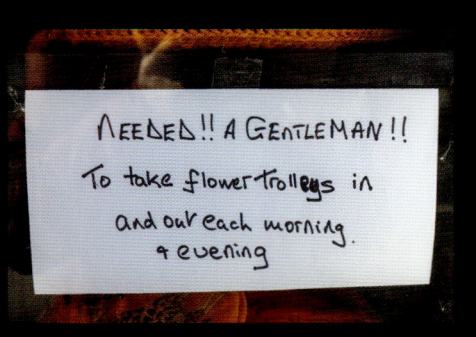

NEEDED!! A GENTLEMAN!!
To take flower trolleys in
and out each morning
& evening

Stockbridge sits at the heart of the beautiful Test Valley. One of the smallest towns in Britain, it is surrounded by beautiful landscapes and has a population estimated at less than 600. The clear, chalk streams of the upper River Test flow through the town and are perfect for fly fishing. The oldest fly fishing club in England, the Houghton Club, is based at the Grosvenor Hotel *(right)* and angling shops are on hand to supply all the necessary equipment.

There is a good selection of independent shops and restaurants in the town for those whose interests veer from the piscatorial – or for those who'd like a nice meal and a drink after a long day by the river.

The broad High Street *(above)* at Stockbridge reflects its history as a drovers' road. It was part of the through-route for drovers bringing cattle and sheep from Wales. The thatched Drovers House at the west end of the High Street was originally a pub and a restored inscription on the front wall is written in Welsh.

A popular local food festival, the Trout 'n About, is held in the town on the first Sunday in August each year, with over one hundred stalls taking over the High Street. Live music, craft demonstrations and circus skills add to the fun of the day.

The River Test branches into multiple streams as it passes round and through the town, providing many beautiful places to sit and watch the world go by. A few minutes' drive from the centre, The Mayfly in Fullerton *(left & right)* is a popular stopping point with fine views of the river from its terrace.

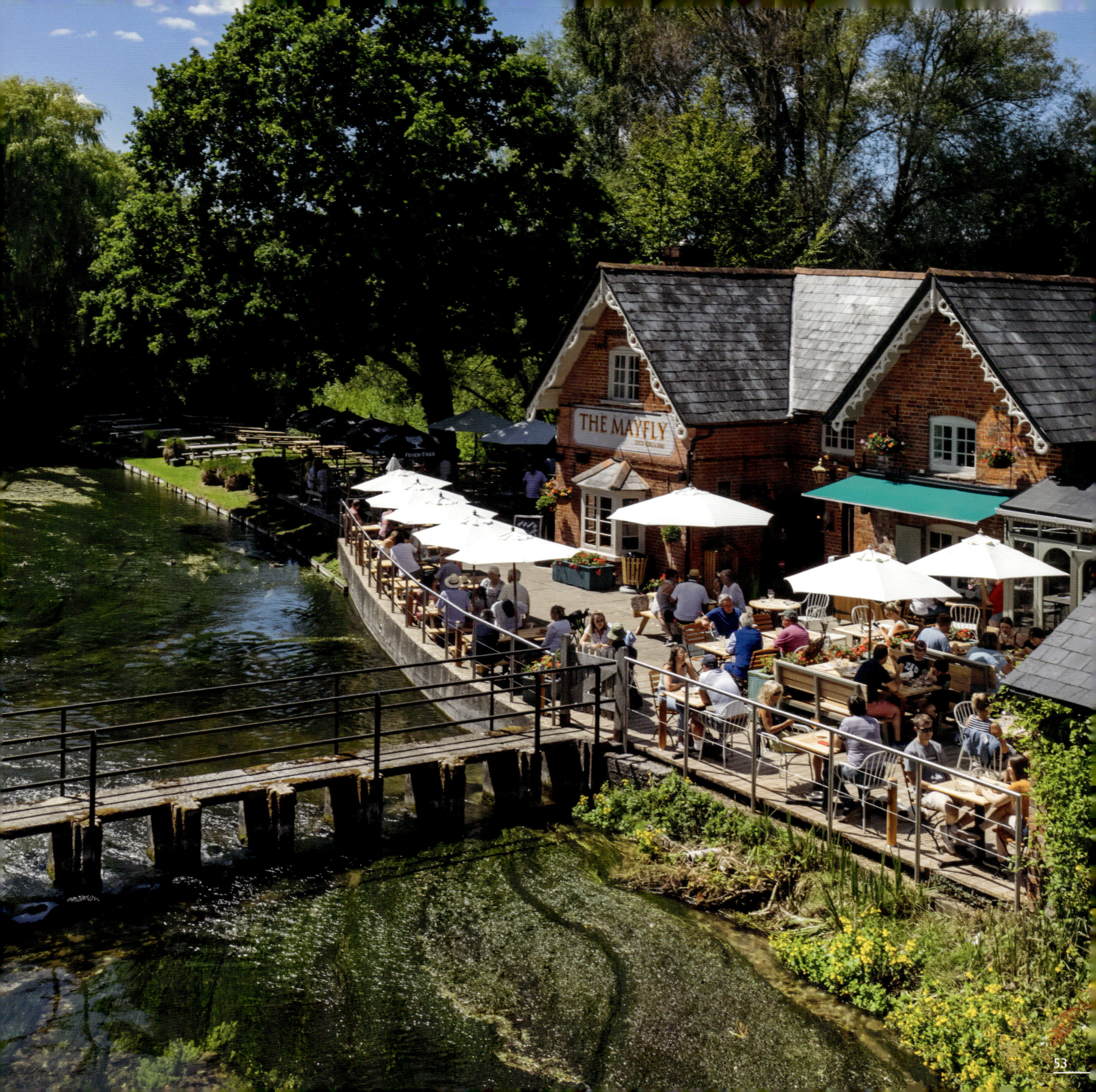
THE MAYFLY

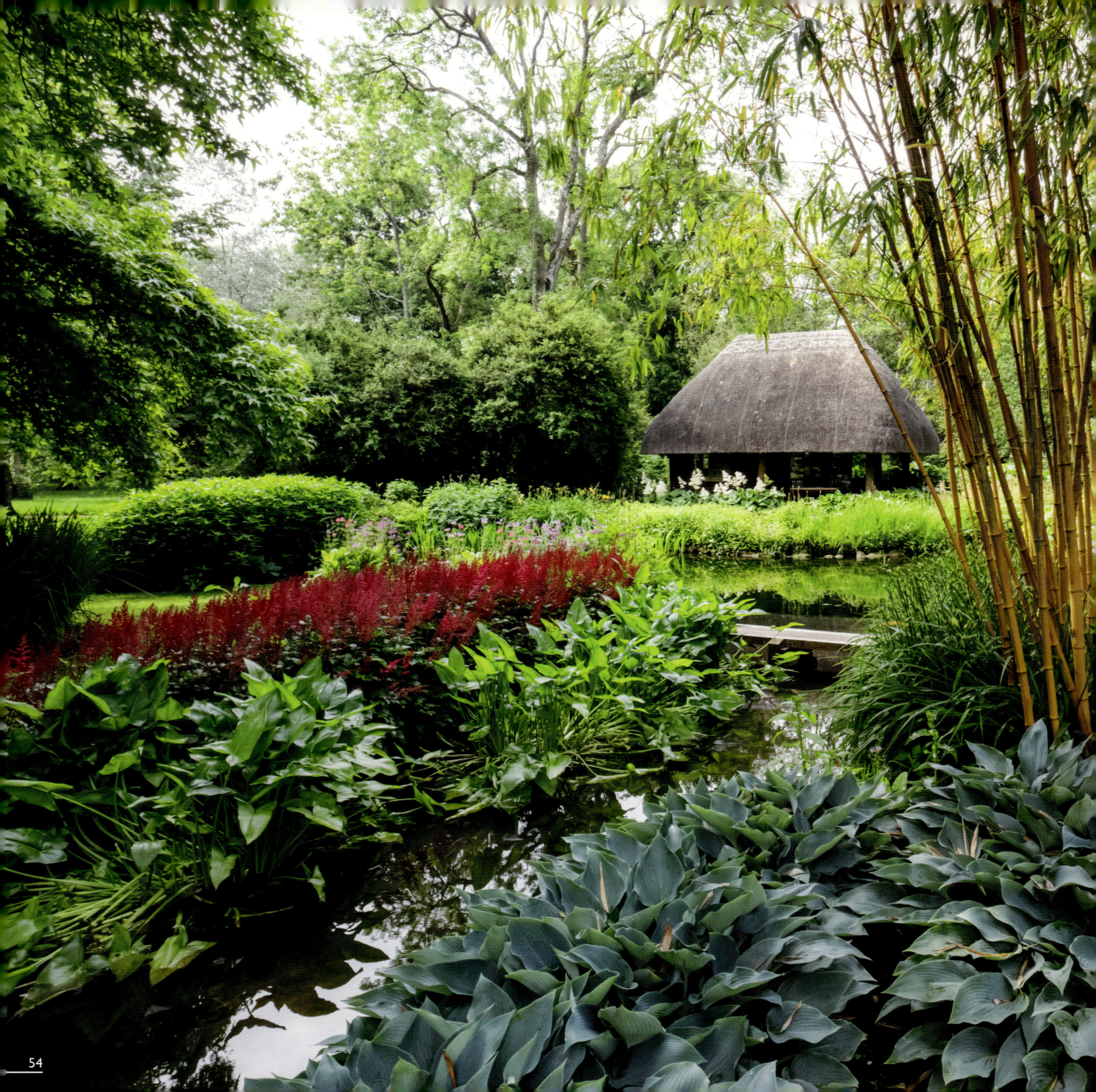

Just north of Stockbridge is the Longstock Park Water Garden, which opens to visitors seasonally. Covering an area of six acres, the gardens were created by the Beddington family at the start of the 20th century.

John Spedan Lewis, founder of the John Lewis Partnership, owned the Leckford Estate on the opposite bank of the river and added the water garden to the estate during the Second World War. He spent much of his later life here enjoying the tranquillity of the atmosphere and the diversity of the plant life. There are plant species from around the world, with more than forty different types of water lily.

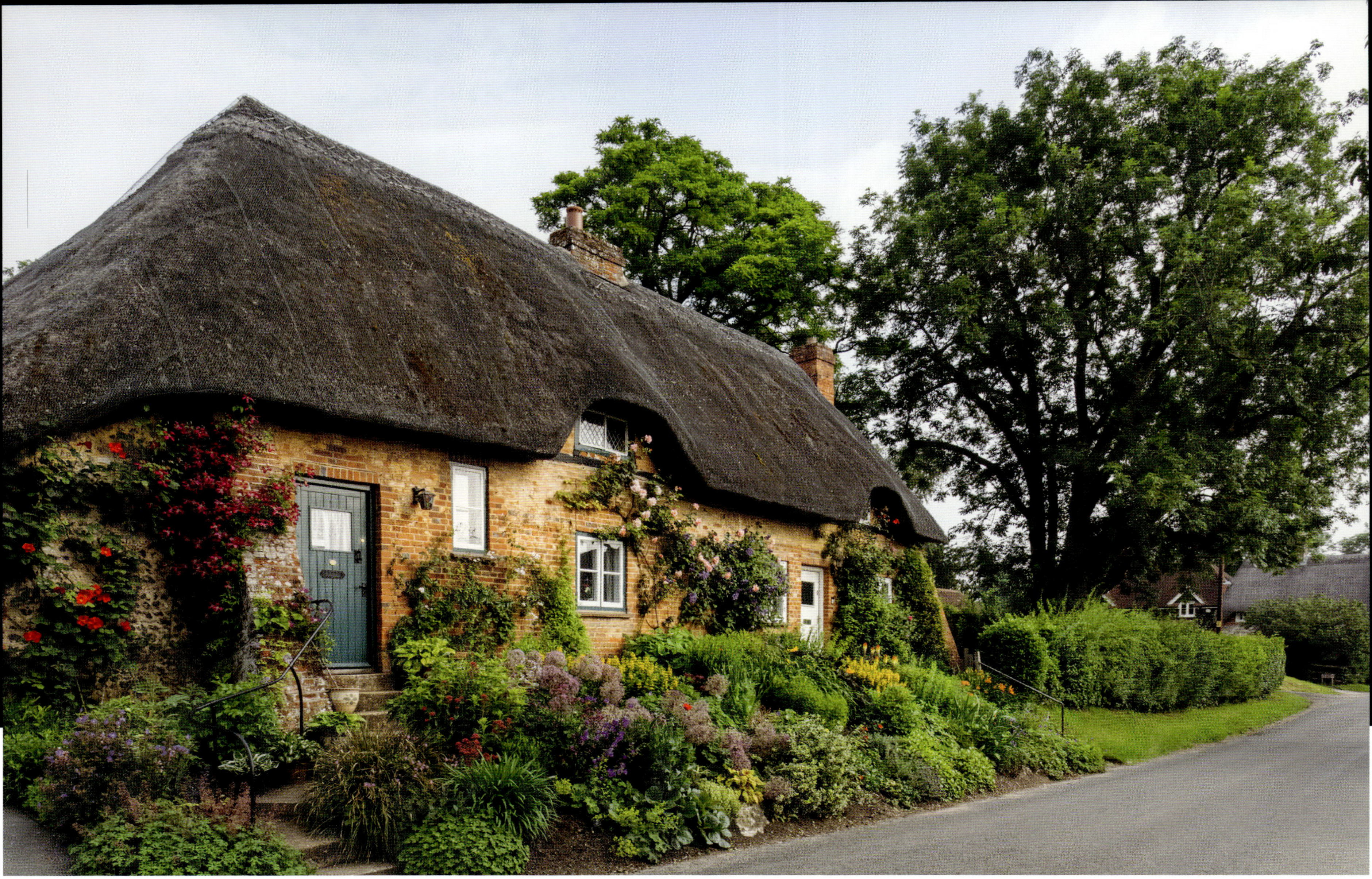

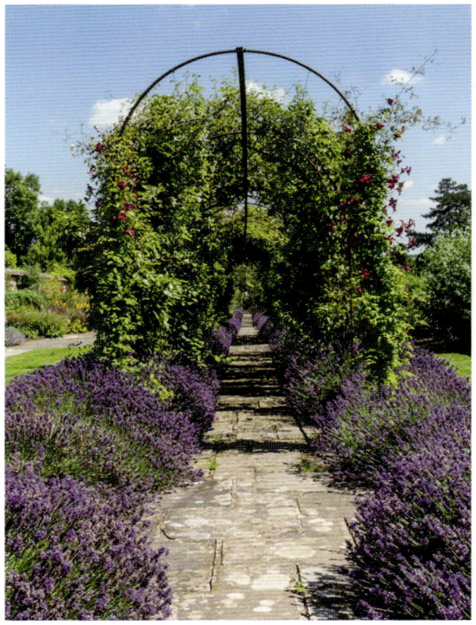

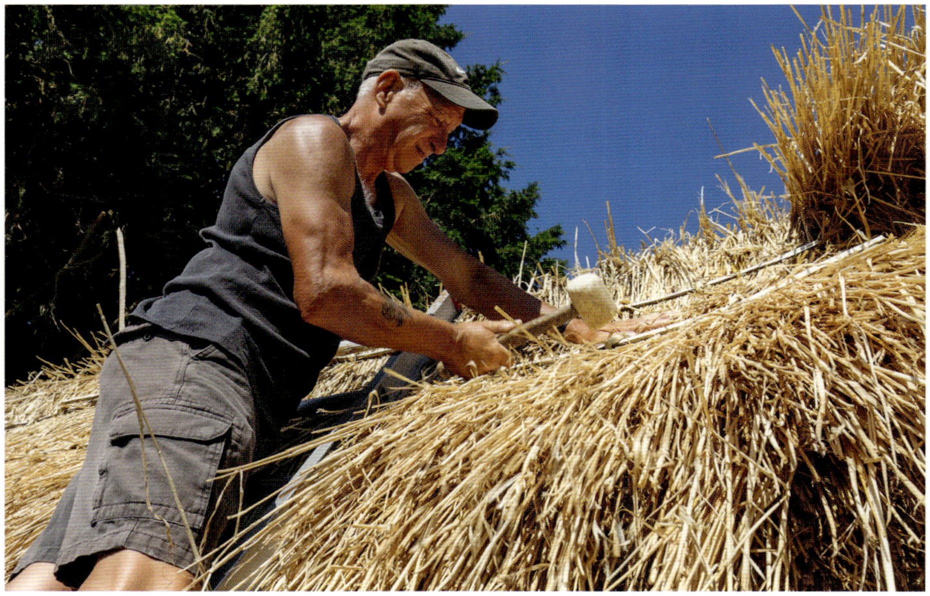

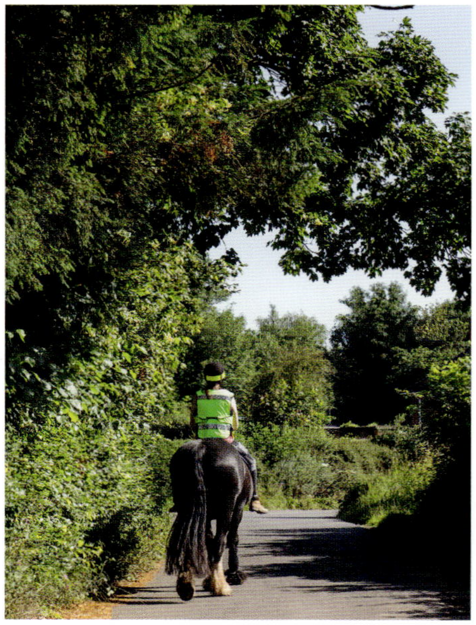

Longstock village lies on the western side of the River Test, with a population of around 450. Home to the Leckford Estate and Longstock Park Water Garden, it also has a number of picturesque thatched cottages *(top left)*.

The Leckford Estate is now officially the Waitrose & Partners Farm. Various farming and food production activities take place on the 2,800 acres of land, with a focus on the use of ethical and sustainable methods. A local farm shop, café and plant nursery are also on site. Between May and October, chalk stream trout fishing is available on the estate's stretch of the River Test *(above & p.58/9)*.

Bottom left (from L-R): Longstock Plant Nursery. Thatcher, Paul Williams. Horse riding.

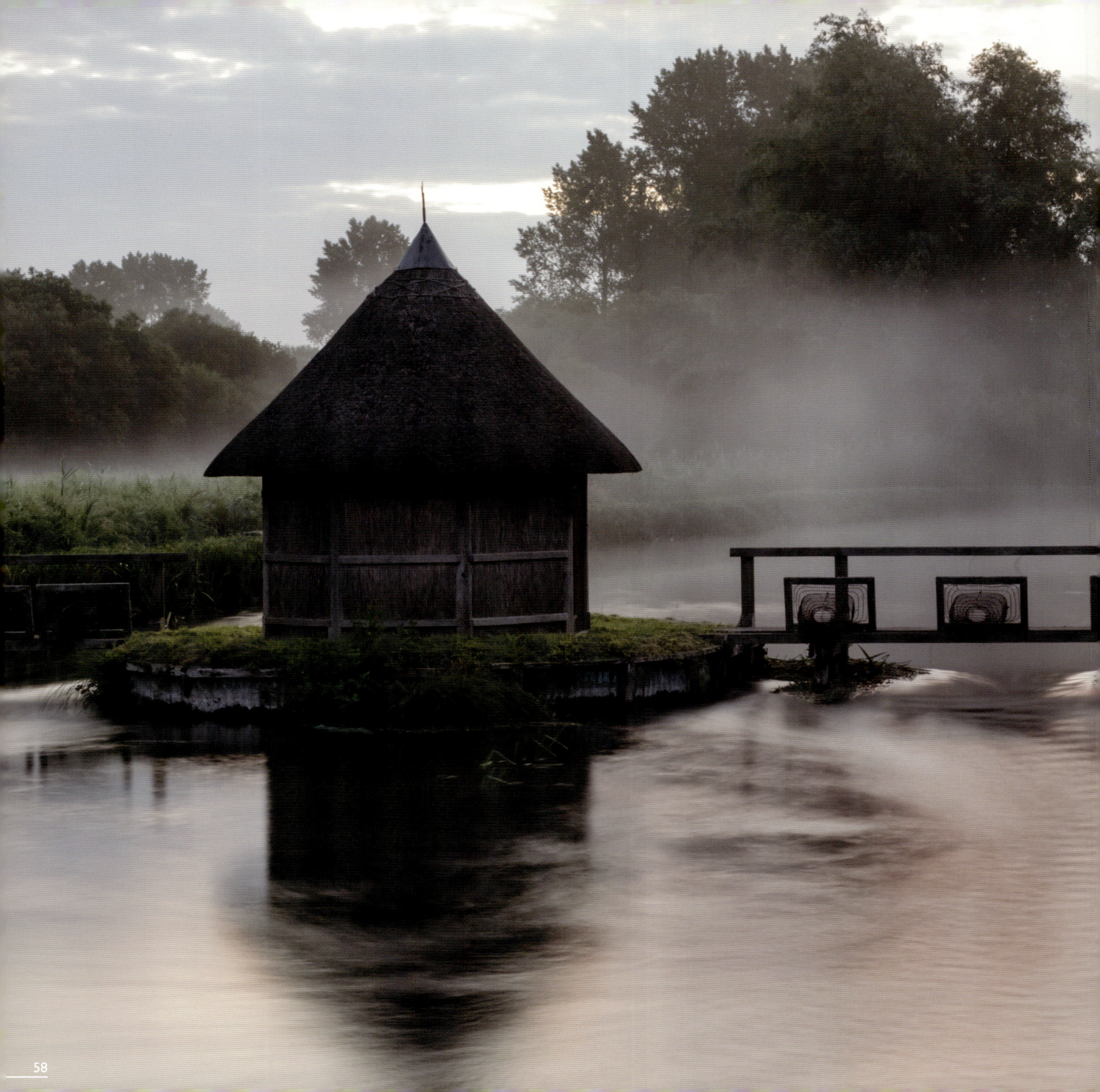

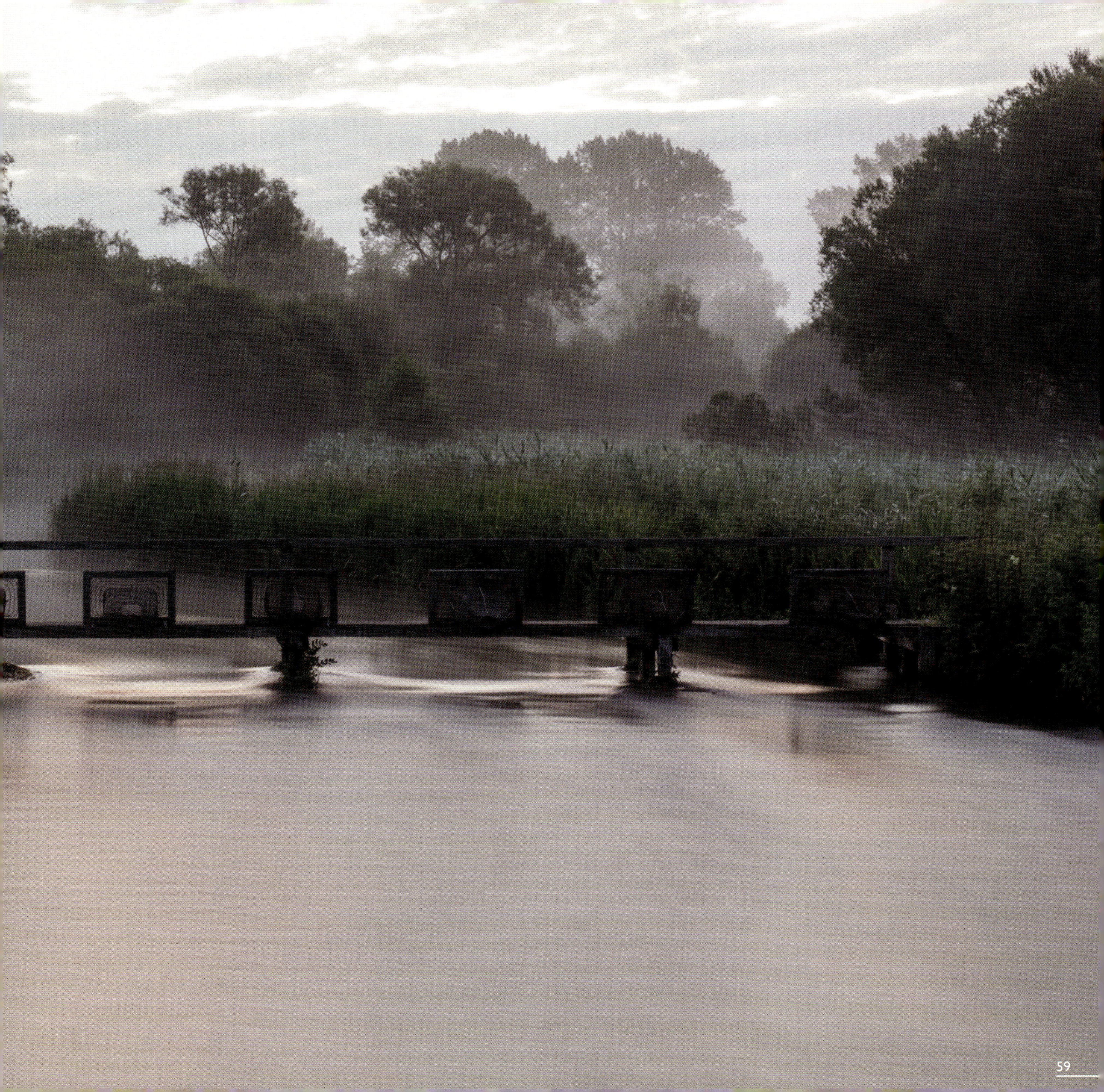

Following the valley of the River Test upstream leads to Wherwell *(above & right)*, a quintessential English village with attractive thatched cottages. A professionally thatched roof can last up to fifty years with good maintenance, depending on various factors including how steep the pitch is and what material is used, although the average is nearer thirty. The roof ridge needs more regular care, as it receives the most wear. Some cottages may feature a thatch finial; a straw ornament that sits on the ridge and gives a property an individual look as well as demonstrating the thatcher's skills.

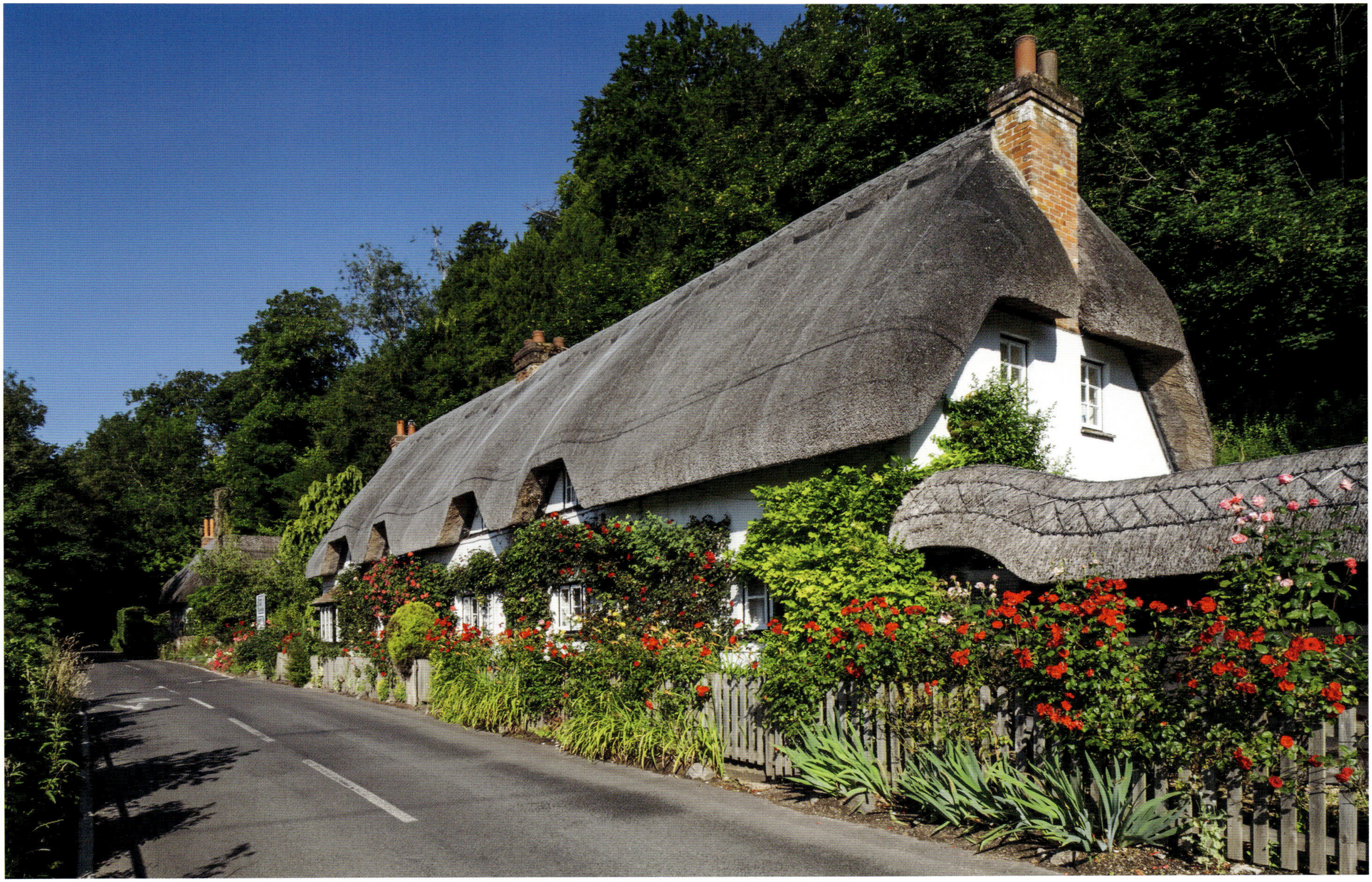

Wherwell sits on the Test Way, a forty-four mile walk along the route of the river that starts on the high chalk downs at Inkpen and leads down to Southampton Water. The walk is divided into eight sections, and each provides a good day out.

Visitors to the village may hear tales of the cockatrice, a mythical beast that is said to have terrorised residents in days gone by. Four acres of land were offered to the man who could slay the beast. Eventually imprisoned in the dungeons beneath the local priory, it resisted all attempts on its life, until a man named Green lowered down a metal mirror. On seeing its reflection, the cockatrice fought its perceived rival until exhaustion set in, when it was killed. A cockatrice weathervane, which used to sit on the local church, is now in Andover Museum and there are four acres of land in the nearby forest known as Green's Acres.

62

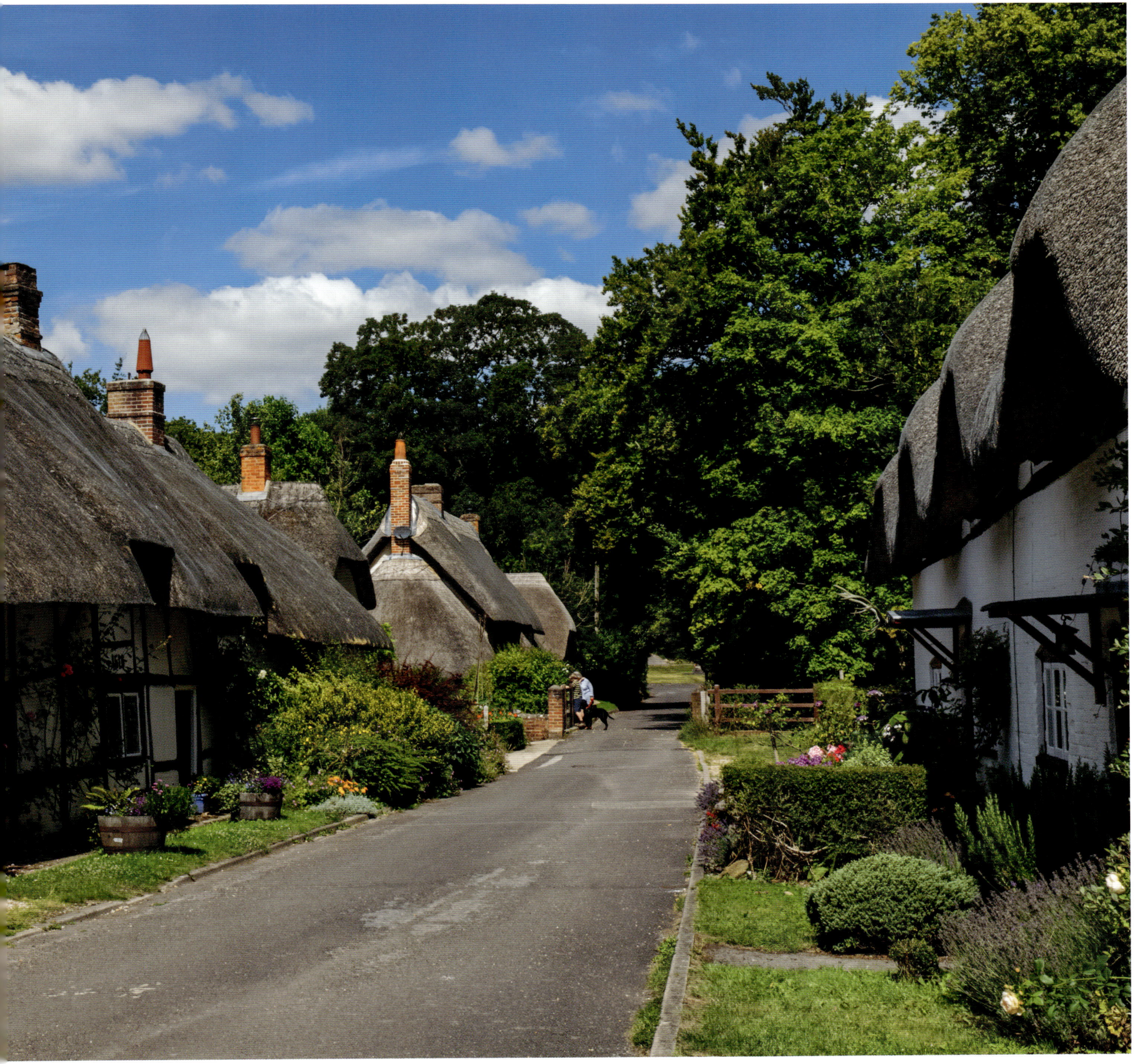

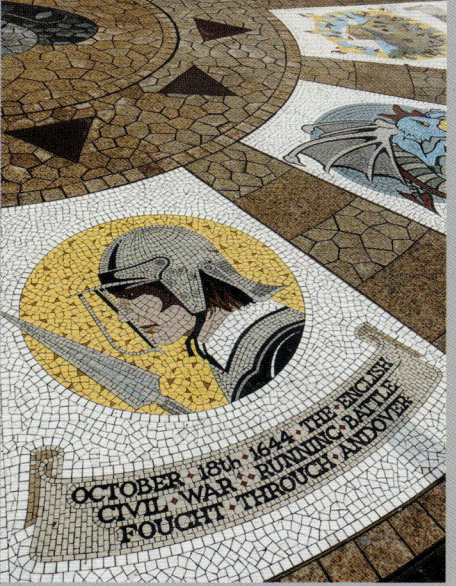

The market town of Andover sits on the River Anton, which joins the River Test five miles to the south. In the 18th century, it became an important stop for stagecoaches travelling between Exeter, Salisbury and London, with a variety of daily and weekly services totalling an estimated thirty each day. The railway station opened in the 1850s and this linked the town to London via Basingstoke. The Time Ring Mosaic *(top & above left)* in the High Street depicts events from Andover's history and was created by Alan Potter. The Wherwell cockatrice is amongst the illustrations that circle the central design.

Right & above right: St Mary's Church, Andover.

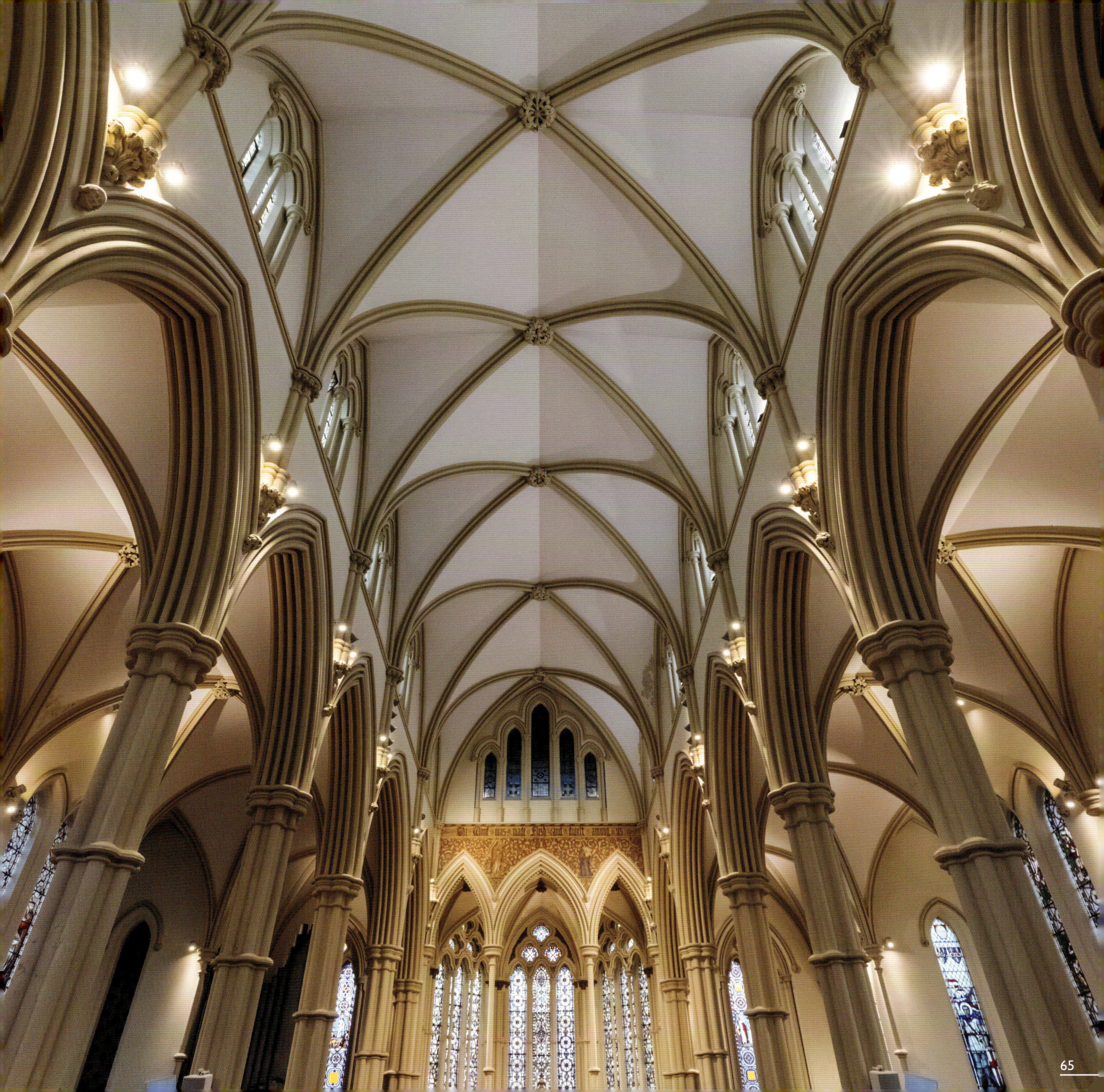
The Word was made Flesh and dwelt among us

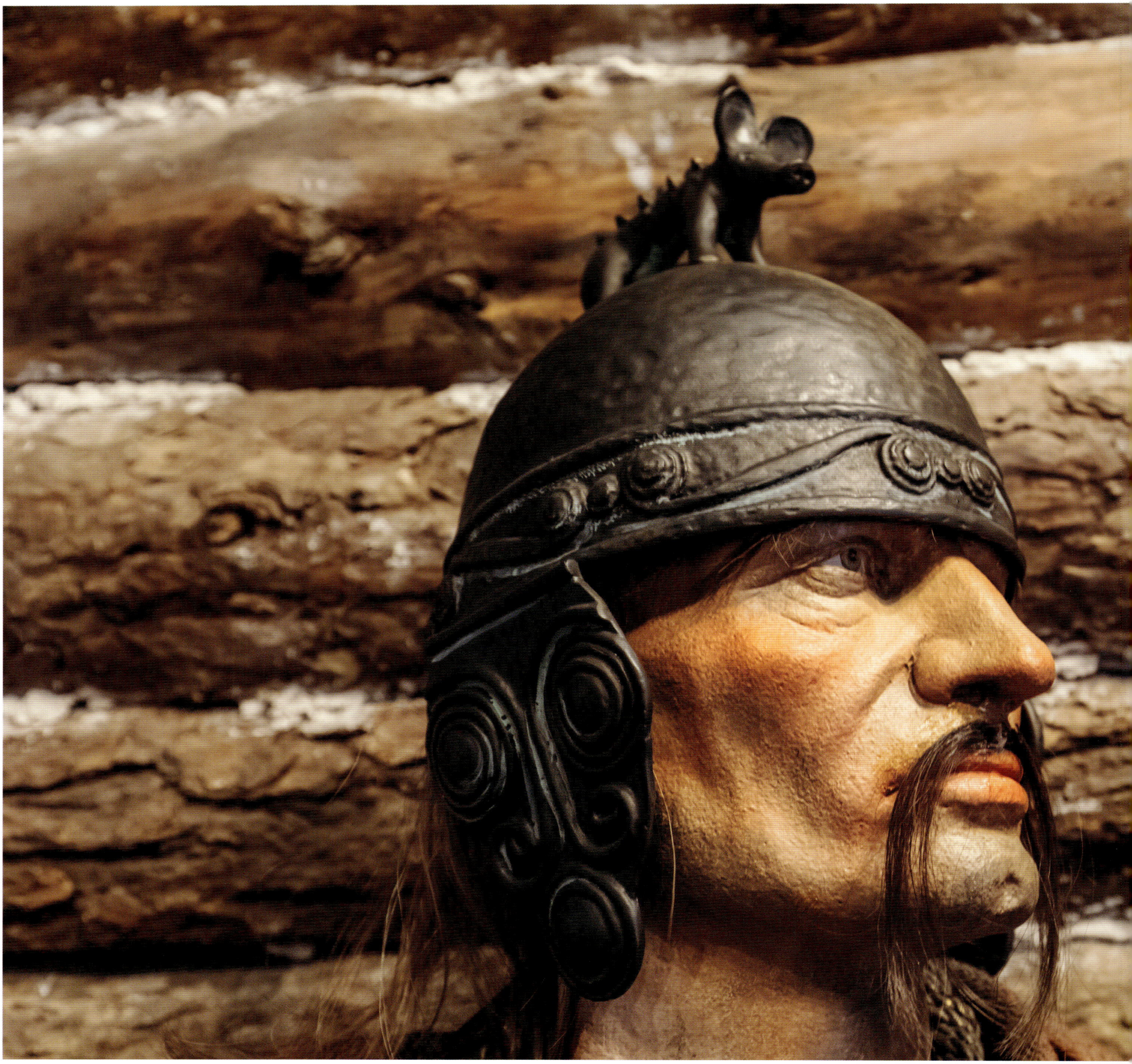

Housed within the same Georgian building as Andover's main museum in Church Close is the Museum of the Iron Age, which tells the story of the Danebury Hill Fort seven miles to the south-west. The site at Danebury has been well-studied and visitors to the museum can find out how people lived their lives more than two thousand years ago. Archaeological finds have included more than 180,000 pieces of pottery and nearly quarter of a million other artefacts made of iron, bronze, bone and stone. A selection of these is on display at the museum.

Also close to Andover, in Middle Wallop, is the Army Flying Museum where visitors can discover the history of aviation in the British Army from its earliest days. More than thirty-five fixed wing and rotary aircraft are on display, with exhibits including a General Aircraft GAL48 Hotspur and helicopters by Westland and Bell.

The museum is adjacent to the Army Air Corps Centre and the first Wallop Wheels and Wings event, held in July 2021, used its airfield to showcase around forty classic aircraft alongside vintage cars and motorbikes.

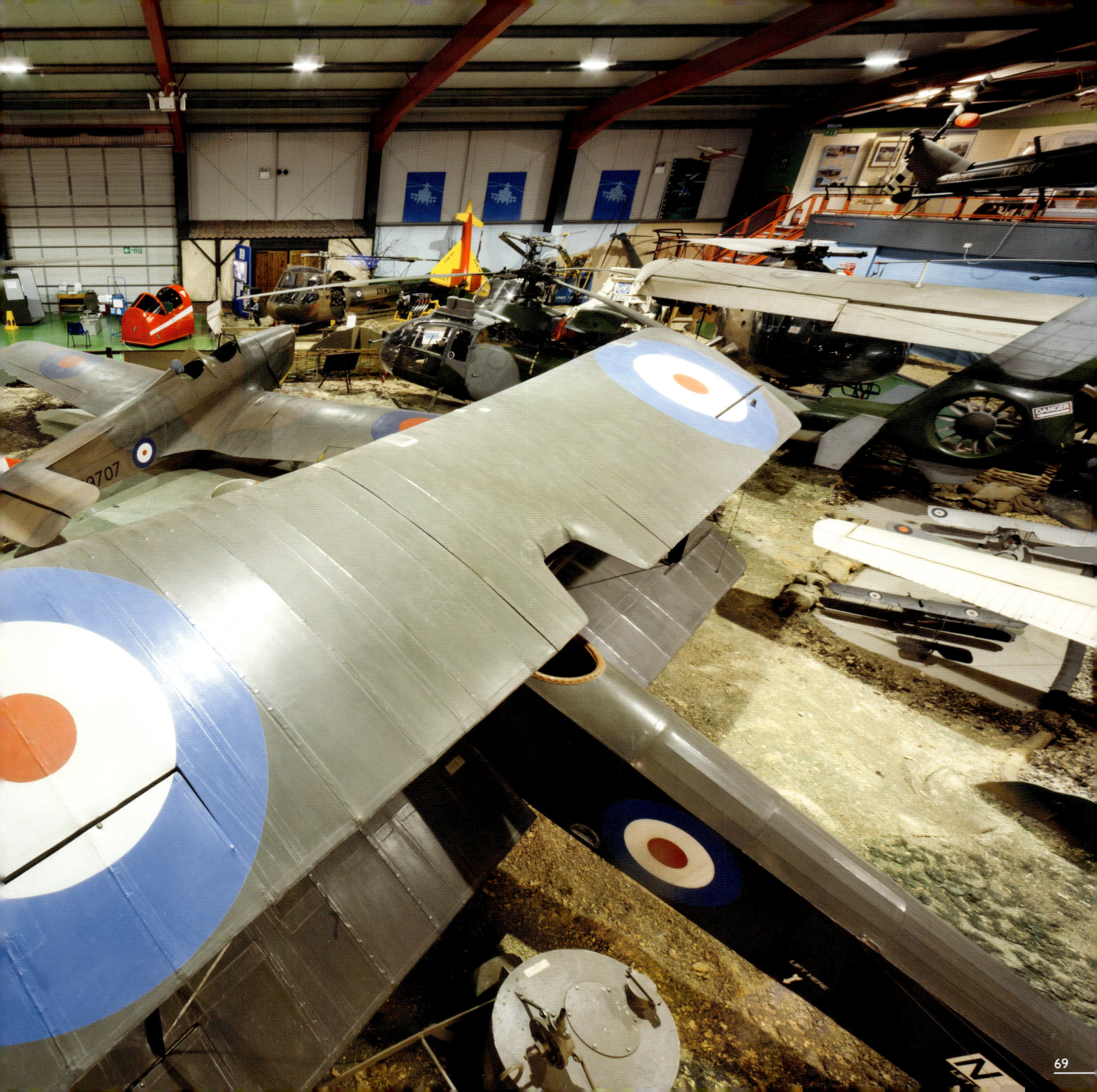

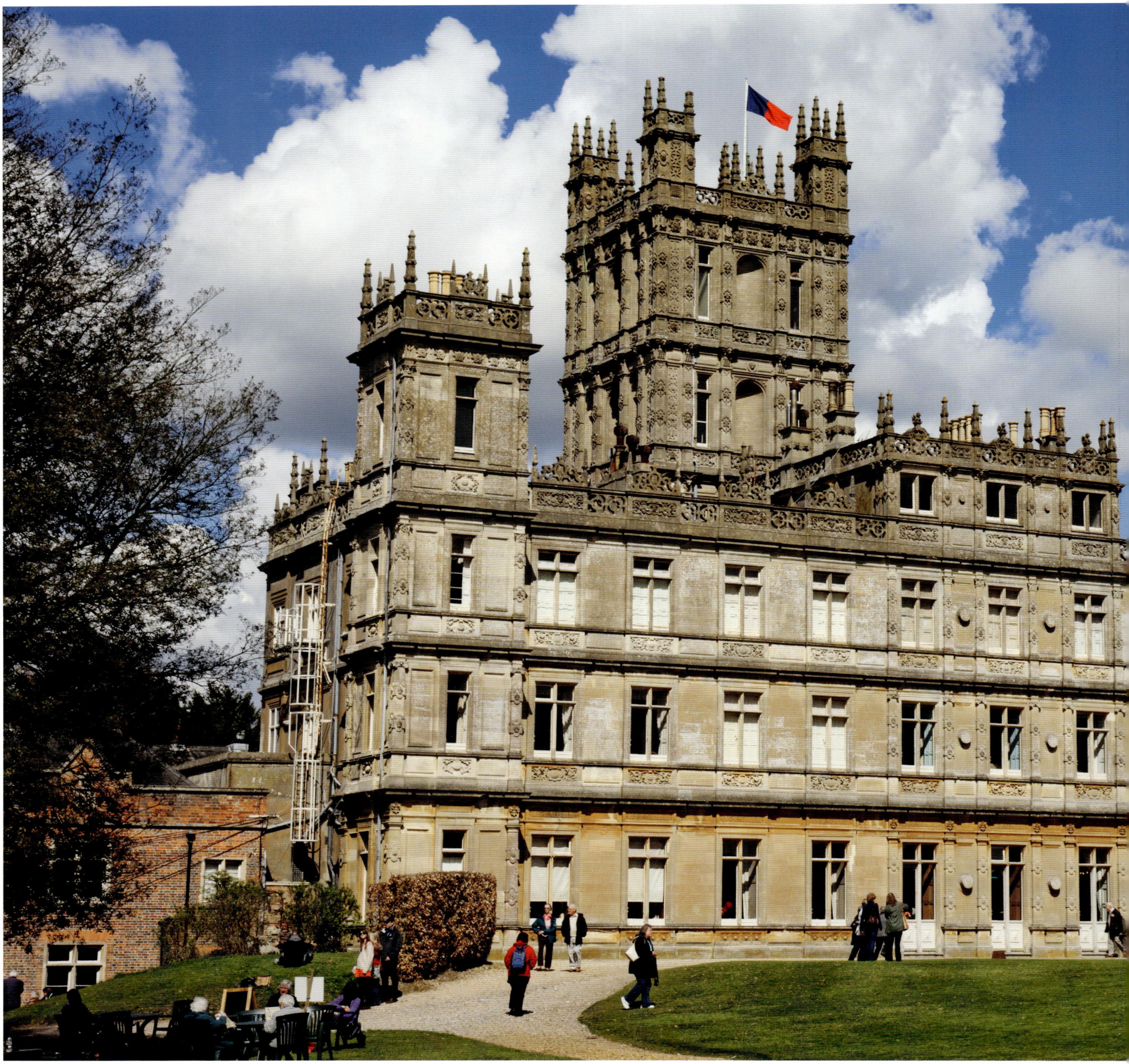

Now world-famous as the setting of Downtown Abbey, the beautiful Highclere Castle is home to the Earl and Countess of Carnarvon. Largely renovated in the 1840s, this country house is an example of Jacobean Revival architecture that was popular in the Victorian period. It was designed by Charles Barry, who was also architect for the Houses of Parliament.

The castle opens to visitors and hosts a variety of special events throughout the year. The current Earl's great-grandfather discovered the tomb of Tutankhamun with Howard Carter in 1922, and the Egyptian exhibition at Highclere tells the story of how this came about and displays a fascinating collection of antiquities.

A popular filming location, Highclere Castle has appeared in many television and film productions but is most famous for its starring role in Downton Abbey with many of the interior rooms being used for filming, as well as the instantly recognisable exterior views of the house and grounds.

Highclere is on the northern border of the county of Hampshire and nine miles to the south is Whitworth Silk Mill. Originally built in the early-19th century, the mill was no longer financially viable by the 1880s and was sold at auction to a local draper for his son James. The mill survived and became known for producing silk linings for the famous Burberry raincoat. By the 1980s, it had fallen into disrepair but was rescued by the Hampshire Building Preservation Trust and is now open as a working museum.

Visitors can see the historic layout of the weaving shed and its Victorian machinery, including the creel, which is thought to be the oldest of its type still in use. Skilled weavers use traditional techniques to produce fine quality items, many of which are sold in the mill's shop. Open throughout the year, Whitchurch Silk Mill also offers a programme of exhibitions and events.

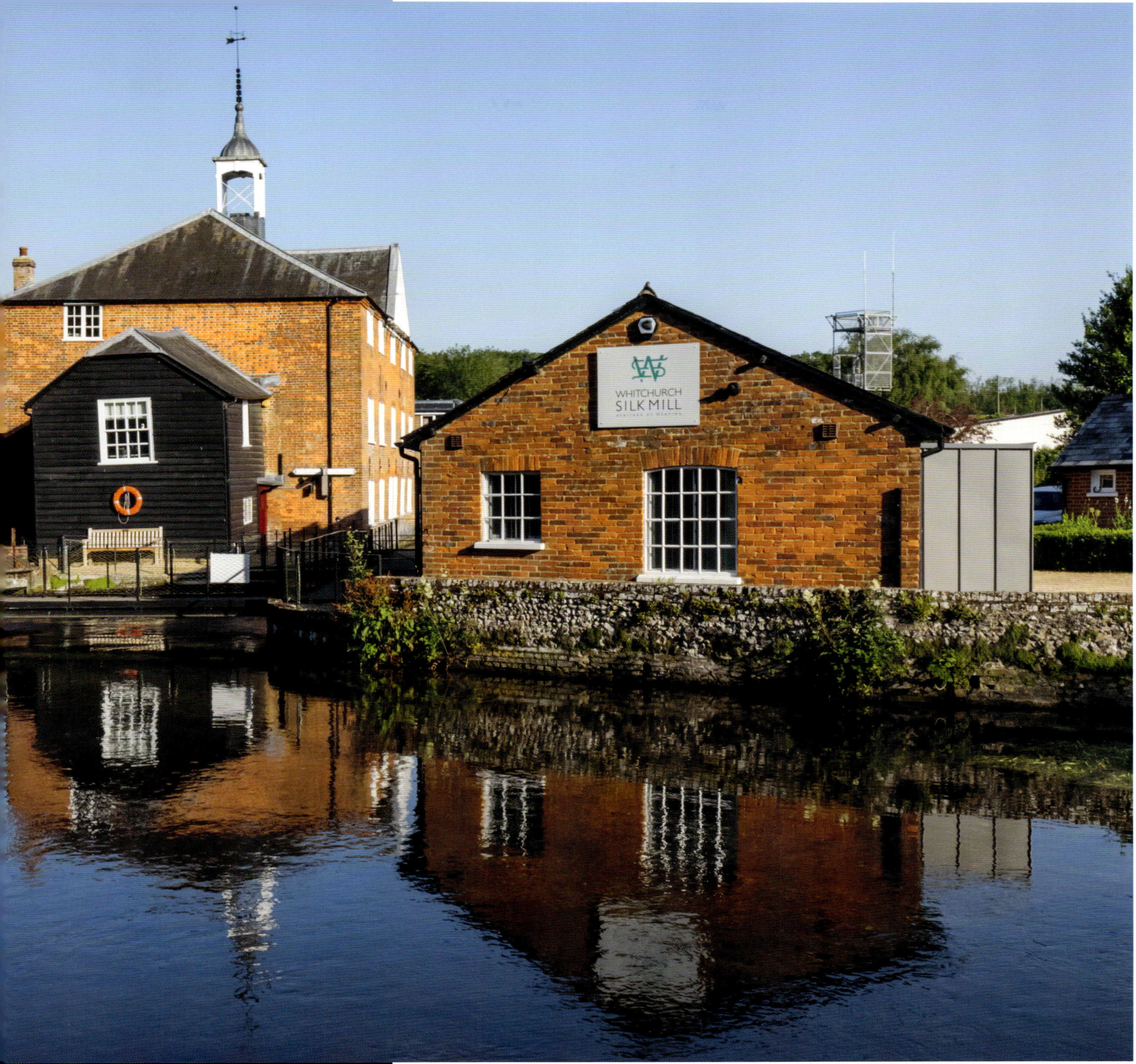
WHITCHURCH
SILK MILL

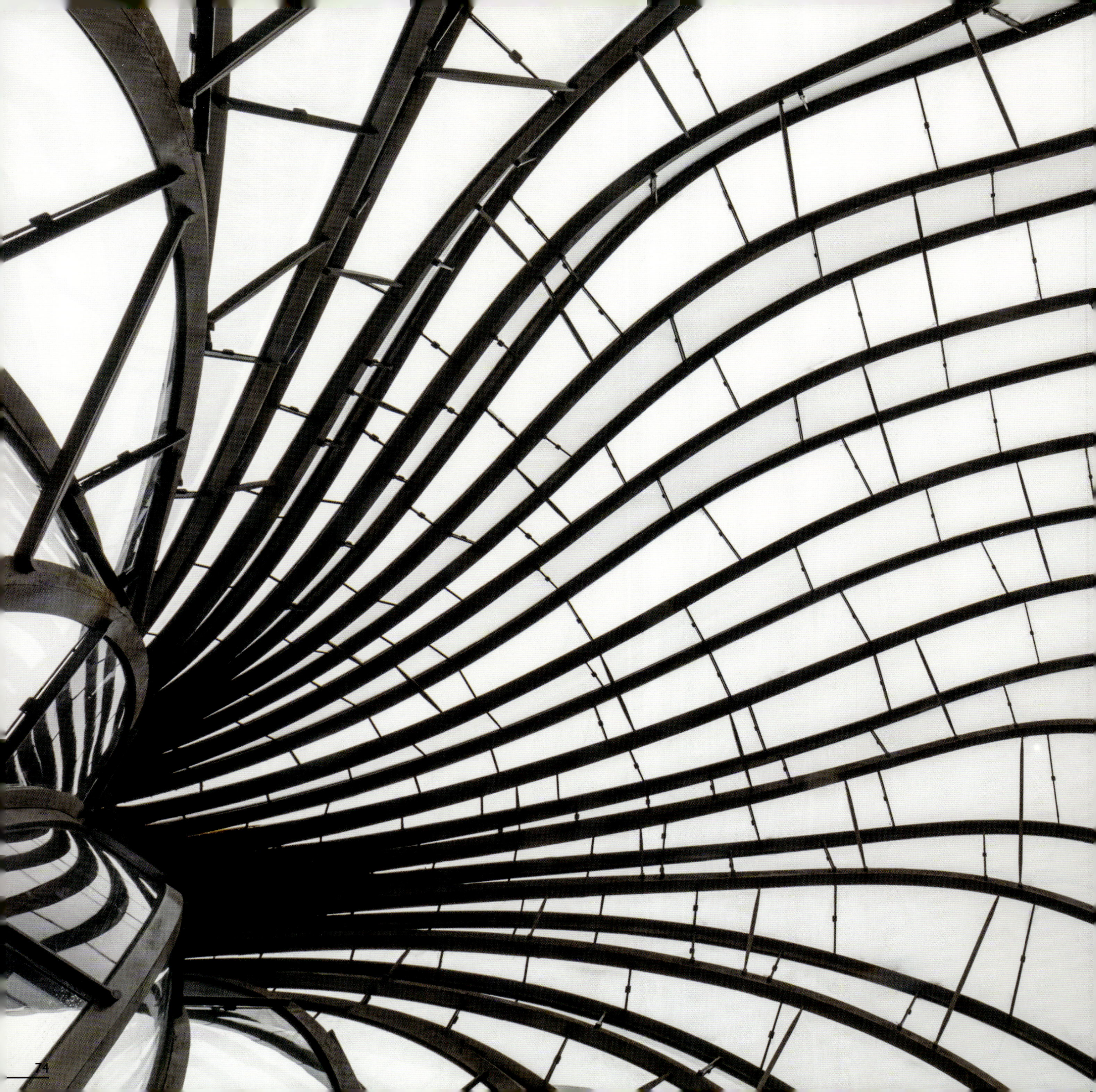

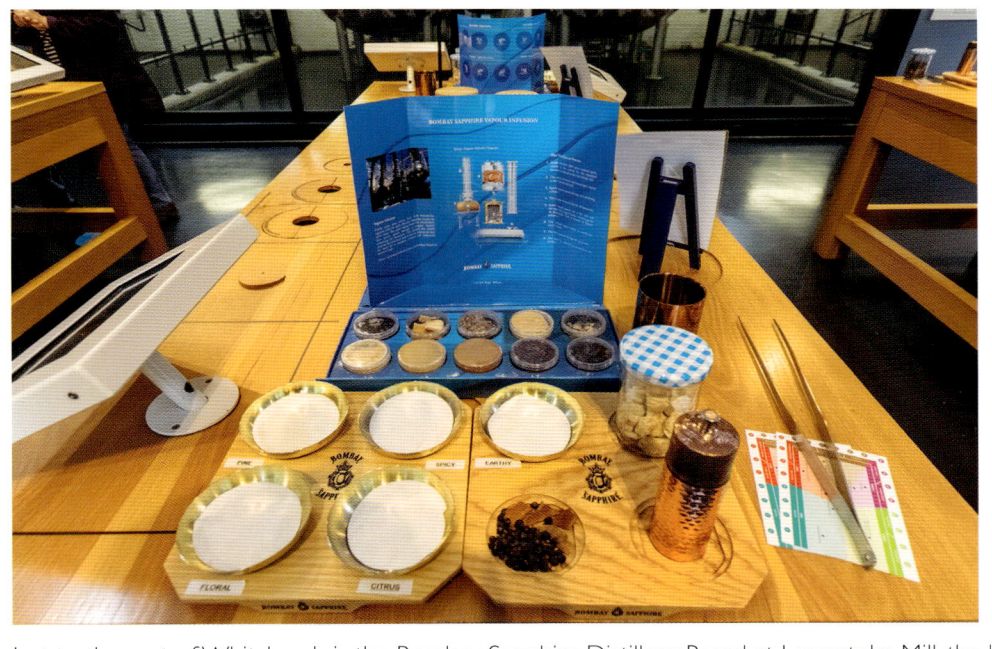

Just to the east of Whitchurch is the Bombay Sapphire Distillery. Based at Laverstoke Mill, the history of the site spans nearly a thousand years, with a mill recorded here in the Domesday Book of 1086. The mill produced paper for bank notes from the early 18th century and also made the paper for the world's first postal order. It ceased paper production in the 1960s and was bought by the Bombay Spirits Company in 2010, opening to the public four years later.

The dramatic glasshouses *(left & above right)*, in which plants are grown and used as botanicals in the production of Bombay Sapphire Gin, were designed by the Heatherwick Studio who also designed the Olympic Cauldron for London 2012. Visitors can tour the distillery to see how the gin is made and there are opportunities to taste the result.

Continuing east, the road leads to Basingstoke, the largest town in Hampshire with a population of around 110,000. An old market town, it saw rapid expansion in the 1960s and is now an important economic centre, home to the UK headquarters of companies including the Automobile Association and various IT, banking and insurance brands.

Above: The Family by Mike Smith (1993).
Left: The Haymarket Theatre. *Middle left:* Jane Austen by Adam Roud (2017). *Far left:* The Malls Shopping Centre.

The borough of Basingstoke and Deane has a large collection of public art that ranges from statues and sculptures to seating and glasswork. The Triumphal Gates *(above right)* by Peter Parkinson and Richard Quinnell mark the entrance to the town centre and include sixteen decorative panels with images of local importance.

The Holy Ghost Cemetery is just north of Basingstoke station and provides a peaceful space at the heart of the bustling town. Local figures buried there include the clothing manufacturer, Thomas Burberry. There were two chapels on the site, with the first dating to the 13th century. The Holy Trinity Chapel *(left)* was added to the original building by William, Lord Sandys of the Vyne in the 1520s but fell into ruin after the Civil War.

Above left: Vue Cinema, Festival Place.

78

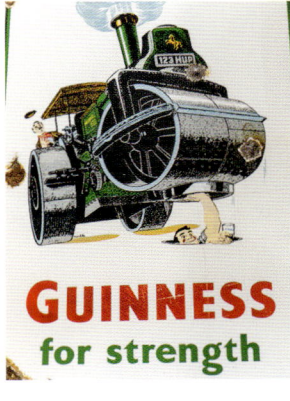

Milestones is Basingstoke's museum of living history based at the leisure park just outside the town centre. Opened in 2000, it has a network of streets with houses, shops and vehicles that tell of specific times in Hampshire's history, focussing on the Victorian era and the 1930s.

An exhibition of more than 260 teddy bears, collected by Mr W Simpson and dating back over one hundred years, has recently been added.

On the eastern edge of Basingstoke is the village of Old Basing, known for its attractive period architecture. The road that passes through the centre is called The Street *(above)*. This stretches for a mile from Basing House in the west, passing St Mary's Church before crossing under the main railway line and ending at the Village Hall.

The writer and artist, Edward Lear includes the name of Basing in a limerick in his *Book of Nonsense*, published in 1846.

Top & right: Built in the 1530s, the Tudor Great Barn at Basing House is now a venue for weddings and other events.

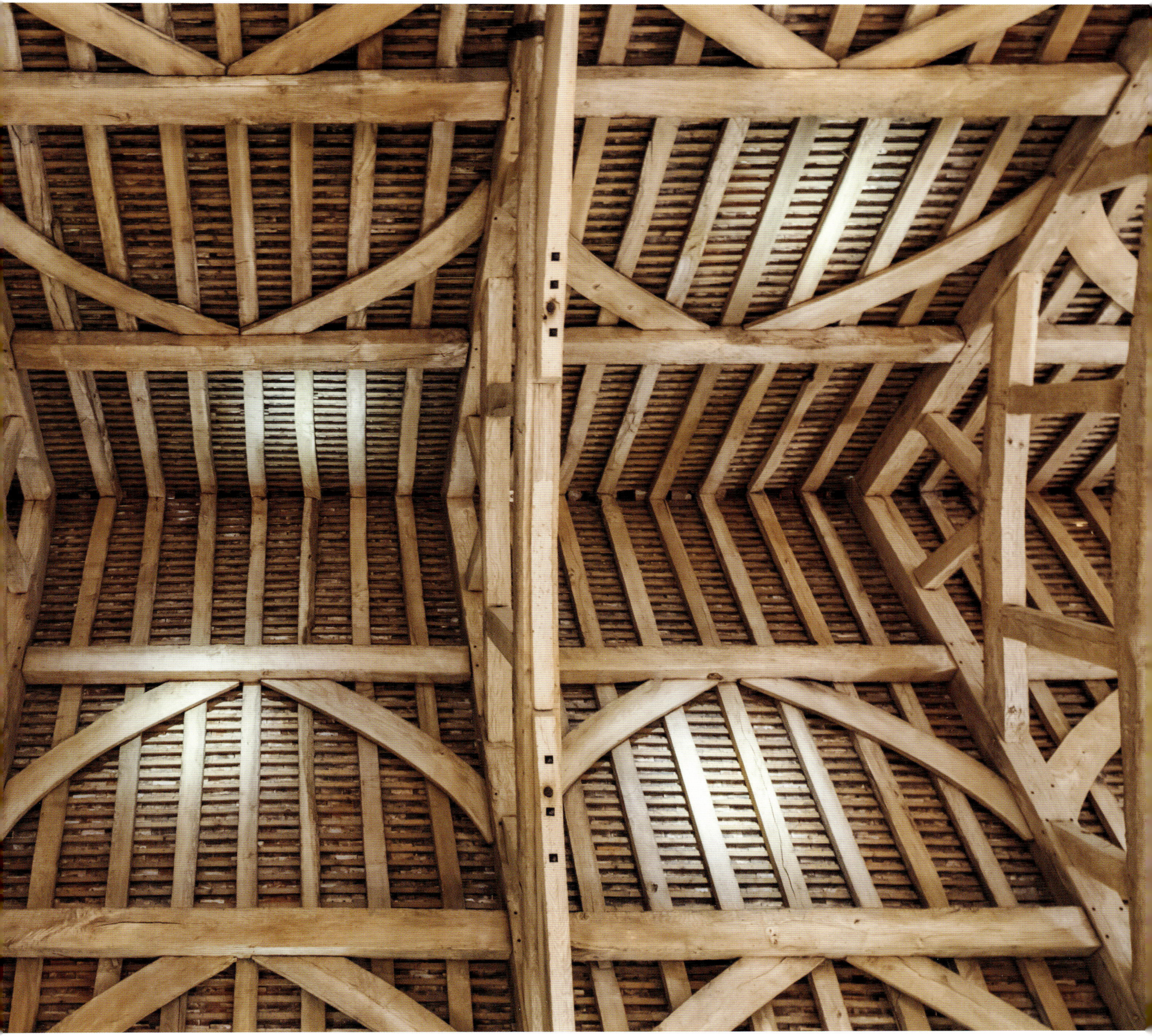

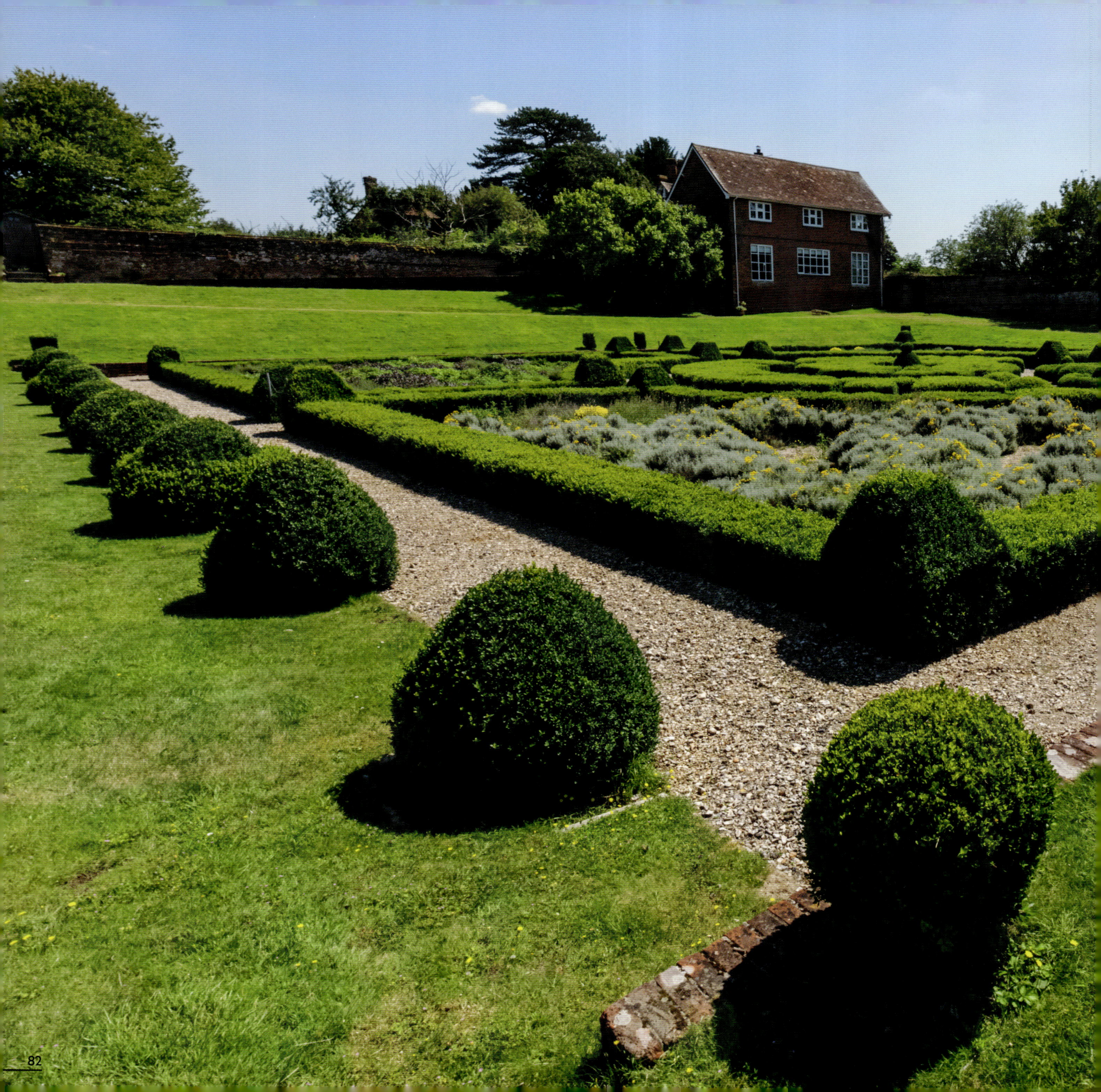

Basing House was originally built as a castle in the 12th century and the earthworks that defended this are still visible. A new palace was built on the site in the 16th century by Sir William Paulet and it rivalled Hampton Court in size and magnificence. Royal visitors were frequent during the Tudor period. The Paulet family were Royalists and Basing House was finally stormed and ruined by Cromwell's men in 1645, leaving only the foundations of a once great residence *(bottom)*.
The ruins and gardens are now open to the public.

Left & above: Knot Garden.

Below: Entrance gate.

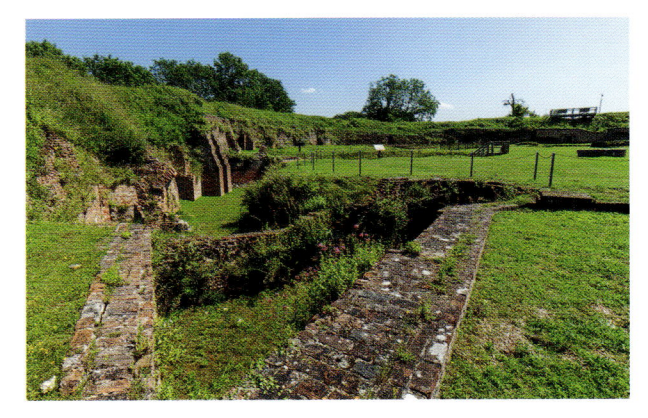

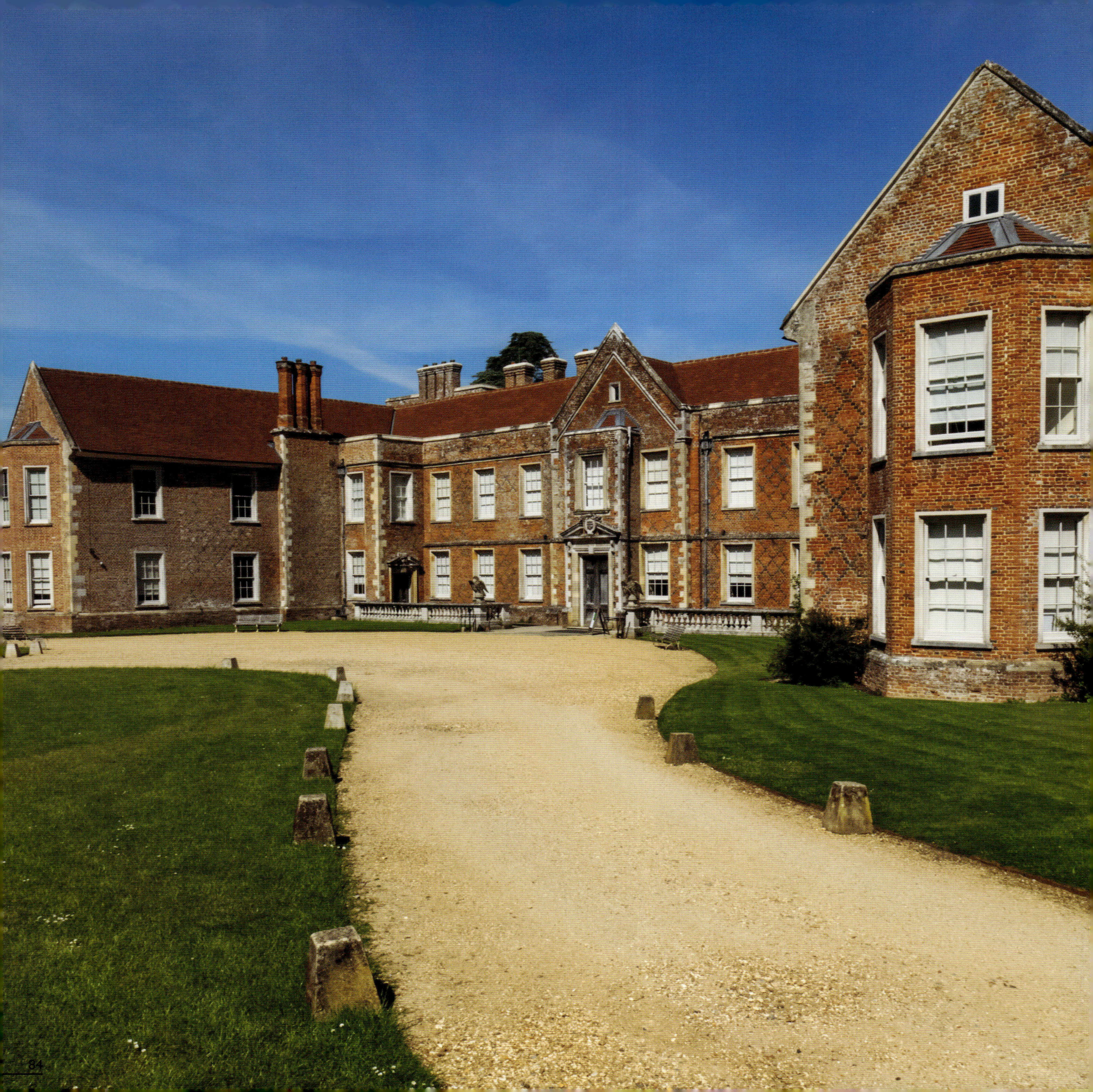

North of Basingstoke is The Vyne, a Grade I listed country house that is now cared for by the National Trust. A number of smaller medieval buildings were converted into an impressive Tudor palace by William, Lord Sandys of The Vyne in the early 16th century. It covered an area three times its present size and was one of the most important houses in the county.

A wealthy barrister named Chaloner Chute bought the estate in the 1650s, reducing the size of the palace and modernising it to create a more friendly family home. The classical portico *(top left)* was added at this time. The interior includes the impressive Palladian Staircase Hall *(above left & right)*, which was built for John Chaloner Chute who lived here in the mid-18th century and was a close friend of Sir Horace Walpole.

Above middle: The Saloon.

Although Basingstoke is a busy town on the main corridor linking London to the west, the surrounding landscape provides opportunities for country walks with a varied mix of woodland, rural lanes, arable fields and grazing for livestock.

87

The Basingstoke Canal was built to connect Basingstoke with the Wey Navigation which in turn linked to the River Thames at Weybridge. It was completed in 1794 but later became derelict. Twenty years of work by restoration teams in the 1970s and 1980s led to the re-opening of a thirty-two mile section which stretches from the Wey Navigation junction to the Greywell Tunnel, six miles east of Basingstoke centre.

The canal is now a haven for wildlife and provides diverse habitats perfect for species such as kingfishers and dragonflies.

Odiham Castle sits by the Basingstoke Canal near to Greywell Tunnel. Also known as King John's Castle, it was built by the monarch during his sixteen-year reign at the start of the 13th century. It is said that it was from Odiham that King John set off to travel to Runnymede where he added his seal to the Magna Carta in 1215. A commemorative plaque, designed by Daniel Bowhay, was placed at the castle on the 800th anniversary *(far left)*.

Having lost its royal status by the 15th century, Odiham Castle became a hunting lodge but was classed as a ruin by the early 1600s.

Alton is a lively town with a population of around 20,000. The centre has a variety of historic buildings *(right)* and modern shops, and a market is held in the High Street each Tuesday.

The town is associated with the dark tale of Sweet Fanny Adams who was murdered here in 1867 and her grave can still be seen in the cemetery *(top right)*. The Curtis Museum of local history, which stands beside the unusual granite war memorial *(above left)* in Crown Close, is a good place to find out more about her story *(above right)*.

The writer, Jane Austen lived in nearby Chawton and a blue plaque in the town shows the site of her brother's bank *(top left)*.

91

The village of Chawton has become a place of pilgrimage for Jane Austen fans from around the world. Jane lived here for the last eight years of her life, although she died in Winchester in 1817 having gone there to seek medical treatment in her final days.

The house in Chawton where she lived with her mother, sister and family friend is now called Jane Austen's House *(top)* and has been a museum since 1949. Her six novels were written or revised here, and visitors can see the table *(above left)* at which she sat to create the works that still resonate so strongly with readers today. *Above right:* Jane Austen's bedroom.

p.93: Church of St Nicholas with statue of Jane Austen by Adam Roud.

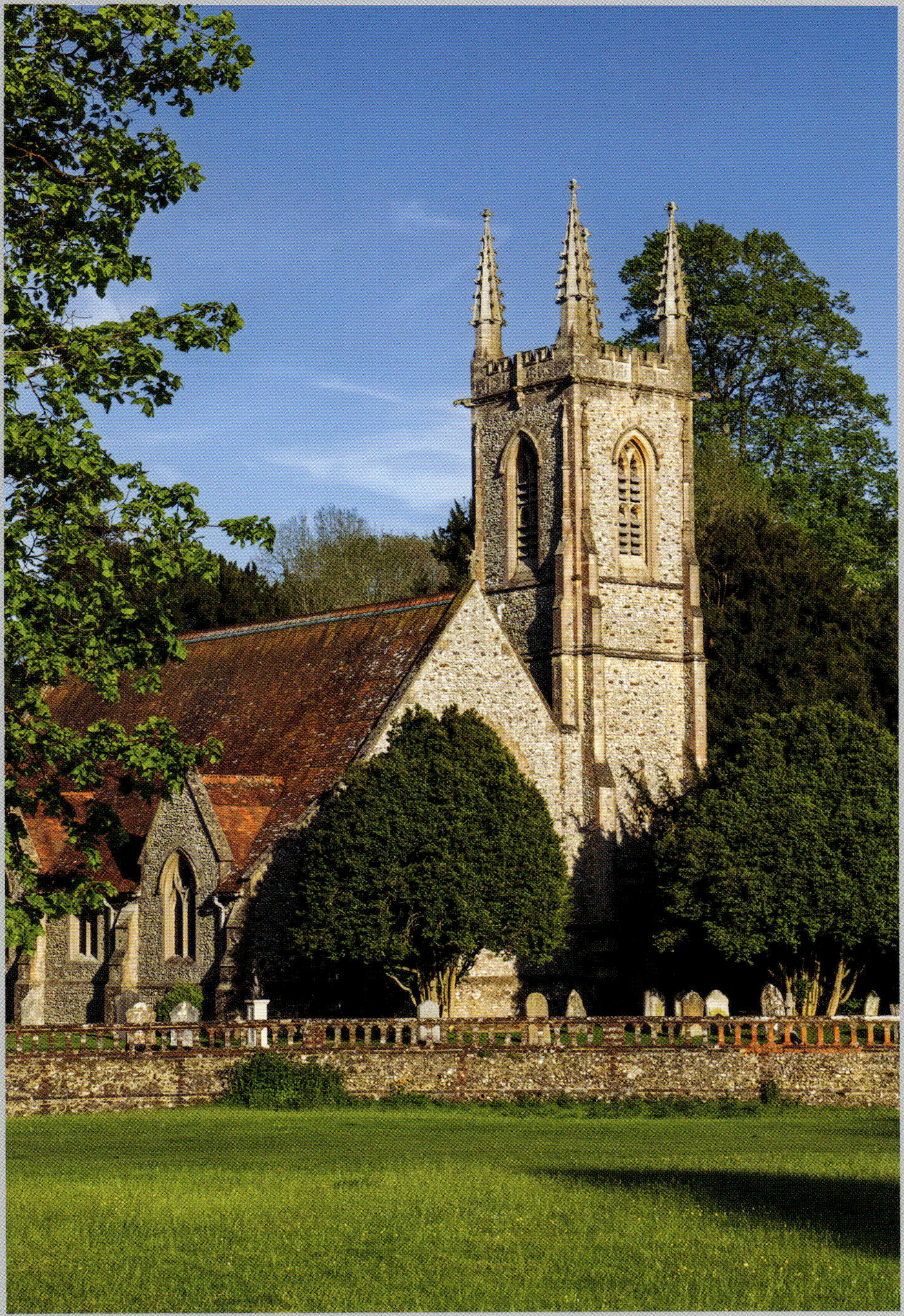

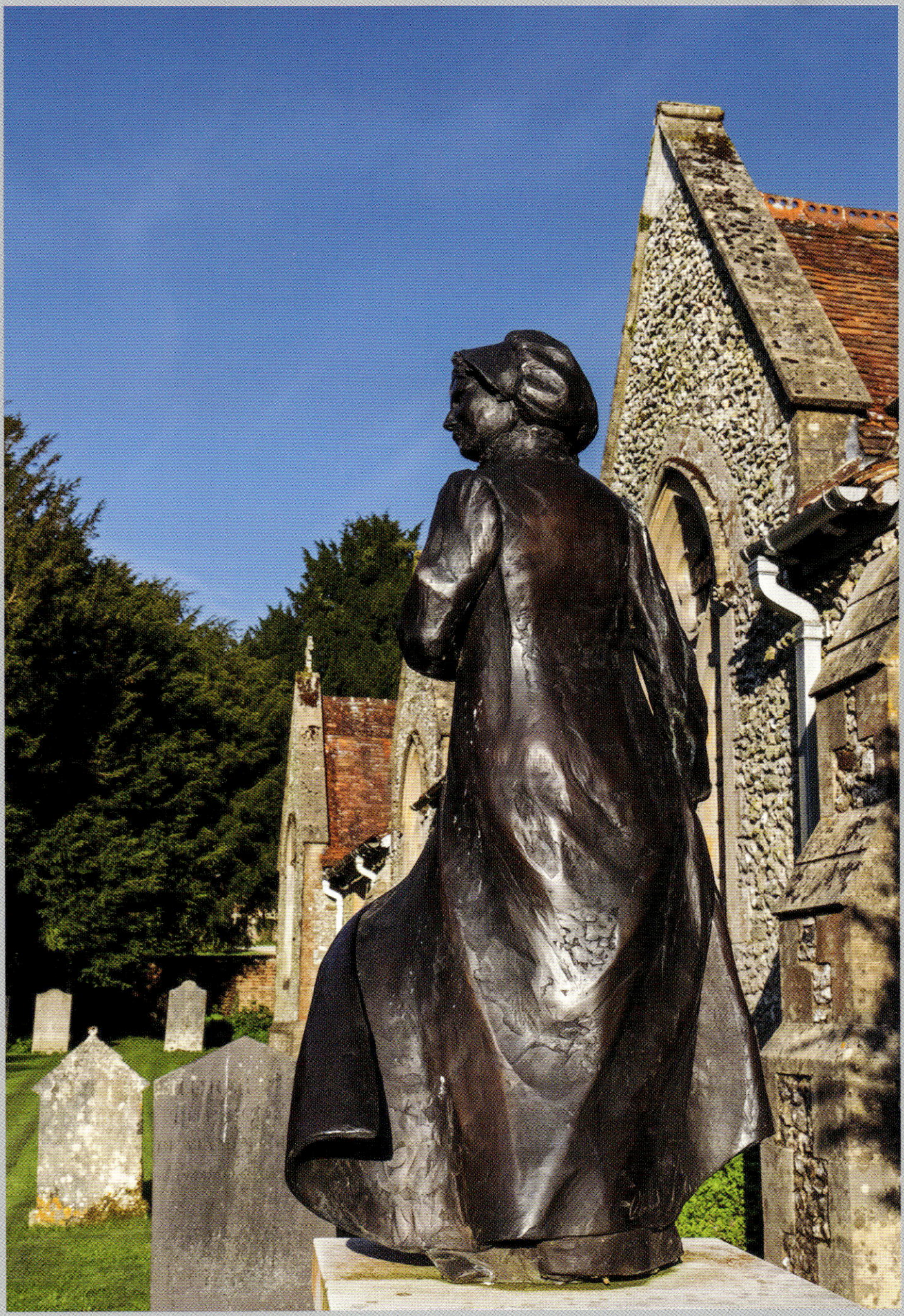

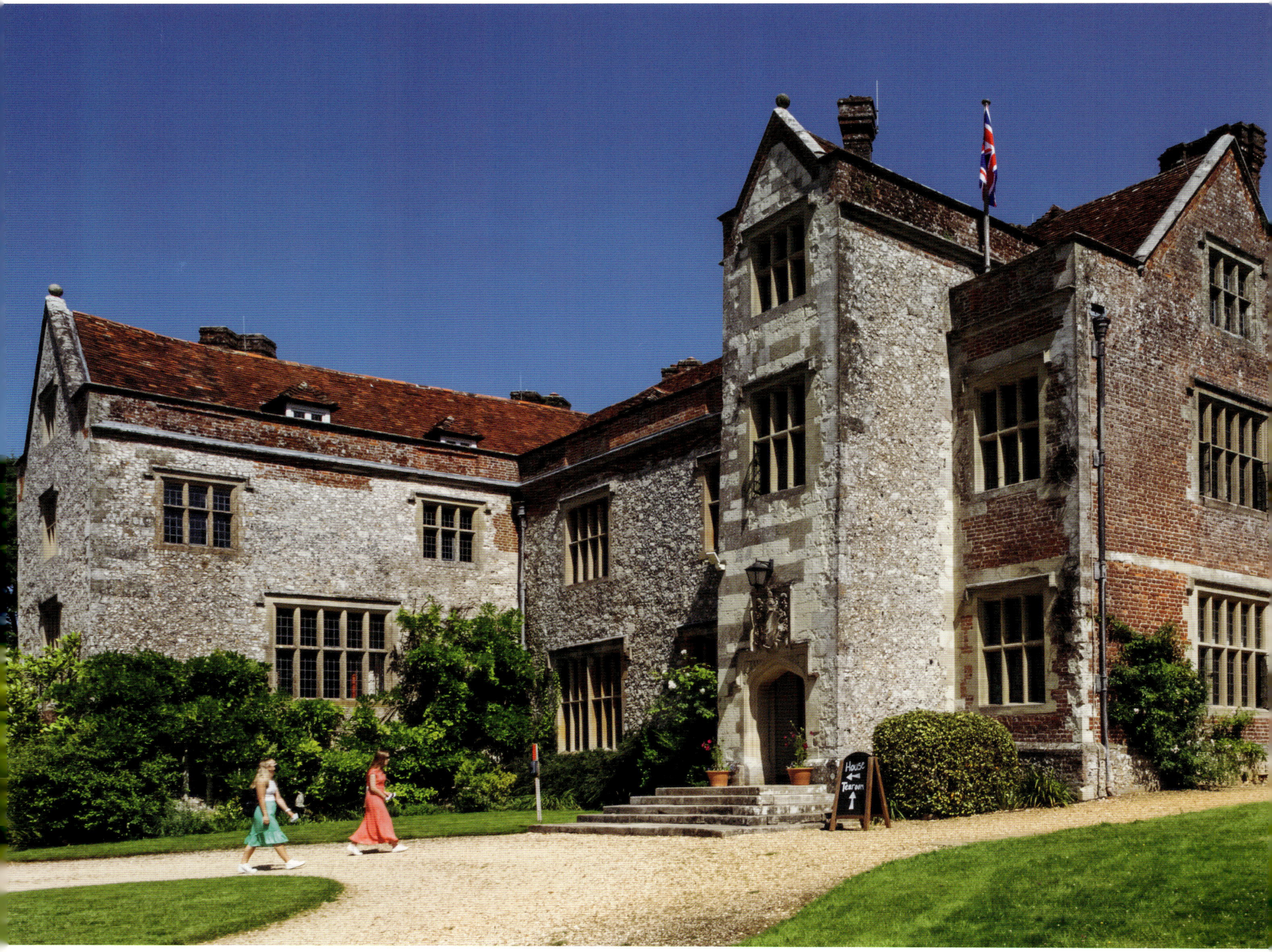
House
Tearoom

Chawton House *(left)* is an Elizabethan manor house once owned by Jane Austen's brother. It has recently been restored and is now a study centre for the research and understanding of early women's writing, with an important library of more than 9000 books and manuscripts. The house also opens to visitors for tours and events.

Paintings include a portrait of actor and writer, Mary Robinson (1758-1800) by John Hoppner *(above right)*. First editions of some of her works can be found in the library.

Top left: Portrait of a Lady *(detail)*, possibly Sarah Harriet Burney by Thomas Lawrence (circle of). *Top right:* The Great Staircase. *Above left:* Heraldic stained glass window.

95

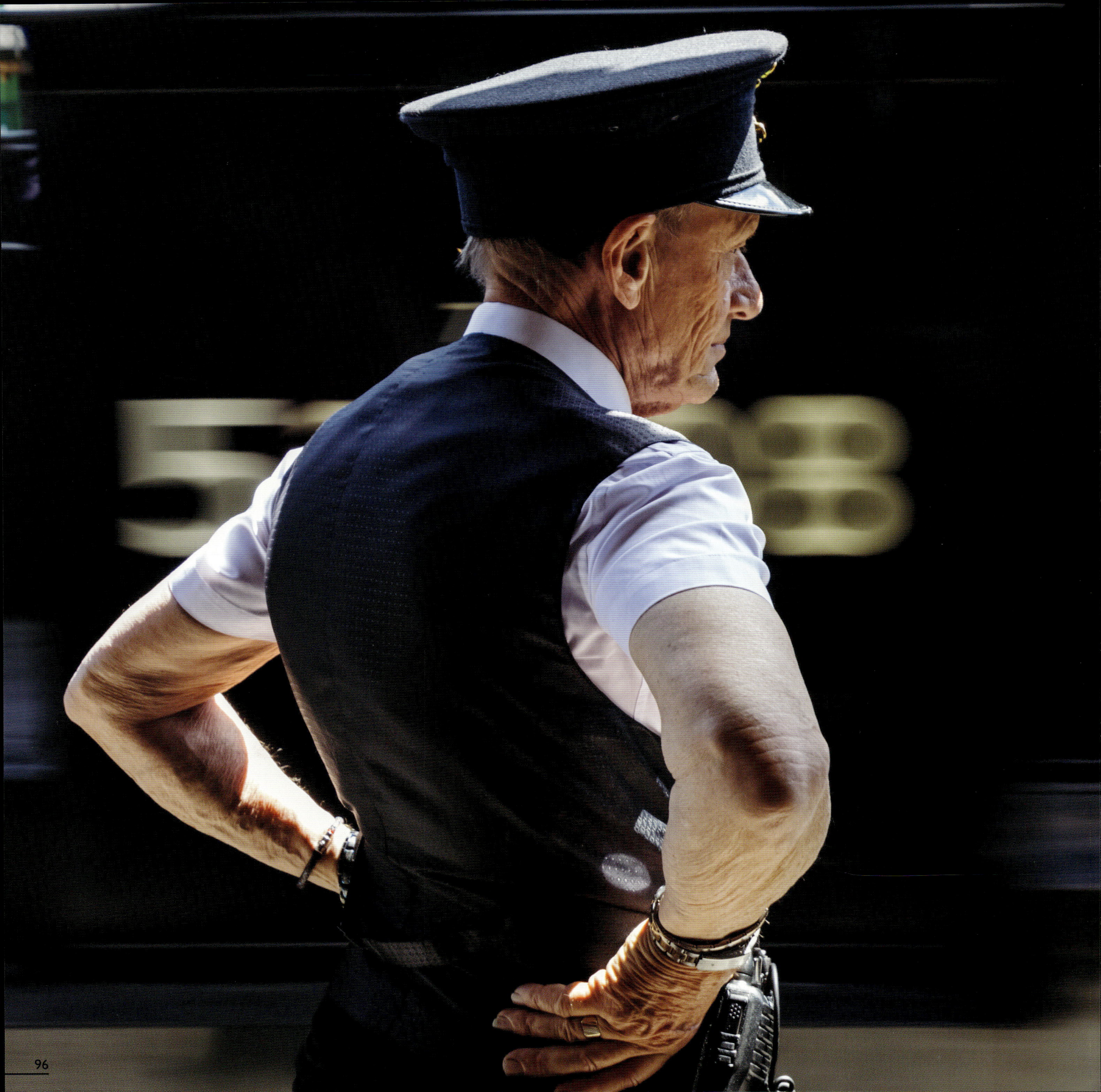

The Watercress Line is a heritage railway that runs for ten miles from New Alresford to Alton, where it links to the main rail network. There are four stations on the line, one at each end with others at Medstead & Four Marks and Ropley. The line was bought from British Rail in the mid-1970s and re-opened in stages, with the final section to Alton opening in 1985.

Once a quiet country station, Ropley *(pp.96-97)* became the loco shed for the railway after the preservation society took over and is now a hive of activity where visitors can see ongoing restoration work and find out more about how the railway operates. Handyside Bridge *(top right)*, which allows visitors to view the trains from above, used to be at King's Cross station and appeared in the Harry Potter films before being reinstalled at Ropley in 2009.

97

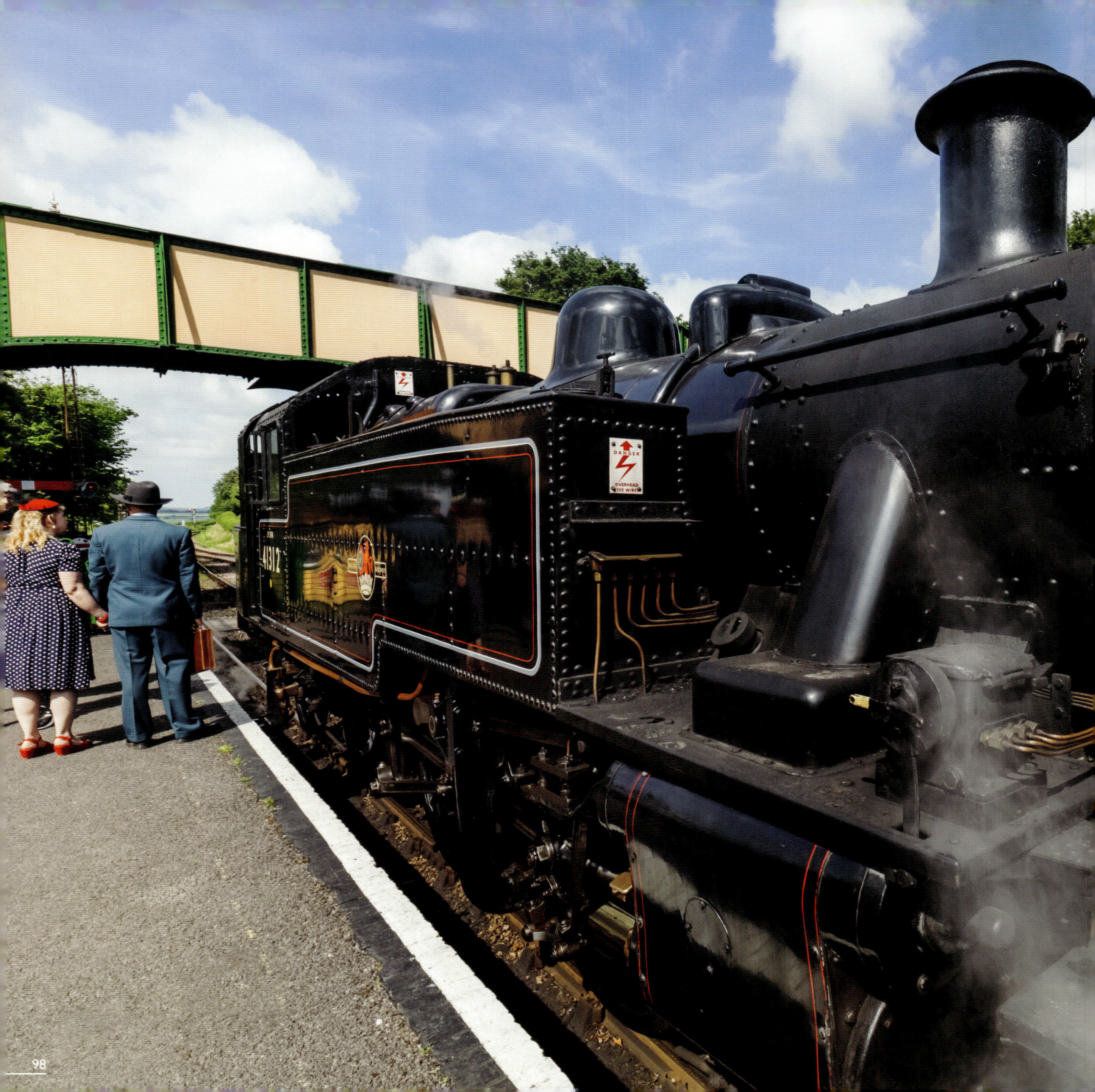
41312
DANGER
OVERHEAD

The name 'Watercress Line' comes from the railway's historic role in transporting the local watercress crop to London and the line is more formally called the Mid Hants Railway. Although there are some permanent employees, the operation relies on a band of 450 volunteers to run its scheduled services and numerous special events.

pp.98-99: Ropley Station and Signal Box.

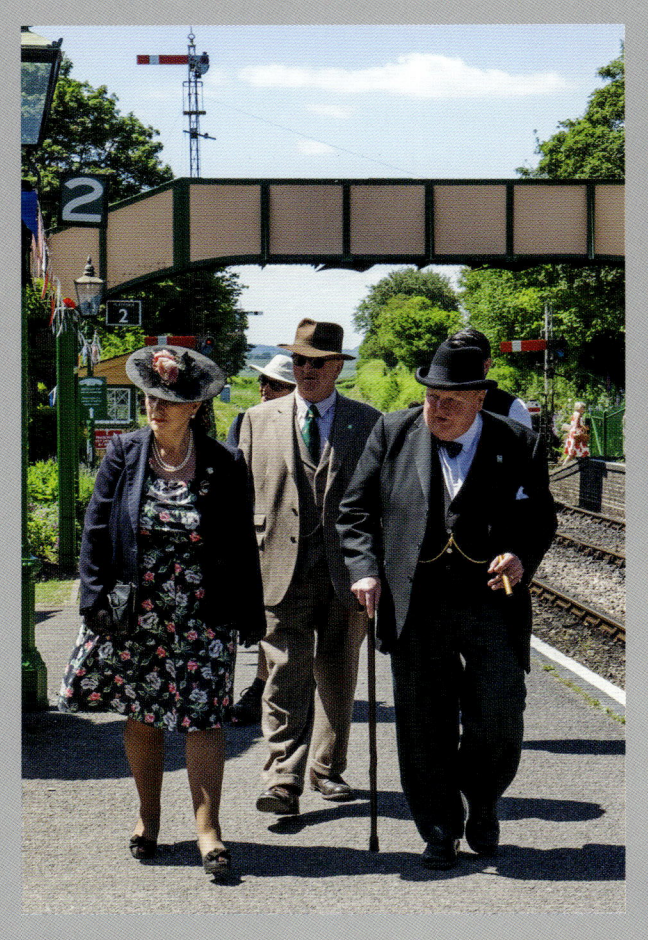

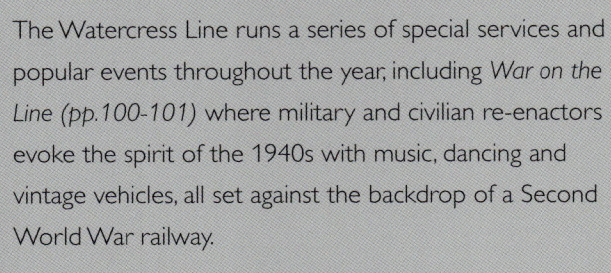

The Watercress Line runs a series of special services and popular events throughout the year, including *War on the Line (pp.100-101)* where military and civilian re-enactors evoke the spirit of the 1940s with music, dancing and vintage vehicles, all set against the backdrop of a Second World War railway.

Other popular events are *Day Out with Thomas (p.97)* and the spectacular *Steam Illuminations*, featuring a train illuminated inside and out by thousands of digitally-controlled LED lights.

Right: Singer, Stephanie Belle at Ropley Station.

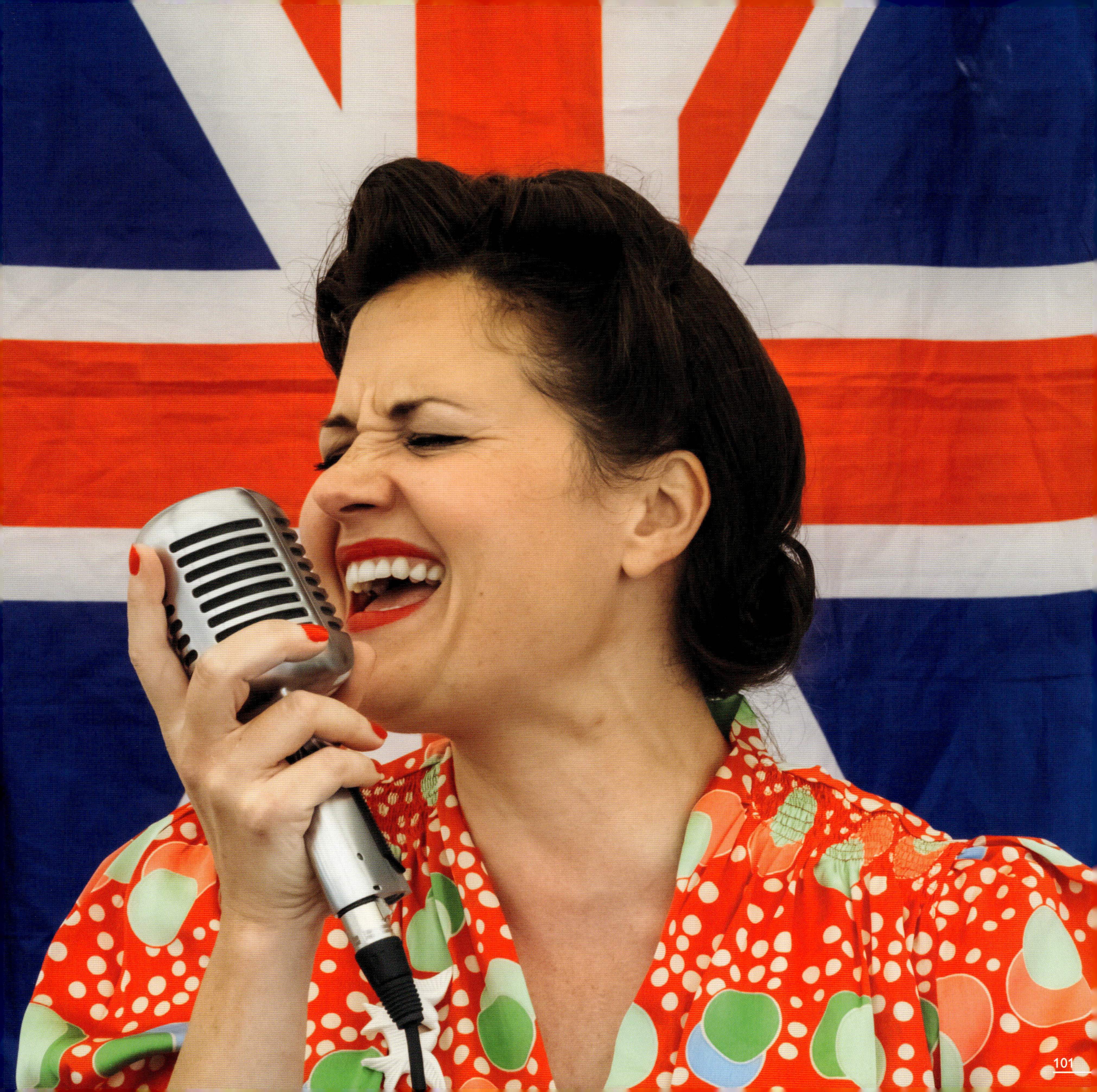

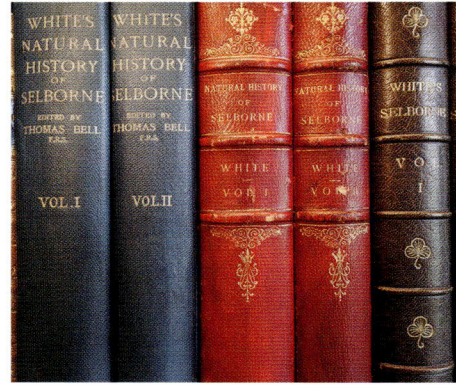

South of Alton is Gilbert White's House *(left)*, former residence of the renowned 18th century naturalist *(top)* whose ground-breaking observations of the natural world were recorded in his book, *The Natural History of Selborne (middle)* which has been continuously in print since 1789. Now a museum, the house also holds the Oates collection, which tells the stories of explorers Frank Oates and his nephew, Lawrence.

The St Francis of Assisi window *(above)* at St Mary's Church in Selborne was installed as a memorial to Gilbert White in 1920.

The lavender fields of nearby Hartley Park Farm fill the air with scent in the summer months. The fields are open to visitors during the flowering season but the shop is open throughout the year and offers a wide range of products, some of which are created from lavender grown on the farm.

South of New Alresford is the small village of Hinton Ampner, which lies on the north slope of a chalk ridge on the edge of the Hampshire Downs and is also in the South Downs National Park. The surrounding landscape has a variety of footpaths ideal for walkers and nature lovers. The woodlands are carpeted with bluebells in the spring but are attractive throughout the seasons.

Top left: Flower trough outside the Hinton Arms.

Right: Oilseed rape field.

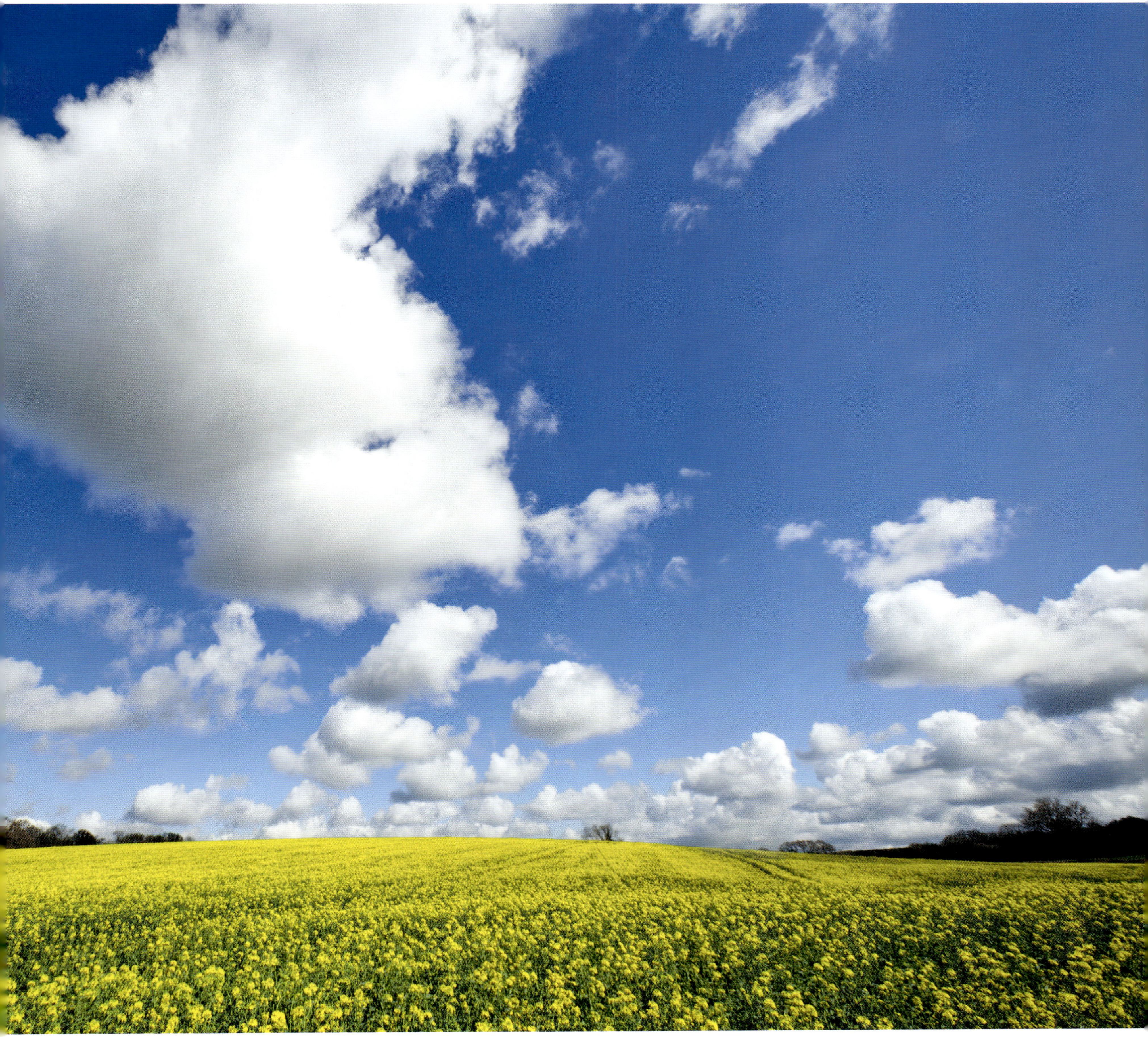

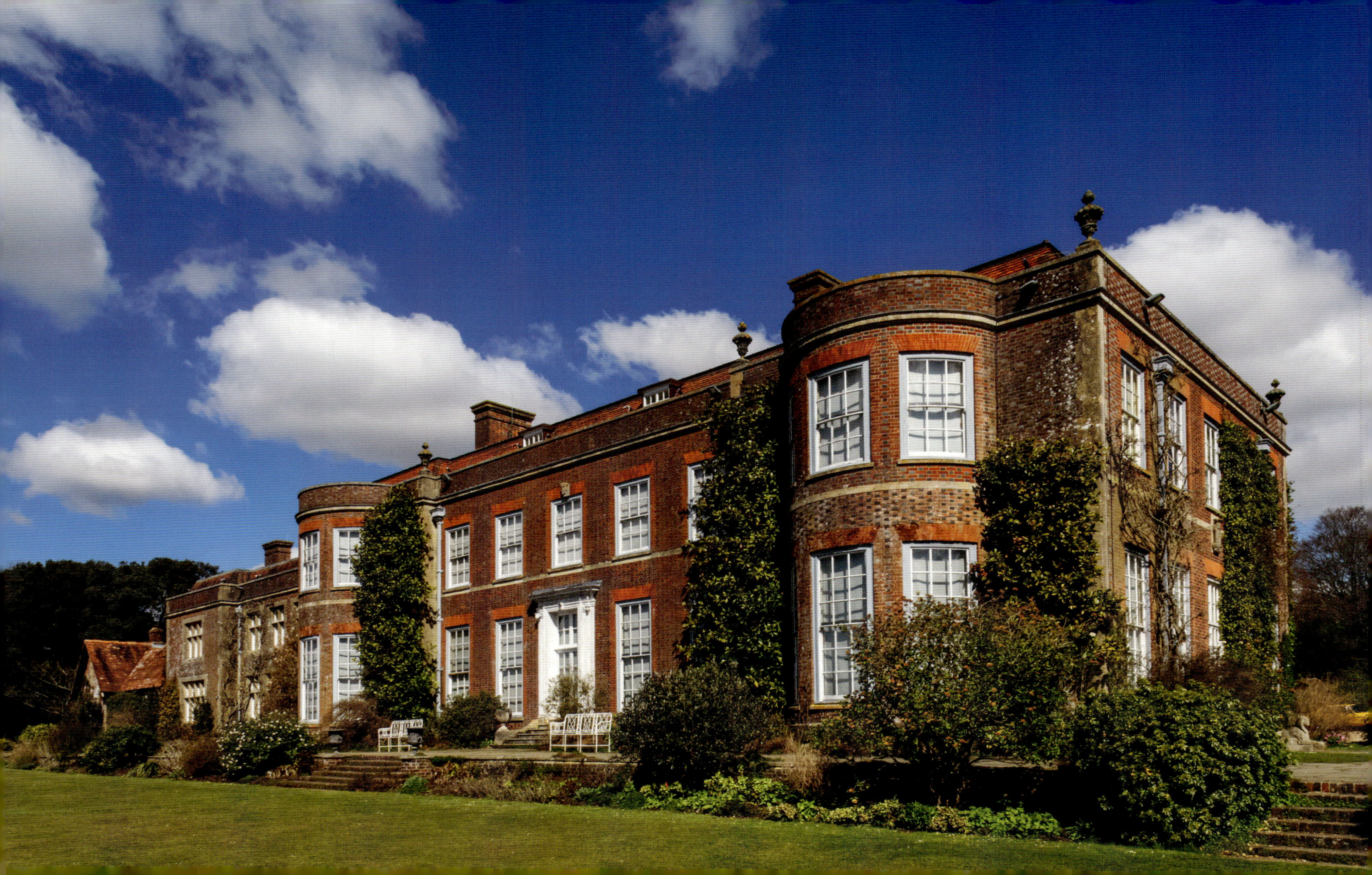

As well as being the name of the village, Hinton Ampner is also a country house estate *(left)* owned by the National Trust. The original building on the site was a 16th century manor house but this was demolished in the 1790s, although the stables and parts of the walled garden remain. A Georgian house was built in its place, which was later encased by a Tudor Gothic extension in the 19th century. Further renovations were completed after the Second World War by Ralph Dutton, 8th Baron Sherborne who had inherited the house in 1935. An enthusiast of the Georgian era, he changed the exterior to give a more 18th century look and collected features from the period for the interior. The newly-finished house was badly damaged by fire in 1960 but was rebuilt over the following three years. Dutton gave the estate to the National Trust on his death in 1985.

Clockwise from top left: Staircase. Library, source of the 1960 fire. The Study. The Grounds, with All Saints' Church. Dining Room with Robert Adam ceiling. The Drawing Room.

DEFIBRILLATOR
GILLIE G'S
SALE
Except for loading and unloading

The ancient market town of Petersfield is set in the beautiful countryside of the South Downs National Park. Founded in the 12th century, the town later grew in prosperity due partly to its location at the crossing of busy historic transport routes and it became an important centre for coaches travelling on the London to Portsmouth road.

A variety of fairs and festivals are held throughout the year and the Musical Festival, which takes place in March, dates back to 1901. Petersfield Museum is based in the former Courthouse and focuses on the social history of the town and surrounding area.

Sheep Street *(left)* is located just off the market square and a blue plaque *(bottom right)* marks a house which has had several notable owners, including John Small who was a 19th century cricketer. An 18th century statue of King William III *(top right)* by Henry Cheere stands in The Square and a more recent addition to the town's public art is a sculpture of a shepherd *(middle right)* by Andy Cheese which is in the Rams Walk shopping centre.

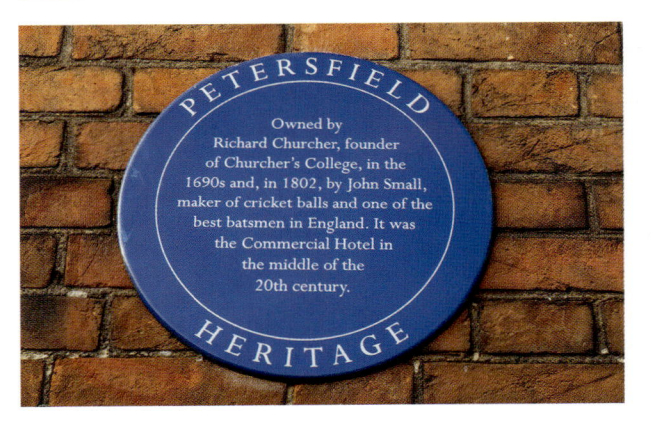

109

raditional Farmin
armony with Na
millfa
Rump
Sirloin
fillet
fore Rib
Rolled Backrib
Neck Clod
Topside
Silverside
Thick flank
Hindquarter flank
Thick Rib
Chuck steak
Braising steak
Skirt
Shin
leg
Brisket
Mill Farm Organic
Quality Beef, Lamb and Pork
BONELESS CHUMP CHOPS
SIRLOIN STEAK

A traditional town market is held in The Square at Petersfield every Wednesday and Saturday and there are also a variety of specialist and seasonal markets throughout the year. The Farmers' Market takes place on the first Sunday of the month and showcases seasonal produce grown locally in the county.

COURTYARD GA
Fowler &Smith
No 32
BROAD
STREET
ALRESFORD
Fowler &Smith
are
Open
Please come in

Our circuit of the heart of Hampshire ends in the town of New Alresford, also known simply as Alresford, with its attractive pastel houses and range of independent shops. Following major fires in the 17th century, much of the town had to be rebuilt, resulting in the elegant Georgian buildings seen today. There are a number of illustrated boards dotted about the town which tell of its history and the 'Millennium Trail' is a self-guided walk that links all these together.

Famous for its production of watercress *(bottom right)*, Alresford has been called the watercress capital of England and a festival to celebrate this peppery-flavoured plant is held on the third Sunday in May.

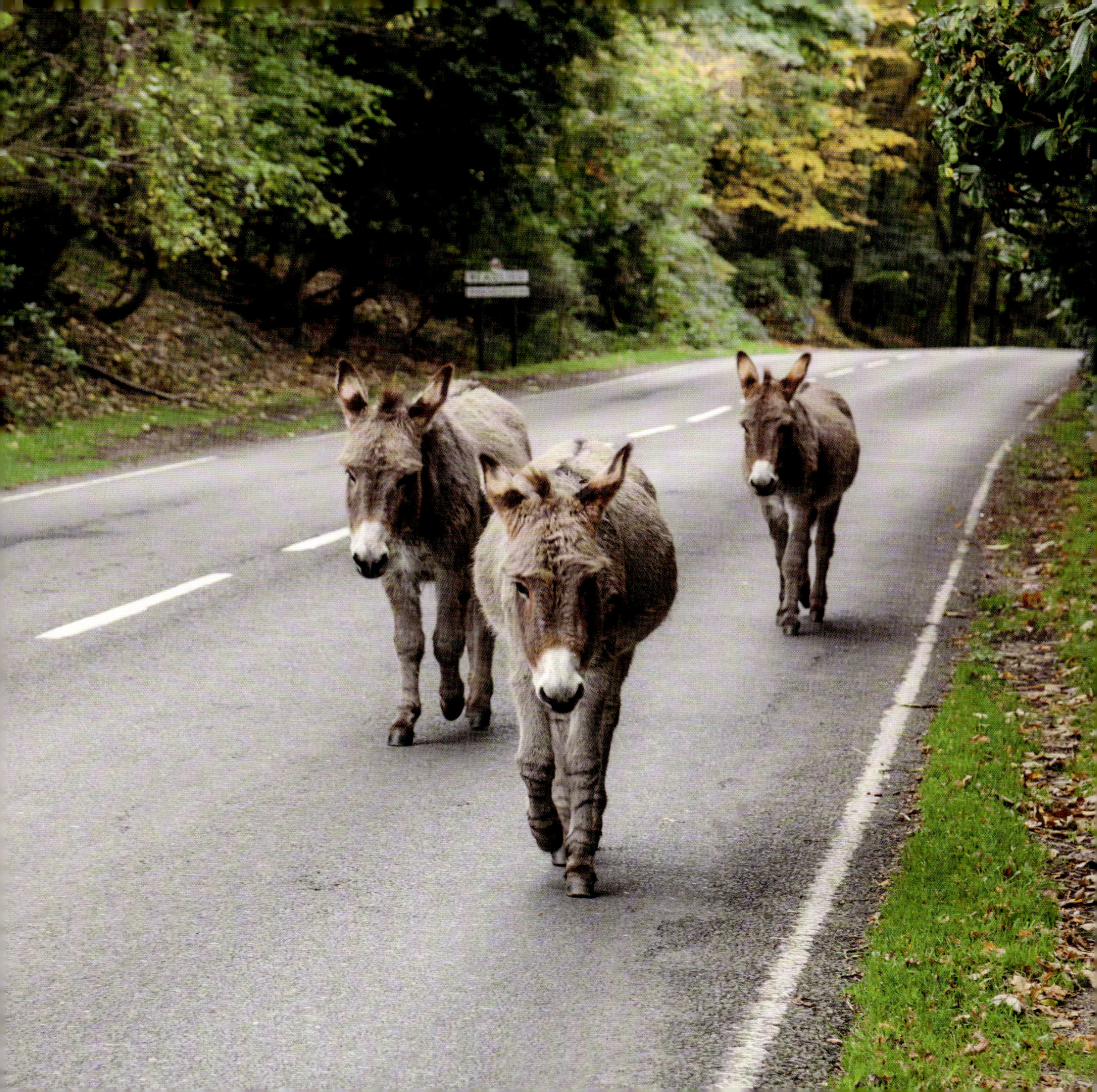

NATURE UNTETHERED

The New Forest is an important area of unenclosed heath, woodland and pasture situated predominantly in the southwest of Hampshire. In 2005, more than 550 square kilometres of this land was designated as a National Park, seen as important to national heritage and deserving of special protection.

William the Conqueror proclaimed the area a royal forest in 1079 and it was recorded in the Domesday Book of 1086 as *Nova Foresta*. William was a keen huntsman and introduced a strict system of Forest Law to protect the vegetation and the animals he wanted to chase for sport. This prevented the local inhabitants, or commoners, from fencing their lands. In return, they were given the right to graze their animals freely.

The ponies, donkeys and other livestock that can be seen roaming the New Forest today not only attract tourists in their own right but, by grazing the land, they also help to create the beautiful scenery that surrounds them, as their ancestors have done for 2000 years. Wildlife thrives in the varied habitats and the list of species that can be spotted is extensive, with birds including the Dartford warbler, stonechats and crossbills. The climate is warmer than much of Britain, which makes it appealing to reptiles, including grass snakes, smooth snakes and venomous adders. Fortunately, adders tend to disappear into the undergrowth at the slightest sound of human approach.

In autumn, pigs roam the forest, eating acorns from the forest floor. This is the result of an ancient right known as 'Common of Mast' or pannage, which again dates to the time of William I.

The unique environment of the New Forest has inspired writers and artists over the centuries, with many visiting or living here to create their work. Sir Arthur Conan Doyle is famous for his Sherlock Holmes novels but also wrote other adventure novels, including *The White Company*, which tells of a band of archers in the Hundred Year's War and is partly set in the forest. Conan Doyle bought a second home in Minstead, near Lyndhurst, towards the end of his life and is buried in the local graveyard.

The girl who was the inspiration for Alice in Lewis Carroll's, *Alice's Adventures in Wonderland* and *Alice Through the Looking Glass*, moved to a country estate near Lyndhurst in the 1880s after her marriage. Her full name was Alice Pleasance Liddell and she is buried at St Michael and all Angels church in Lyndhurst.

Augustus John was already a well-known artist when he moved to a house near Fordingbridge in 1927. He worked here until his death in 1961 and a bronze statue in the town celebrates his link to the neighbourhood.

The long history of the New Forest has evoked a number of spooky tales, with the ancient woodland, quaint pubs and long-ruined abbeys providing perfect backdrops for the stories. Palace House and the ruined Beaulieu Abbey are a particular hotspot and there have been many reports of ghostly monks and unexplained wafts of incense.

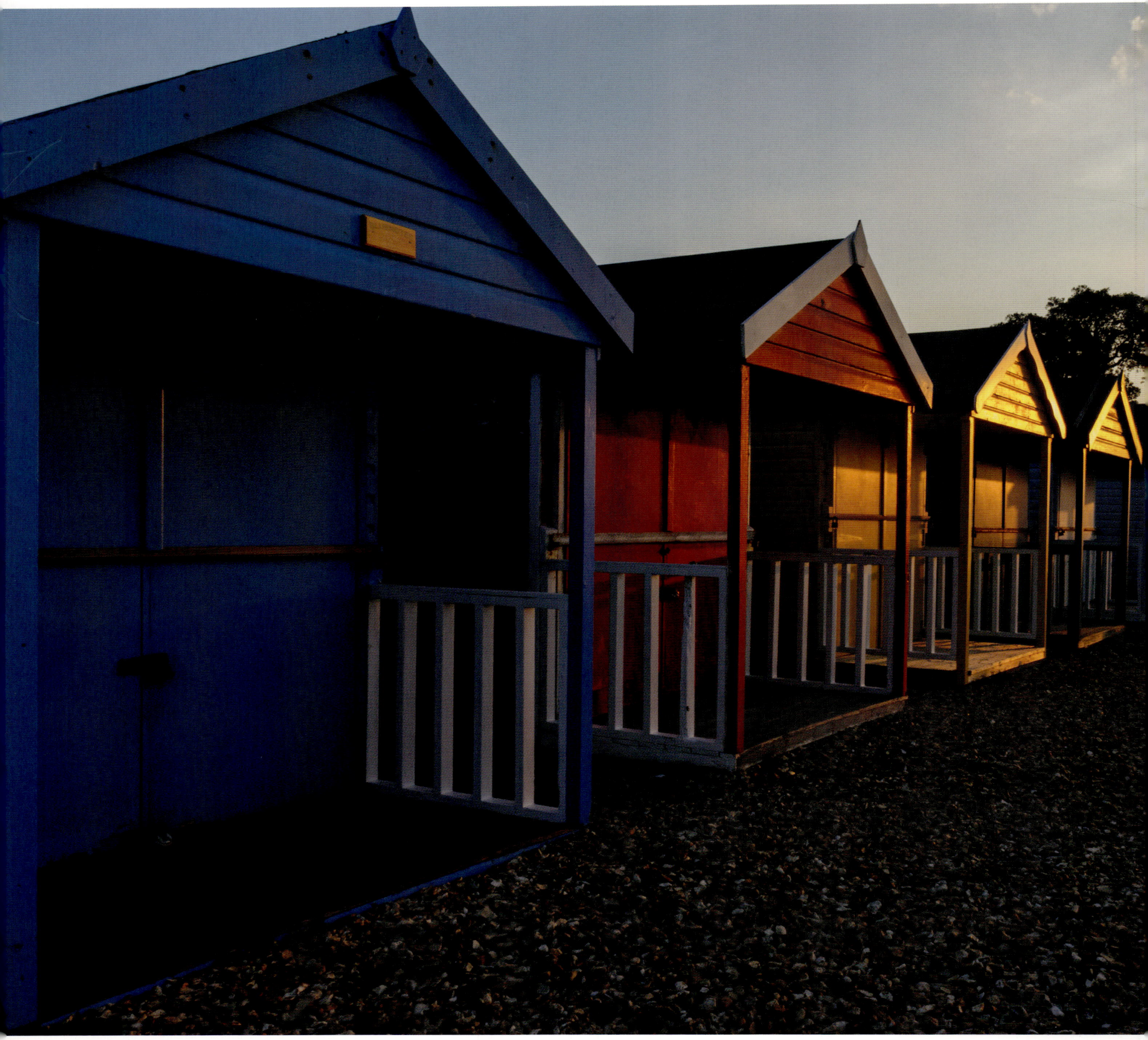

Overlooking the Solent and at the south-eastern corner of the New Forest National Park is the coastal village of Calshot. The beach *(left & bottom right)* is part of a shingle spit that stretches for a mile out into the mouth of Southampton Water. A big activities centre is located here, based within a World War II hangar that originally housed flying boats for the Calshot Naval Air Station, and this offers cycling and climbing facilities, as well as water sports. The famous international race for seaplanes, the Schneider Trophy, was held at Calshot in 1929 and 1931, with the winners achieving average speeds of around 340mph.

At the end of the spit is Calshot Castle *(below & bottom left)*, an artillery fort constructed on the orders of Henry VIII in 1539. Its original role was to guard against possible invasion from mainland Europe and the castle remained as a defensive stronghold for many years. It finally closed in 1961, after being used as a Navy and RAF base, but was later placed in the care of English Heritage and now opens to visitors in the summer months.

117

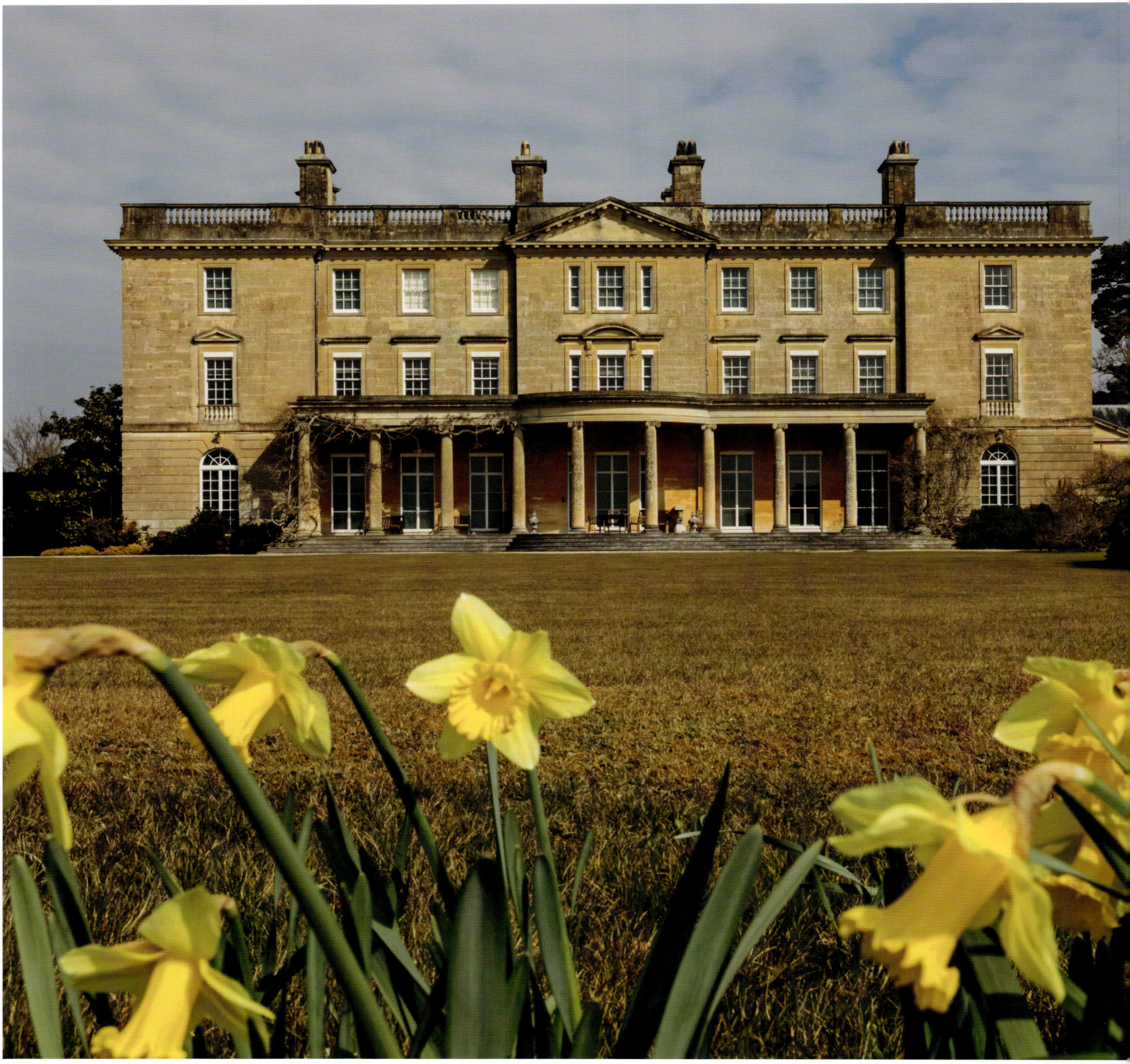

A few miles to the west and on the banks of the Beaulieu River is the Exbury Estate, which was bought by Lionel de Rothschild in 1919.

It was Lionel's vision and passion that created one of the finest woodland gardens in Britain. He also had the necessary resources, employing around 250 men to prepare the woodland for the laying of paths and for the new planting. It was a time of great global discovery, with seeds of exotic plant types being brought from remote locations, so many species had not been seen before. The beautiful gardens *(left)* open to visitors from March to November and the specialist collections of rhododendrons and azaleas are a big draw in the spring.

The 18th century core of the current Exbury House *(far left)* was refaced in Neoclassical style in the 1920s *(left)*. During World War II, it was requisitioned by the Royal Navy and became a headquarters for the Normandy Invasion but was subsequently returned to the Rothschild family and is now occupied as a private residence.

Originally laid out between 1919 and 1939, Exbury Gardens cover around 200 acres and have been open to the public since the mid-1950s. A half mile trail, the New River Walk, is a feature that has recently been added to the gardens and provides viewing points where visitors can watch the wildlife on the tidal flats of the estuary.

There are various ponds *(right)* and water features within the gardens that reflect the changing colours of the surrounding vegetation throughout the seasons. One of these has recently been adapted to encourage dragonflies and was officially opened by naturalist, Nick Baker, in 2021. A narrow-gauge steam railway *(above)* loops around the northern end of the estate.

121

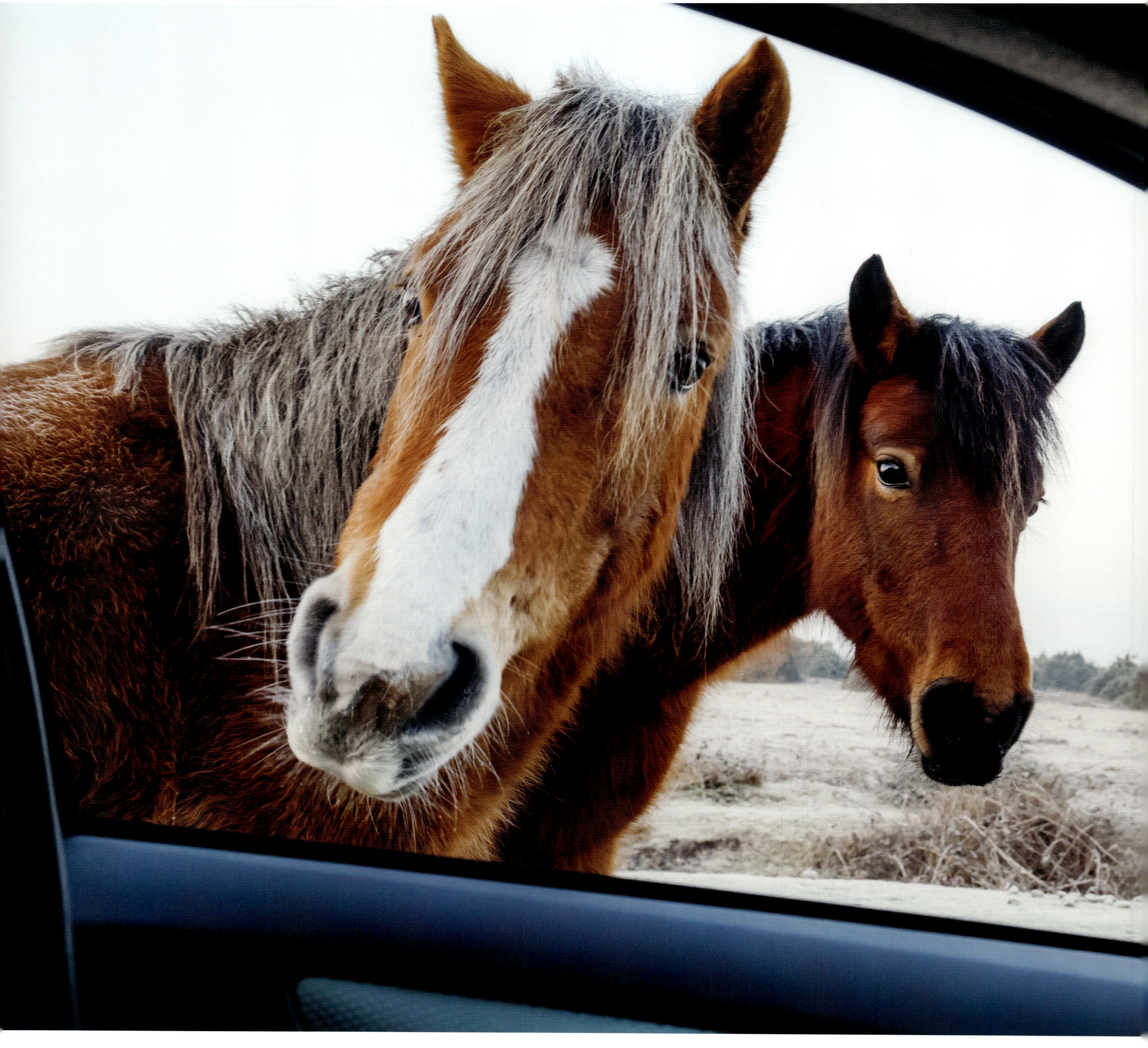

One of the main places within the National Park to see New Forest Ponies is near Beaulieu, where they are a frequent sight grazing by the roadside. They are not to be fed or touched but are a highlight enjoyed by visitors from around the world.

Although they roam freely, they do have owners and are regularly rounded up in what are called 'drifts', so that they can be checked to ensure they are in good health. Pony sales are held in Beaulieu throughout the year and the gentle temperament and intelligence of the breed, as well as their sure-footedness, makes them popular for riding.

Beaulieu is also famous as being home to the National Motor Museum, which has one of the world's finest collections of cars, motorbikes and associated memorabilia. Edward, 3rd Baron Montagu of Beaulieu, founded the museum in 1952. It was a tribute to his father who had been a pioneer of motoring in Britain.

From small beginnings, when the cars were displayed in the front hall of his home, Palace House, the collection eventually moved to a purpose-built museum in the grounds, which opened in 1972. There are now around 250 vehicles plus changing exhibitions of cars from TV and film.

Right: AEC Regent MkIII RT London Transport bus (1950) and three-wheeled BMW Isetta 300 Super Plus from 1962, which has appeared on *Top Gear*.

SHELL
SHELL
ICA
SERVICE BAY
SHELL LUBRICATION
WOADCORNER
SUPER SHELL
SUPER SHELL
SHELL
SHELL
SHELL OILS
2T
MICHELIN
518 ELT

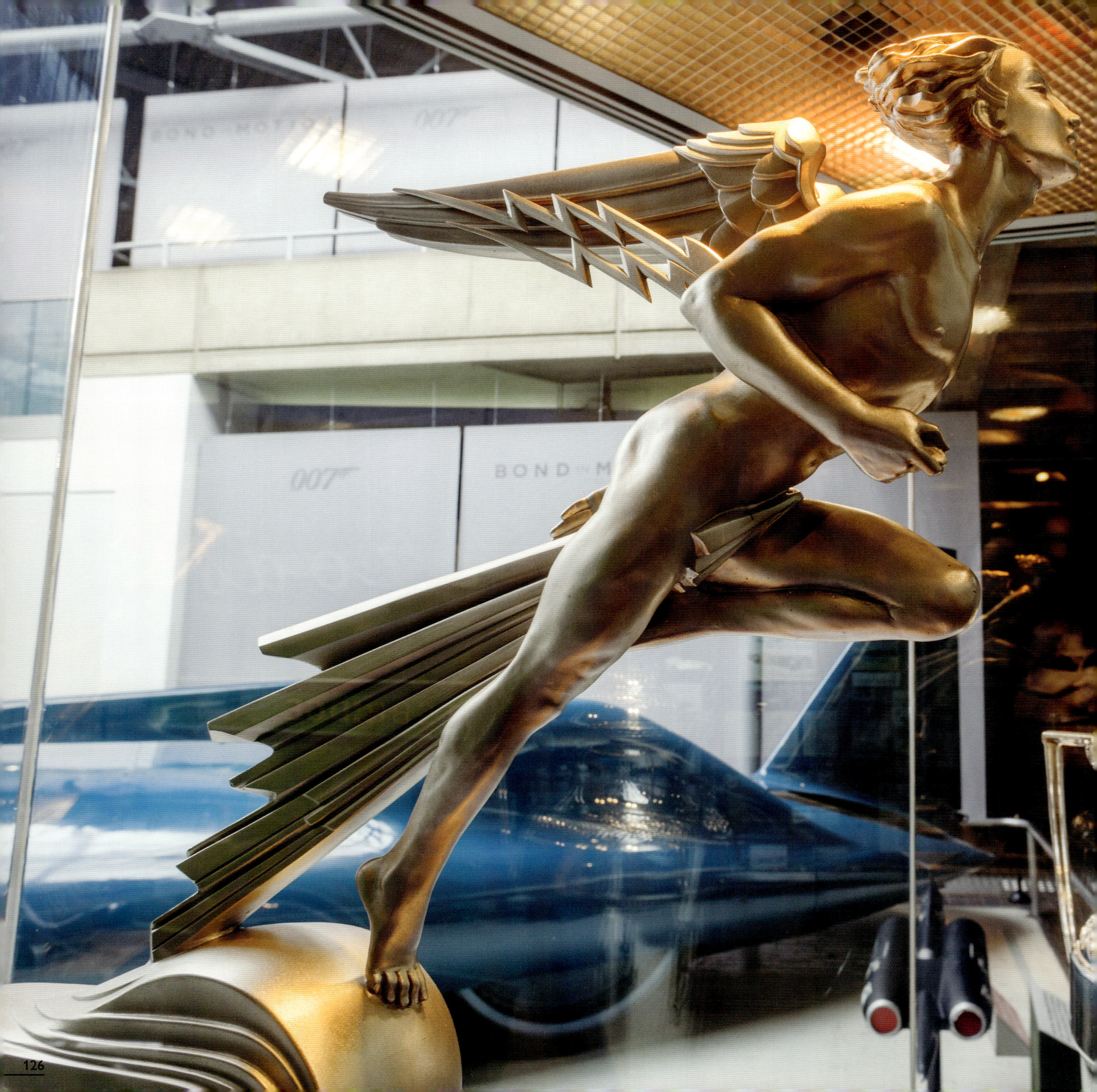
007
BOND

The vast collection of automotive memorabilia in the National Motor Museum's collection includes the Wakefield Trophy *(left)*, which was presented to Henry Segrave in 1929 by Sir Charles Wakefield. Designed by Phoebe Stabler, it depicts Jupiter holding a lightning bolt and marked Segrave's achievement of driving Golden Arrow to reach a record-breaking speed of 231.45 mph in March 1929 at Daytona Beach in Florida. The car had less than 20 miles on the clock when used to set the record and is now in the collection at Beaulieu.

Another man famous for breaking speed records was Donald Campbell and visitors to the museum can see the Proteus Bluebird CN7 *(above)*, a gas-turbine powered car that carried Campbell to the world land speed record in 1964. The car had been badly damaged on a previous attempt in Utah in 1960 but was rebuilt with some modifications and eventually succeeded in reaching speeds of over 400 mph at Lake Eyre in Australia.

128

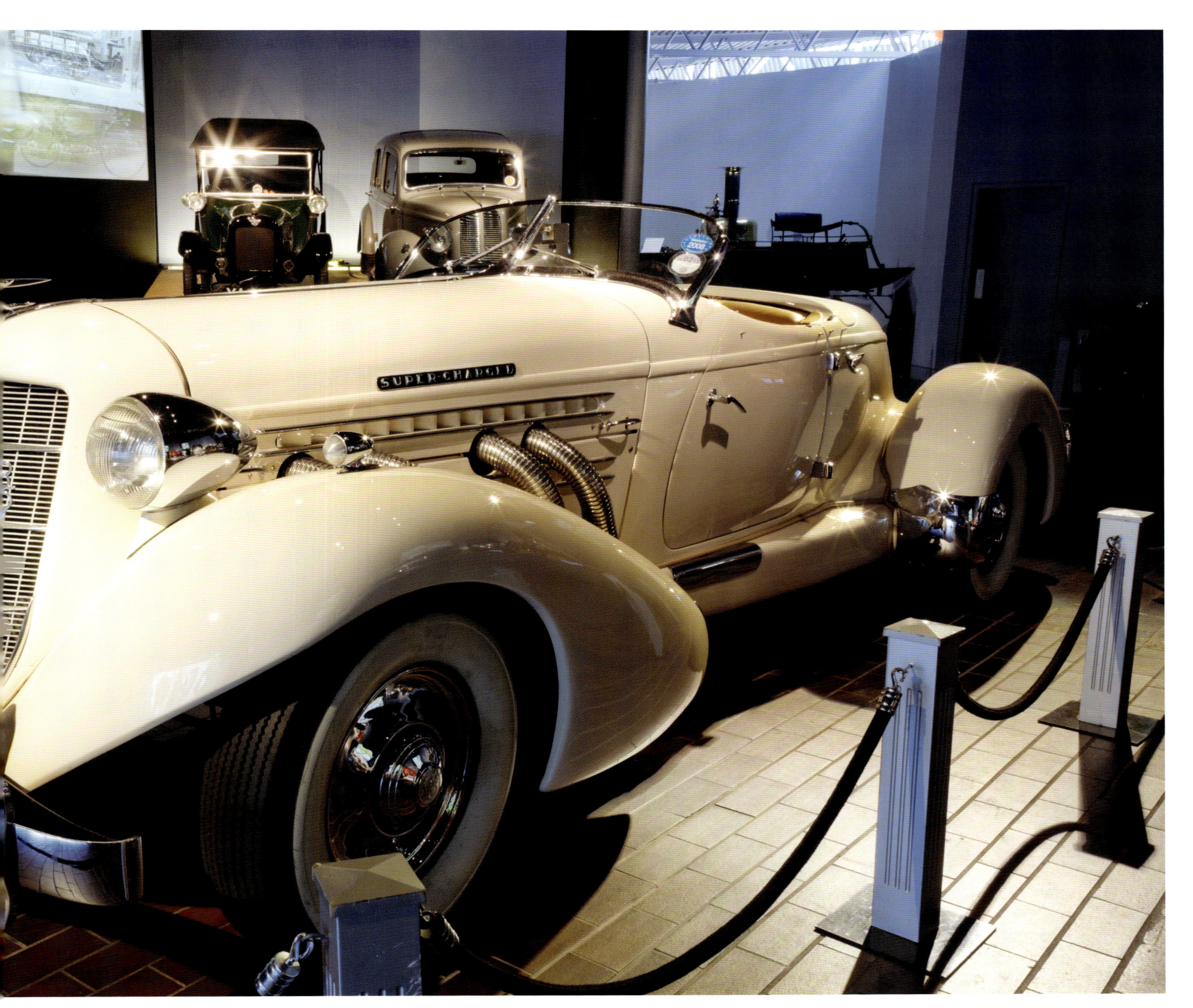

The collection at the National Motor Museum includes cars dating from the earliest days of motoring through to a range of Formula One cars relying on the very latest technology (p.128). A monorail at the museum is the oldest in England and was moved to Beaulieu in 1974. Running for a mile, it offers passengers high level views of the grounds before passing through the roof of the museum, with views over the vehicles below. Visitors can also explore the wider Beaulieu Estate, including Palace House and the early 13th century ruins of Beaulieu Abbey. *Above:* American Auburn 851 Speedster from 1935.

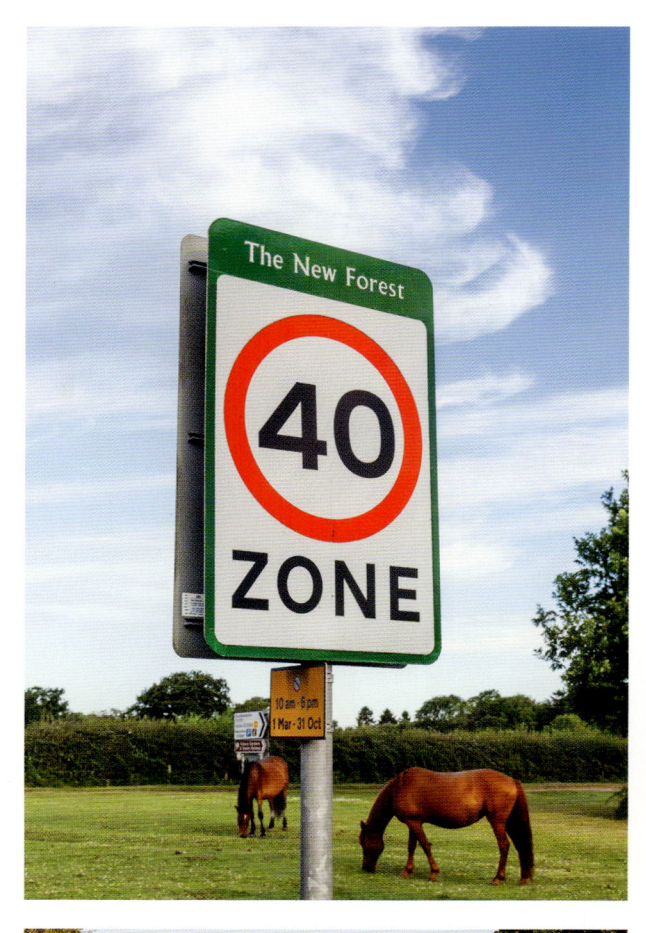

The village of Beaulieu is situated at the head of the tidal Beaulieu River and is largely unspoilt. It has been listed as one of Britain's most attractive villages and initially grew up around the Cistercian Abbey from which it takes its name. The word Beaulieu means 'beautiful place' and, although not large, the village is popular with tourists. The charming high street has some interesting independent shops, including the Beaulieu Chocolate Studio which continues a local tradition of chocolate making.

As well as New Forest ponies, the National Park is also home to several hundred donkeys, and they are often seen strolling along the streets of Beaulieu *(p.131 bottom middle)*.

pp.114, 130-131: Beaulieu and surrounding area.

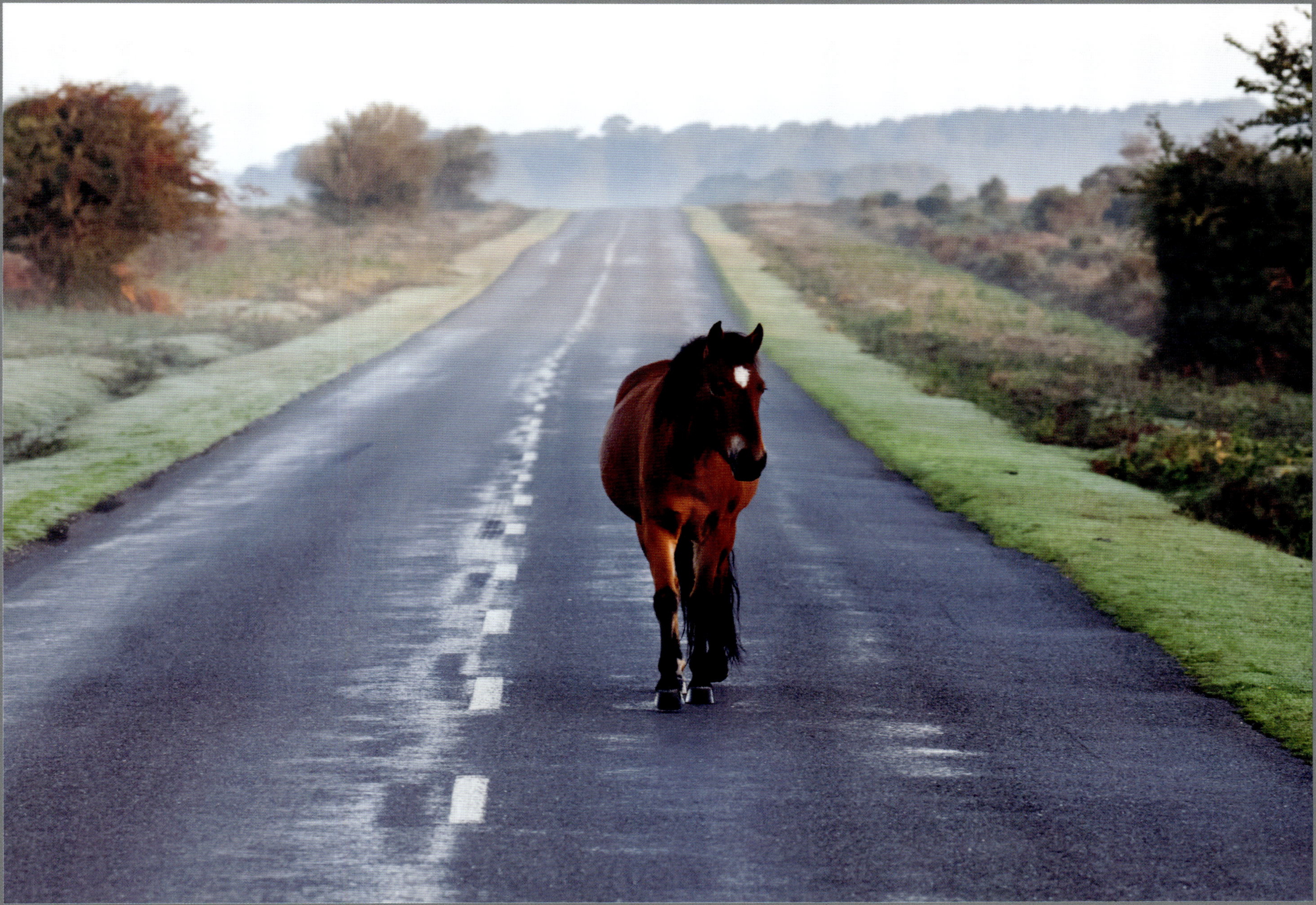

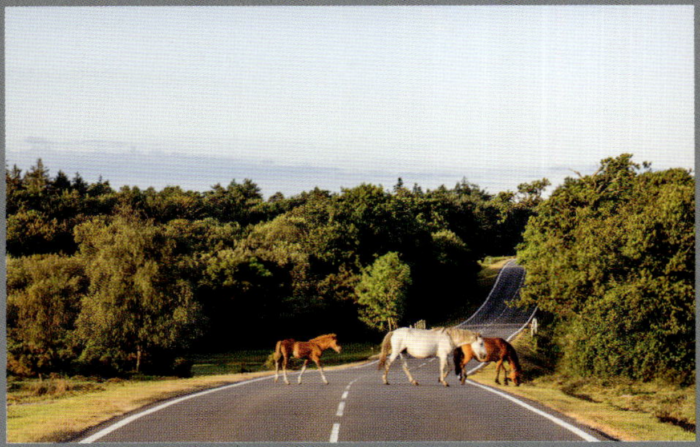

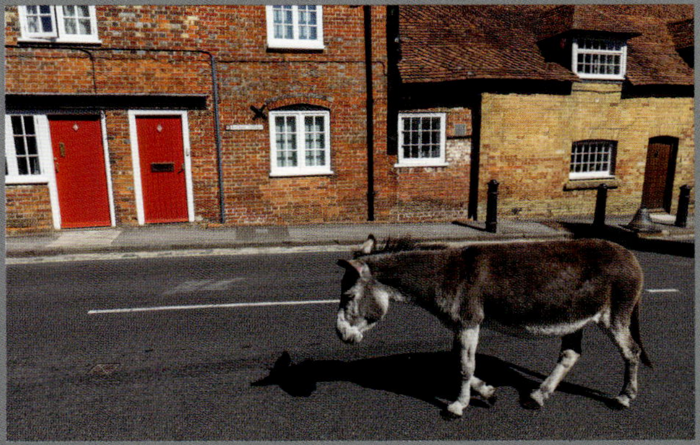

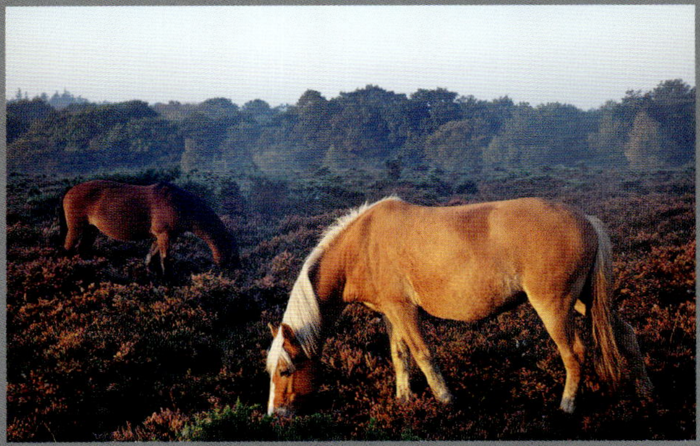

Two miles downstream and an enjoyable stroll along the Beaulieu River path, is Buckler's Hard. Sitting on the west bank of the river, this village has two attractive rows of Georgian cottages that run down towards the water *(top left & above left)*. Its location made it suitable for shipbuilding, which developed from the early 18th century. Many ships were built here including more than forty for the Royal Navy, three of which saw action at the Battle of Trafalgar. Today, visitors are attracted to this picturesque haven, with its Maritime Museum *(above top right & right)* and yacht harbour *(above right)*.

133

Jack & the Wolfe
Antique
Sales
and
QUAY POINT
QUAY POINT
STARBOARD HOME

At the southern edge of the New Forest and looking out to Hampshire's south coast is the pretty market town and port of Lymington. Evidence of settlement nearby dates back to the Iron Age, with Lymington itself beginning as a village in the Anglo-Saxon era.

The town was given its first charter and the right to hold a market in the 13th century and a bustling street market still fills the Georgian High Street on Saturdays. Tourists are attracted to the area around the cobbled Quay Hill, which is home to a range of gift shops, boutiques and brasseries. Adjoining this is Lymington Quay Side, where many sit to watch the boats go by or venture out on a cruise to the Needles or Yarmouth on the Isle of Wight. The town is an important yachting centre with three marinas.

A few miles to the west of Lymington is the large coastal village of Milford-on-Sea, which has a population of around 4700. Although the village's sea air and relaxed atmosphere make it popular with those of retirement age, the summer months attract visitors keen to enjoy the beautiful beach *(above)*, where they can swim, surf and paddleboard. There are good views of the Needles and the Isle of Wight from the western cliffs.

At the centre of the village is a green surrounded by picturesque houses, independent shops and places to eat and drink. A May Day festival takes place over the holiday weekend each year and a Music and Arts Festival follows in the summer. The oldest building in Milford-on-Sea is All Saint's Church, which was largely built in the 13th century. Rumour has it that the window on the south side was used to smuggle beer to the bellringers.

Right: Traditional signpost on the green.

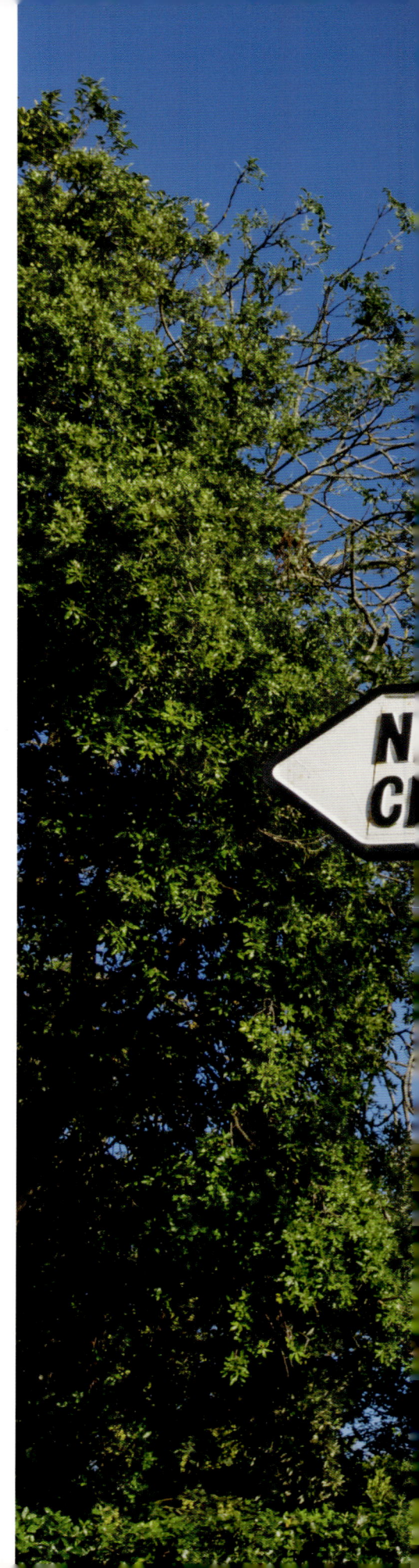

HAMPSHIRE
MILFORD ON SEA
MILTON 3
STCHURCH 9½
LYMINGTON 3½
SOUTHAMPTON 21½

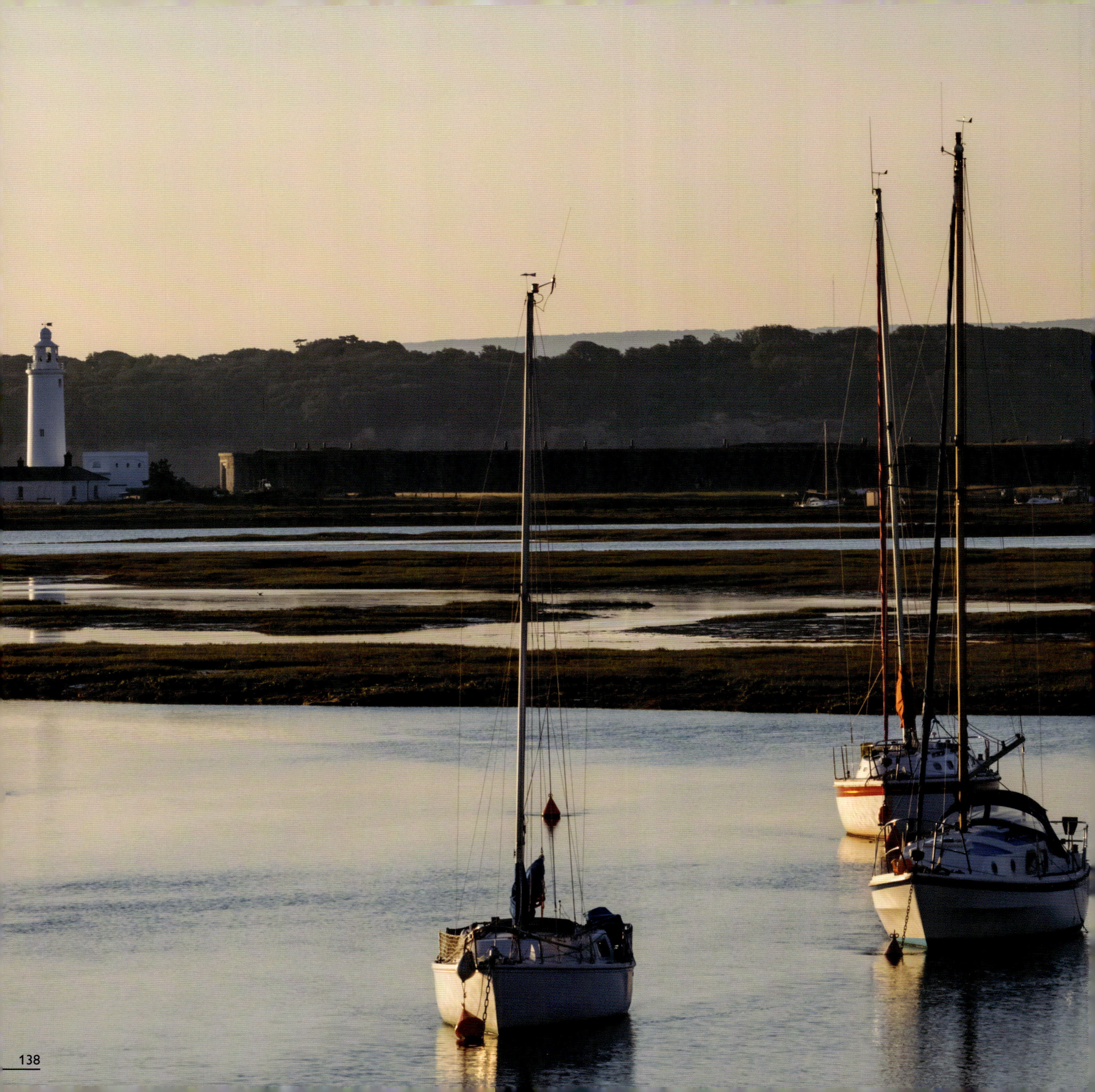

A two mile walk eastwards from Milford-on-Sea leads to the artillery fort of Hurst Castle, which stands alongside Hurst Point Lighthouse at the far end of the shingle spit. For those wishing to avoid the shingle walk, a relaxing ferry ride from nearby Keyhaven offers opportunities to see wildlife on the varied habitats of the surrounding marshes.

By the 18th century, this section of the coast had become a leading centre for salt production, with a line of saltworks stretching from Lymington to Hurst Spit. The industry had started to decline by the end of the century but much of the reclaimed land is now protected as a nature reserve, which provides a habitat for important bird populations and rare plants.

As with the castle at Calshot, Hurst Castle was built on the orders of Henry VIII and was one of his Device Forts and part of his defence programme. Being only a mile from Fort Albert on the Isle of Wight as the crow flies, it offers stunning views along the south coast and across to the island.

Originally built in the 1540s, the castle was modernised in the 1860s, with two armoured wing batteries being added to the east and west. It formed part of Britain's network of defences during both World Wars. Coastal erosion has been an increasing problem for the castle structure and a section of wall on the east wing collapsed in February 2021. Major works were required to prevent further damage and to stabilise this section.

Hurst Point Lighthouse has been guiding vessels through the Solent since it was built in 1867 but is not the first or only lighthouse on the site, although it is the only one that remains in active use.

The original lighthouse was first lit in 1786 but was obscured from some angles, so was joined by a second structure in 1812. Together, they became known as the Low Lighthouse and the High Lighthouse. Following the expansion of the castle in the 1860s, these two lighthouses were rebuilt in different positions. Then, in 1911, the Low Light was left in situ but joined by a new replacement structure.

These two Low Lights can be seen within the West Wing of Hurst Castle, although they are no longer in use *(far left)*.

The still-operational High Light is now called Hurst Point Lighthouse *(right & below)*.

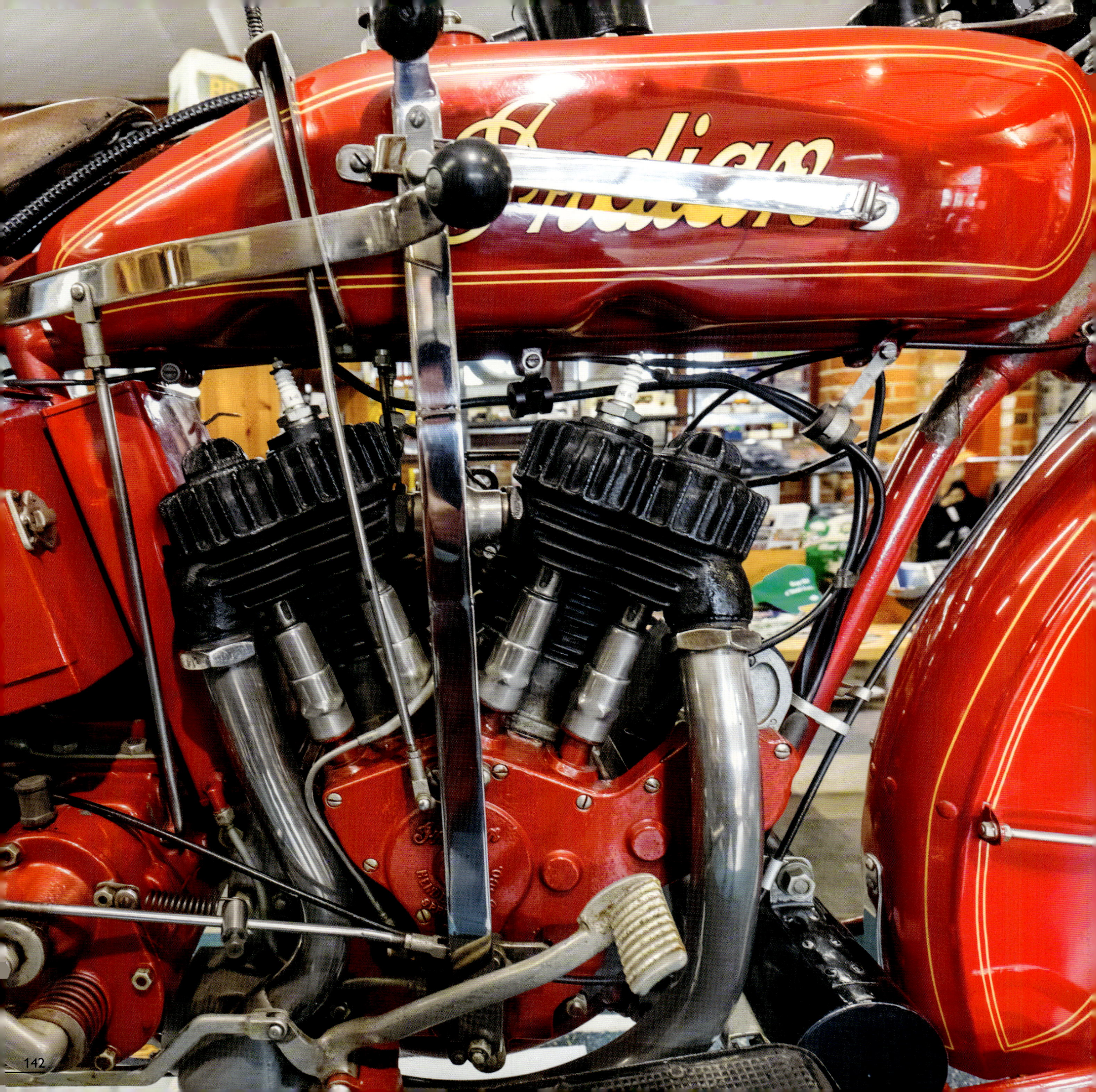
Indian

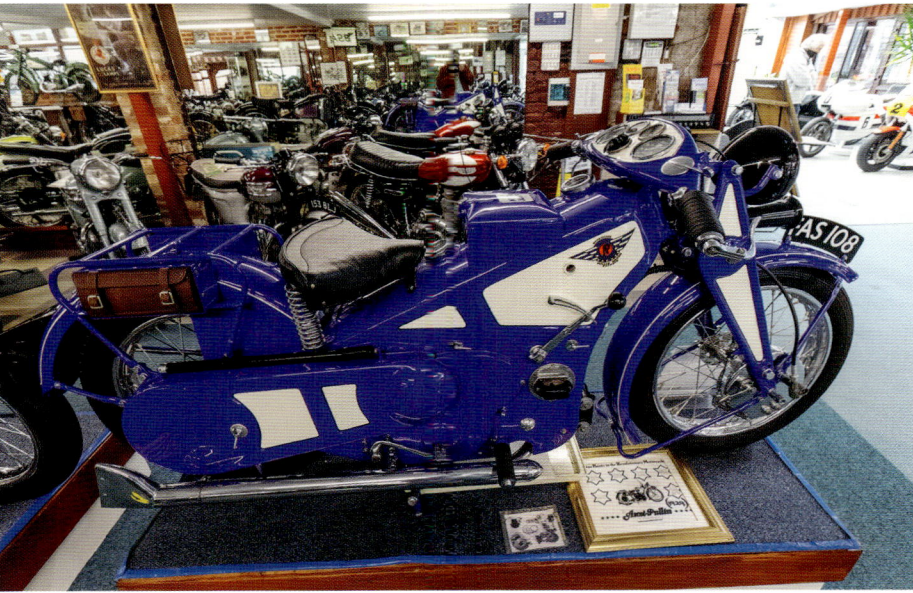

West of Milford-on-Sea is the town of New Milton, home to the Sammy Miller Motorcycle Museum. Sammy Miller MBE is a championship motorcycle rider, with a successful career that has spanned many decades. After setting up his own motorcycle parts business in 1964, he had a few of his racing bikes in the corner and this small collection eventually evolved into a museum that has recently been extended and now houses more than 450 machines, with new models being added regularly. Nearly all the bikes are fully operational and there are demonstrations throughout the year.

144

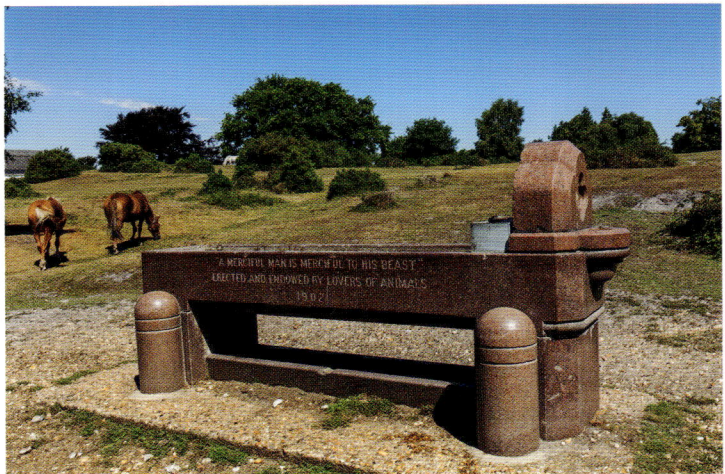

The large, bustling village of Lyndhurst *(left)* is known as the capital of the New Forest and is its administrative centre. At the heart of the village is the New Forest Heritage Centre, which includes a museum, gallery and shop all providing information about the area and how best to enjoy it.

The High Street has a range of independent stores and a popular antiques centre *(top)*, which is home to multiple independent dealers and has two floors to explore. Nearby is the church of St Michael and All Angels, which has stained glass windows by William Morris and Edward Burne-Jones. The small, yew-topped hill of Bolton's Bench just to the east of the village is a well-known landmark that offers views back to the church.

A stone water trough *(above)* at nearby Parc Pale has provided water for the New Forest Ponies since 1902.

Ringwood is a town on the western edge of the New Forest that stands by the River Avon. There has been a weekly market here since the 13th century and this takes place every Wednesday. Nearby is the Furlong Shopping Centre, which is home to independent shops and cafes as well as big name brands that surround a courtyard where music and community events are held.

The Church of St Peter and St Paul *(left)* was rebuilt in the 19th century and contains some notable architectural features and fine stained-glass windows *(far left & right)*.

Below: The Old Cottage Restaurant and The Fish Inn, both in West Street.

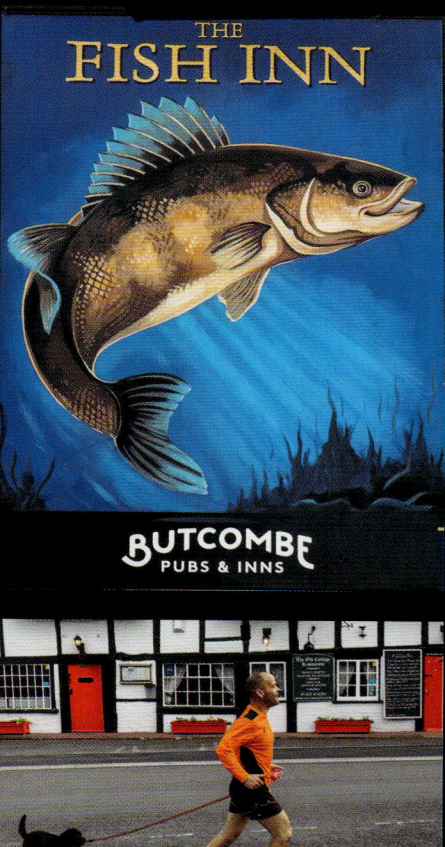

HOLY · HOLY · HOLY

Due north of Ringwood is the town of Fordingbridge, which is also by the River Avon in the west of the county. The town gets its name from the Great Bridge (right), which has seven arches and dates to the medieval period. Sections of the river are popular with anglers getting to grips with the finer points of fly-fishing, while the riverside pub offers respite for those who would rather watch than wade.

The Rufus Stone (below) is found ten miles to the east of Fordingbridge and commemorates the day, in 1100, when King William II was killed by an arrow which possibly glanced off a tree during a hunt.

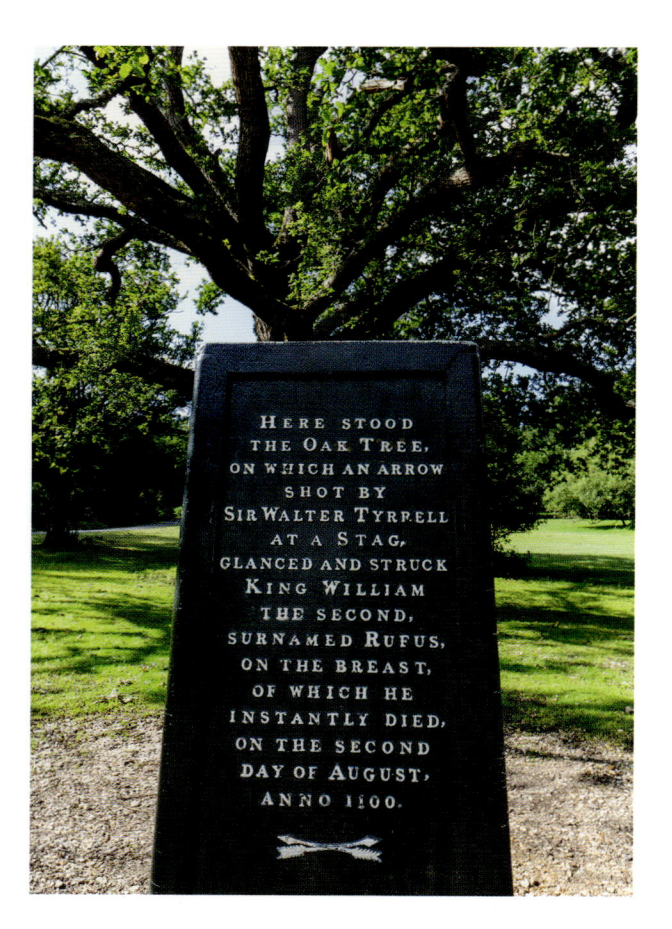

149

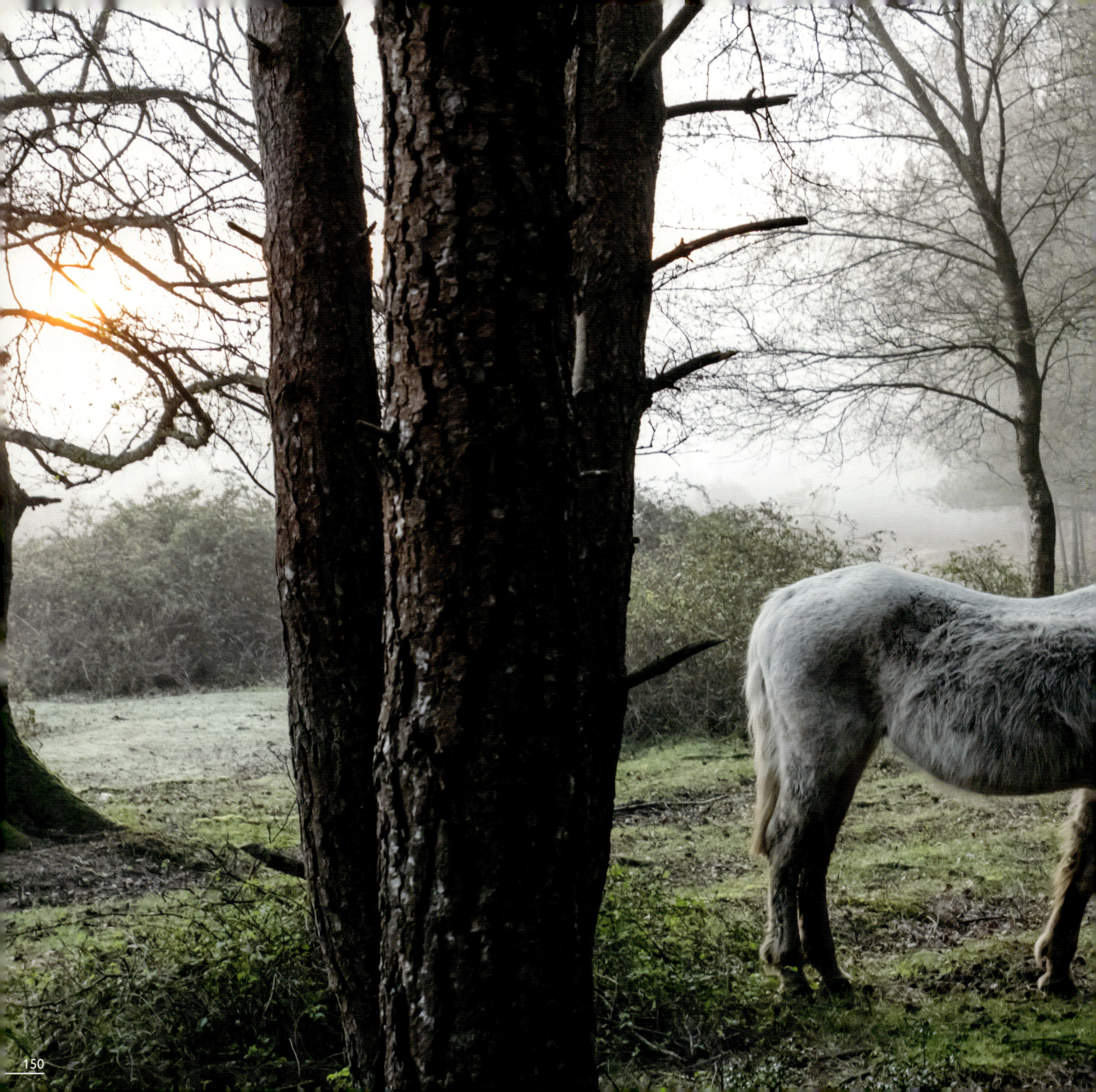

A number of walking paths lead into the New Forest from the Rufus Stone and the Sir Walter Tyrrell Pub is nearby. This is named after an Anglo-Norman nobleman, who is supposed to have been the man who fired the fatal arrow that killed the King. He subsequently fled to Normandy as he feared repercussions. Legend has it that he stopped en route to get his horse reshod with shoes that faced the wrong way, so that he could not be tracked. There has been much debate amongst chroniclers over the centuries as to how much of an accident it actually was and whether Sir Walter was responsible – William was not a popular monarch.

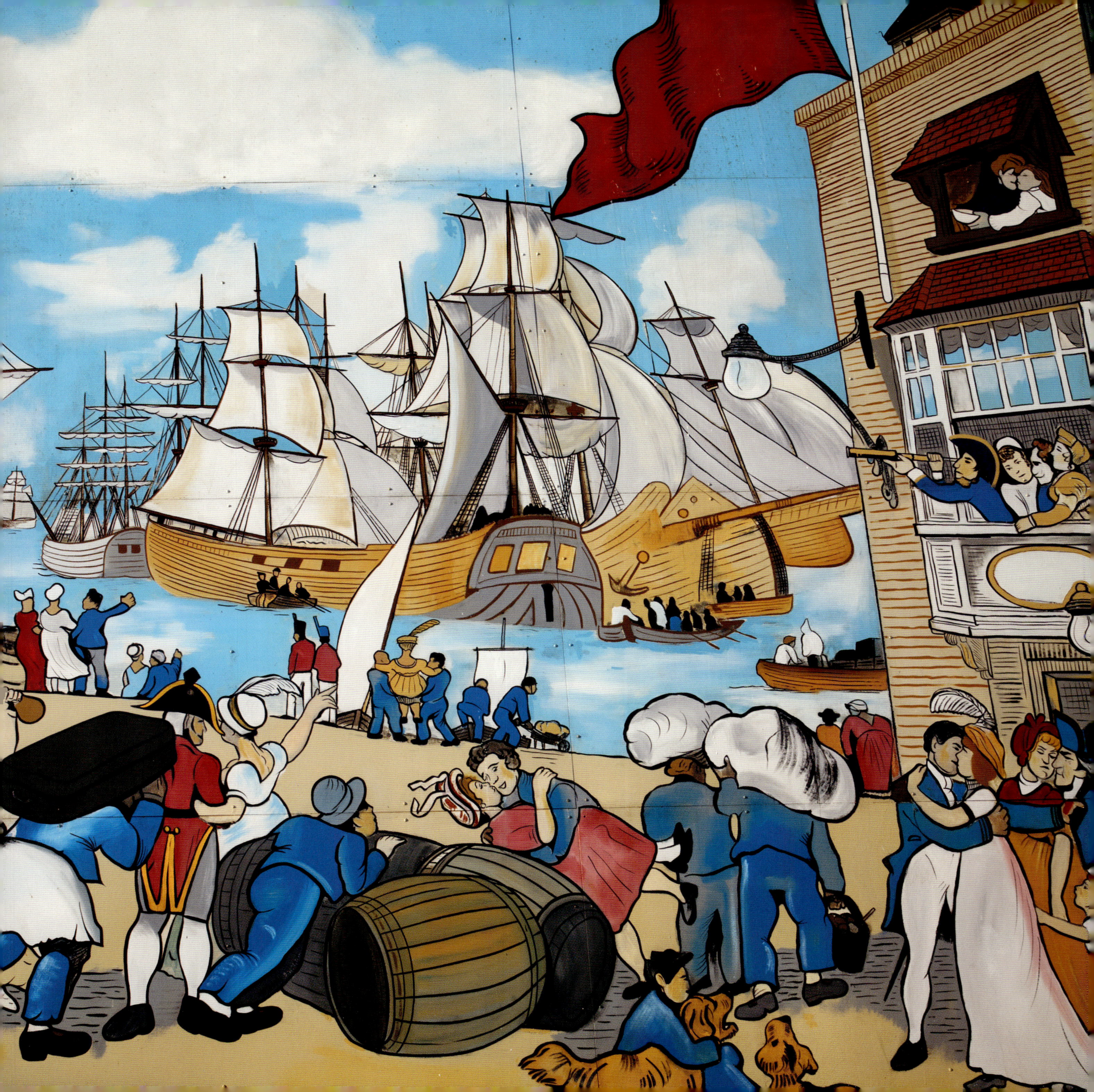

MAGNIFICENT MARITIME

Hampshire's coastline stretches from Chichester Harbour in the east to Highcliffe in the west and has an estimated length of 370 kilometres. As well as the coastal cities of Portsmouth and Southampton, there are nature reserves, beautiful beaches and historic forts to discover.

The character of the coastline is shaped by its location on the Solent, a major shipping lane that runs between Hampshire and the Isle of Wight. Originally a river valley that widened and deepened over many thousands of years, the Solent is now a relatively shallow stretch of tidal water that separates the Isle of Wight from the mainland.

The main two settlements along the coast, Portsmouth and Southampton, both have a population in excess of 200,000, with Southampton being the larger of the two. Portsmouth holds the accolade of being home to the football team who were FA Cup Champions for the longest time, a result of the outbreak of World War II. The cup was presented to Portsmouth as winning team in 1939 but the competition was not held again until 1946. The cup had to be kept safely for the duration of the war and moved around the city before arriving at the Bird in Hand pub in Lovedean, where it was displayed behind the bar by day and moved to a safe haven under the landlord's bed each night.

According to Ordnance Survey, Hampshire has one of the highest numbers of museums outside London, with around fifty to visit. Some, including Jane Austen's House and Gilbert White's House, tell the story of a famous resident, while others focus on the county's strong links with the military. The variety is wide and many a happy day can be spent discovering the fascinating stories they tell.

Ordnance Survey has a long history in the county having been based in Southampton since the 1840s, when a fire in the Tower of London caused the organisation to seek a new home outside the capital. After many years in The Avenue building, they moved to Maybush in 1969 before relocating to their current, purpose-built premises to the west of the city centre. Opened by Prince Philip in 2011, this is used by around 1000 employees and has been nominated for a number of architectural awards. After each move, more work is created as local maps have to be redrawn to show the position of the new headquarters.

Hampshire's coast has a long history of famous residents, with Portsmouth being the birthplace of both Charles Dickens and Isambard Kingdom Brunel. Dickens spent the first few years of his life in the house that is now 393 Commercial Street, and this family home is now a museum.

The sheltered nature of Hampshire's coast makes it one of the warmest and sunniest in Britain. Southampton has held the record for the warmest June temperature since 1976, with thermometers rising to a scorching 35.6°C on the 28th of the month.

An important historic feature in Southampton is Bargate (*above & right*), a medieval town gateway that was constructed around 1180 in the reign of Henry II. In the 1960s, it was described by the historian Nikolaus Pevsner as being 'probably the finest, and certainly the most complex, town gateway in Britain'. It was the main north entrance to the town during the Middle Ages and was a toll gate.

Originally just a single-storey tower, the gateway was extended around a hundred years later with the addition of a first floor and two drum towers, before being extended again at the end of the 14th century. Many alterations and restorations have taken place since then, depending on its use. The first floor was the Guildhall for four hundred years and parts of the ground floor have historically served as a prison. A sketch of the gateway, drawn in 1795 by J M W Turner, is held in the Tate Collection.

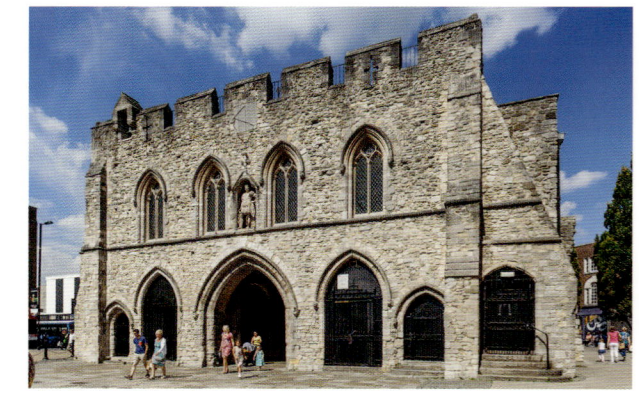

By the end of the 14th century, Southampton was surrounded by defensive walls more than a mile long and, as its name suggests, Westgate (above) was the western entrance into the city. It was important, as it provided access to West Quay which was the main area for maritime activity. Some of the troops from the army of Henry V would have marched through this gate in 1415 on their way to fight in the Battle of Agincourt, as would the Pilgrim Fathers who set sail on the Mayflower in 1620. The gate used to have a portcullis and the grooves it left can still be seen in the stonework.

In the Middle Ages, buildings were sometimes disassembled and rebuilt in a new location. This was the case with Westgate Hall (left), which originally sat nearby at an angle to St Michael's Church. Thought to date from around 1400, it was rebuilt on its current site in the mid-17th century. The hall has recently been restored and is now a venue for weddings, conferences and concerts.

The SeaCity Museum (left) explores the long maritime history of Southampton and tells the stories of its people. There is a strong focus on the RMS Titanic, as the tragic events of 1912 had a devastating effect on the city with more than 500 households losing a family member when the ship sank. A 1:25 scale interactive model of the Titanic shows visitors the detailed layout of the ship.

A painting from 1912 (right), by local man George Fraser, remained unfinished following the disaster. He had seen the ship in dock before she sailed and had planned to add the crowds on the quayside but was too upset to do so.

The museum opened in 2012, marking the 100th anniversary of the Titanic's sailing, and is in a listed Art Deco civic building with the addition of a modern pavilion formed of three interlocking bays.

Bottom left: Model of the RMS Queen Mary.

TITANIC

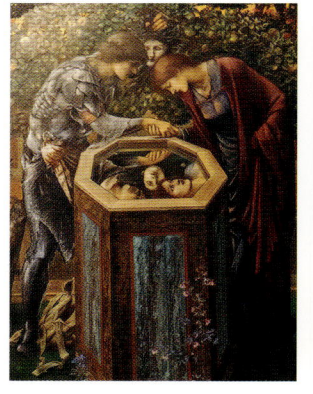

Next to the SeaCity Museum in Southampton's Cultural Quarter is the City Art Gallery *(right)*, which moved to its permanent home in the Civic Centre building in 1939. It currently holds over 5,300 works and this number continues to grow. Although visitors can discover the story of western art from the Renaissance period, the gallery is particularly known for its modern British art with one of the finest collections outside London. A varied programme of exhibitions and events is held throughout the year and entry is free.

Above (clockwise from top left): The Church at Vétheuil by Claude Monet (1840-1926); The Torn Gown by Henry Tonks (1862-1937); Fishermen upon a Lee Shore in Squally Weather by JMW Turner (1775-1851); Spring, the Morning Room by William Rothenstein (1872-1945); Timber Run in the Welsh Hills by Lucy Elizabeth Kemp-Welch (1869-1958); The Baleful Head from the Perseus Series by Edward Burne-Jones (1833-1898).

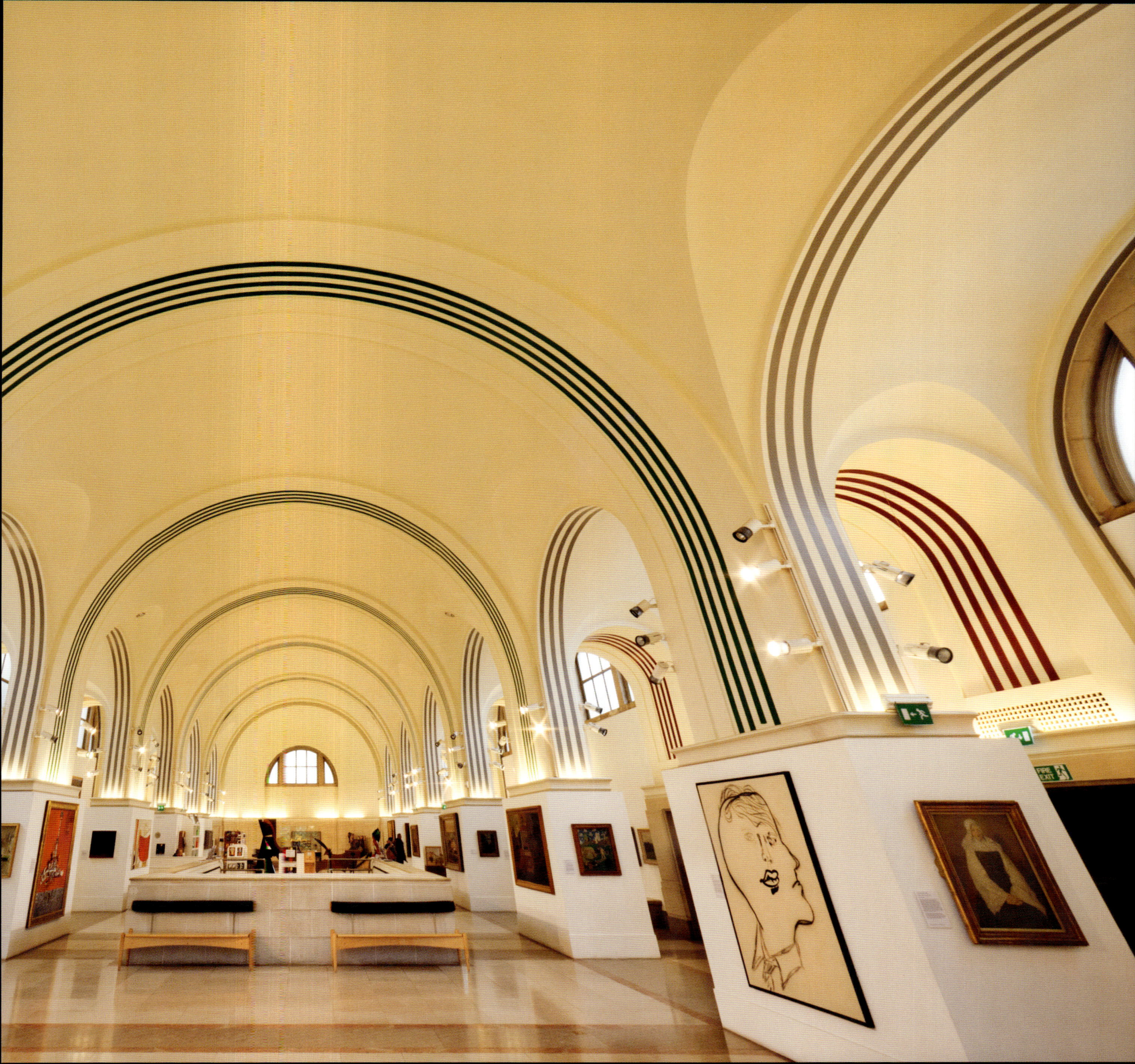

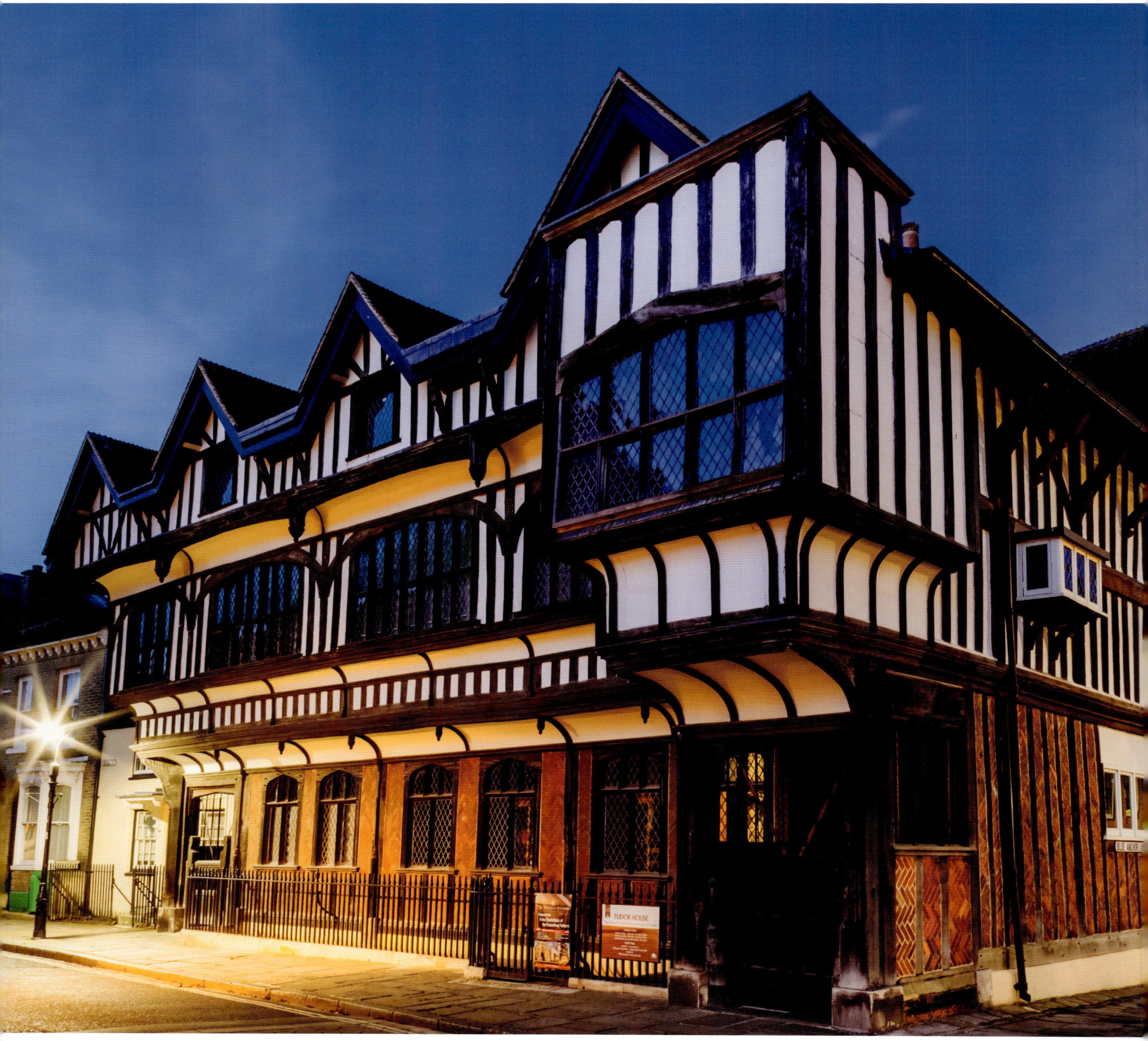
TUDOR HOUSE

The Grade I listed 'Tudor House & Garden' *(far left & left)* sits at the heart of Southampton's Old Town and was built in the 15th century. This historic, timber-framed building is now open as a museum and visitor attraction. There are many interesting objects contained within, including a sedan chair dating from the mid-18th century and *My Tudor Paper Galleon* by Jessica Palmer *(below)*. The garden *(bottom)* was redesigned in the 1980s by Dr Sylvia Landsberg, using the style of planting seen in the 1500s.

The Solent Sky Museum is found near Ocean Village in Southampton and opened in 1984. It tells the aviation history of the city and surrounding area, particularly the story of the Supermarine Works where R J Mitchell designed the iconic Spitfire of which more than 8000 were built in the area.

Over twenty aircraft are on display, including the Supermarine S.6A-N248, also designed by Mitchell, which took part in the Schneider Trophy Air Race held at nearby Calshot in 1929. Since 2017, Solent Sky has been home to the Hampshire Police & Fire Museum.

POLICE STATION
The Uniform
Spitfire at War
1942 - 1945
Supermarine Destroyed
1940
Cunliffe-Owen Attacked
1940
Southampton in Flames
1939 - 1945
Businesses Ruined
1939 - 1940
Churches Bombed
1939 - 1940
FIRE EXIT
N
220
4

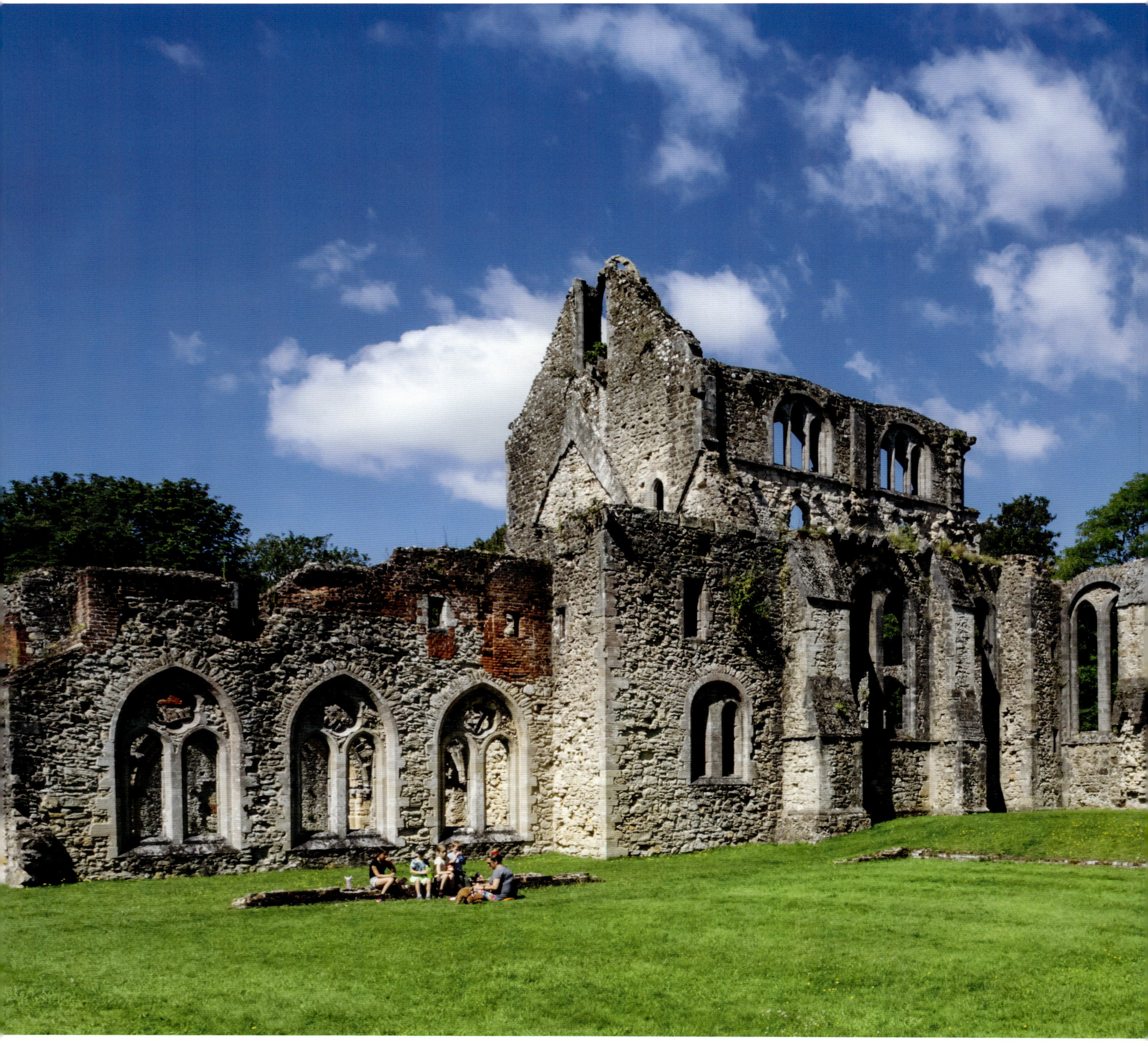

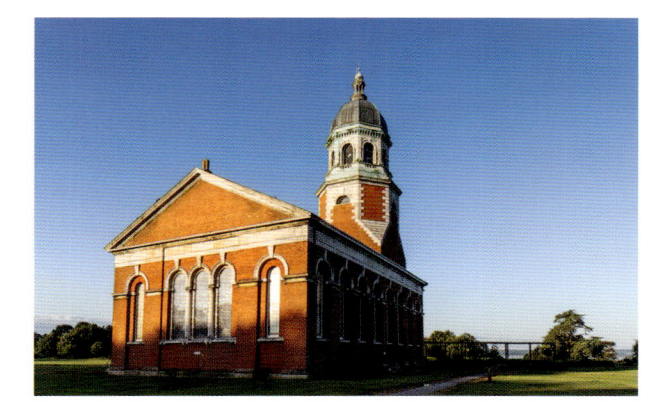

On the east bank of Southampton Water stands the substantial ruin of Netley Abbey *(left)*. Originally constructed in the 13th century, this is the most complete Cistercian abbey remaining in Southern England and is now under the care of English Heritage. During the reign of Henry VIII and following the Dissolution of the Monasteries in 1536, the building was converted into a Tudor courtyard house for Sir William Paulet, a powerful man in the county and a national statesman. It was occupied as a home until the early 18th century, when it was partially demolished and became a picturesque ruin attractive to both artists and writers. It is said that Jane Austen found inspiration here for her novel, Northanger Abbey.

A mile from the abbey is the Royal Victoria Country Park, once the site of a military hospital that was England's longest building. Opening in 1863, it was used throughout the rest of the 19th century and during both World Wars before being demolished in the 1960s. Only the Chapel *(above)* now remains, and this can be visited throughout the year.

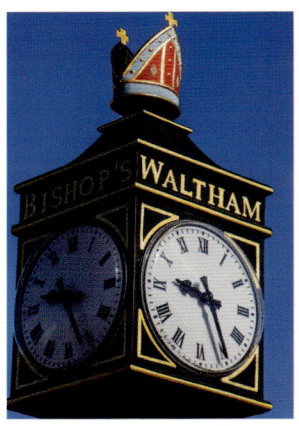

Ten miles inland from Netley, to the north-east, is the medieval market town of Bishop's Waltham and the historic ruins of Bishop's Waltham Palace. This grand residence was owned by the Bishops of Winchester throughout the Middle Ages. They were powerful men, both locally and nationally. A stone palace was originally built here by Henry of Blois, brother of King Stephen, in the 12th century and this was extended in the 14th & 15th centuries.

Regularly a meeting place for royalty, the palace was visited by many monarchs, including Richard I, Henry V and Henry VIII. It was destroyed in 1644, during the English Civil War, having been held for the King. The ruins were later returned to the bishops after the Restoration, with various owners following from the 1860s. The site is now looked after by English Heritage.

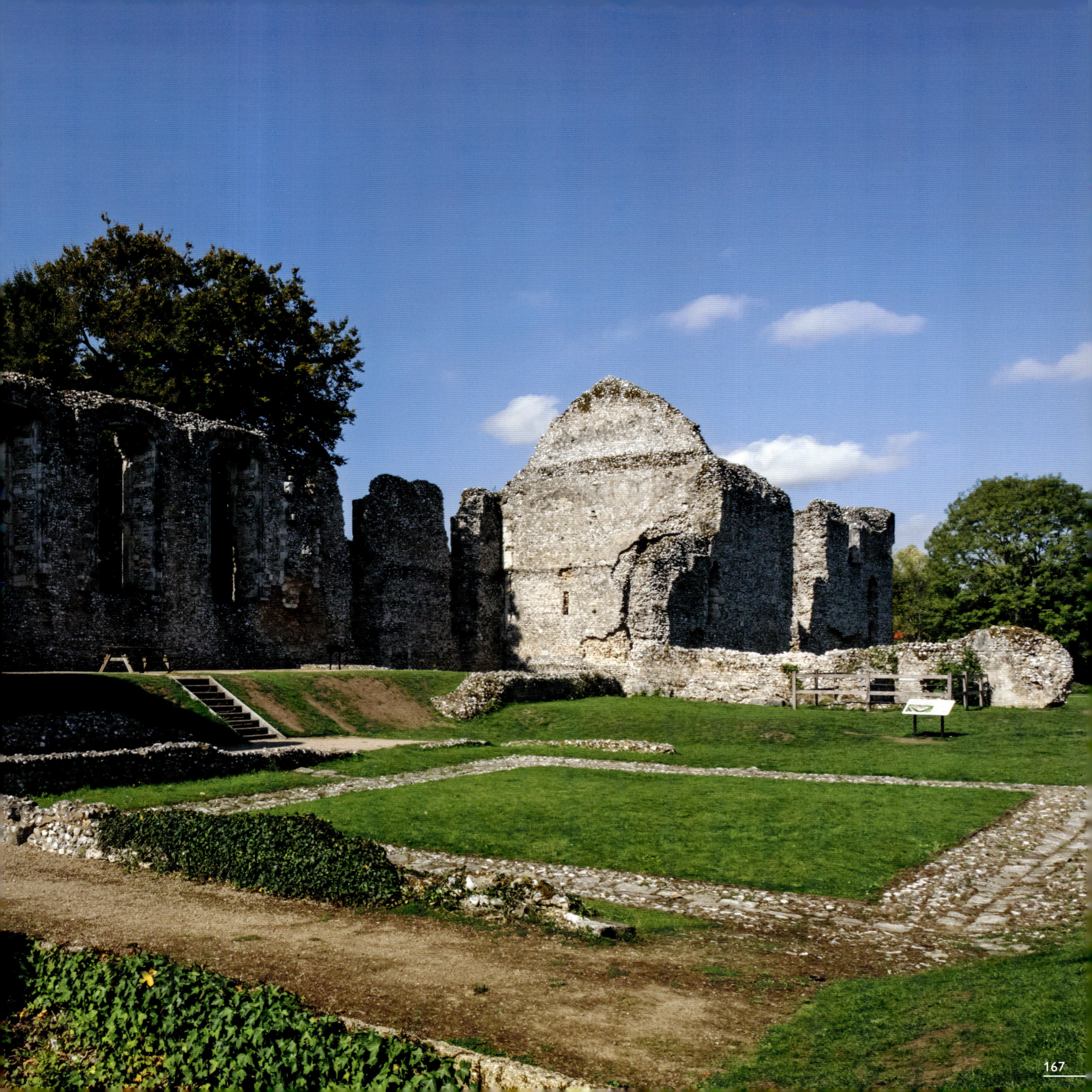

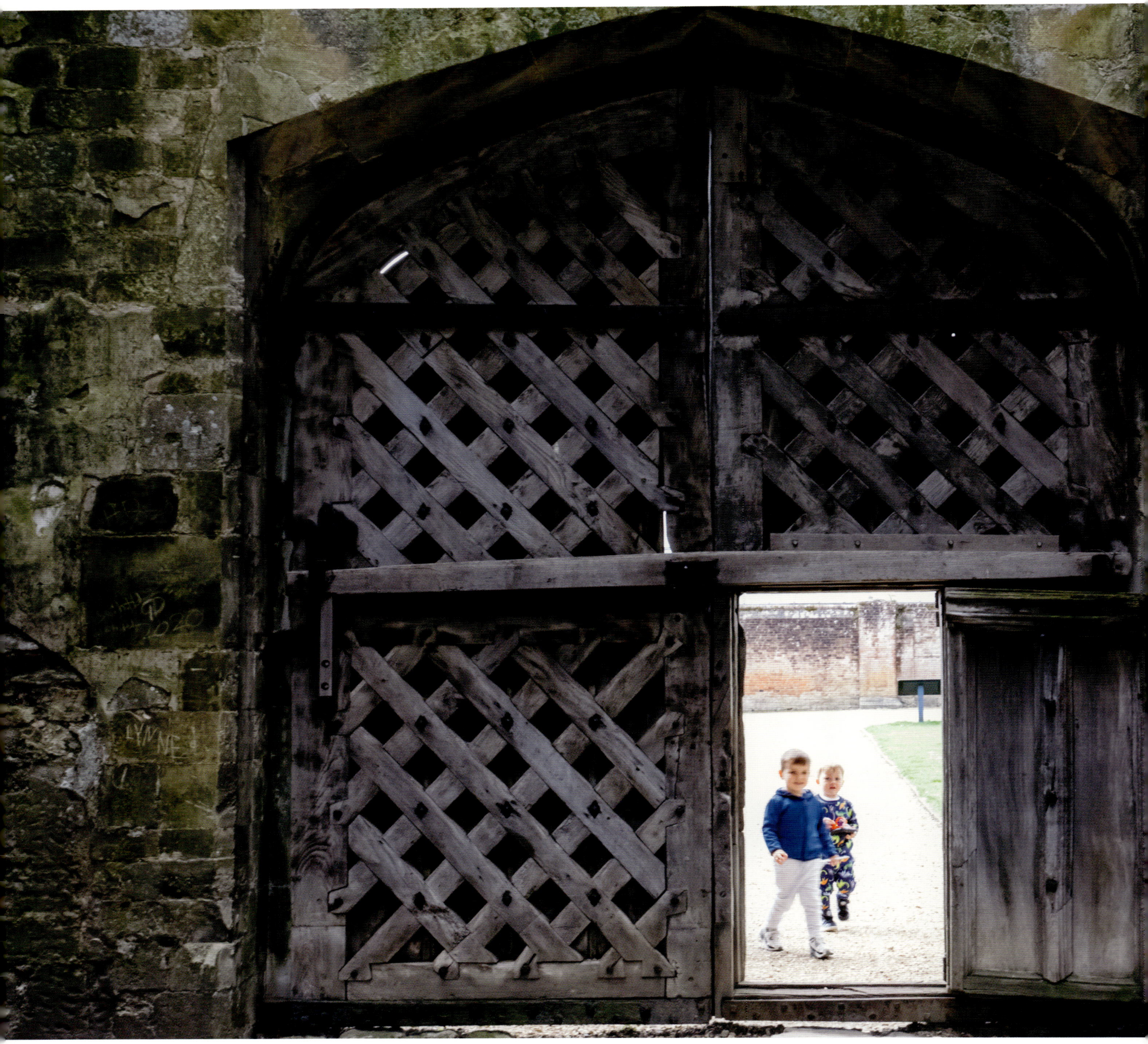

Heading back south towards the Solent and just to the west of Fareham is Titchfield Abbey *(left & above)*, which was founded in the 13th century by the Bishop of Winchester, Peter des Roches. It was home to an order of Premonstratensian canons who lived under monastic vows but were also involved in communal life. They were a scholarly group and owned an impressive library. The library catalogue still survives, and the scale of the listing is unusual for the time.

The abbey was dissolved by Henry VIII in 1537 and converted into a mansion, known as Place House, for Thomas Wriothesley, 1st Earl of Southampton. In the late 18th century, the building was abandoned and much of it was intentionally demolished to create a romantic ruin.

Extensive sections of the building remain, and these include tiled floors from the late medieval period *(above left)*. These were covered over when the abbey was converted into a house and only rediscovered in 1923. Now an English Heritage property, Titchfield Abbey is open to the public.

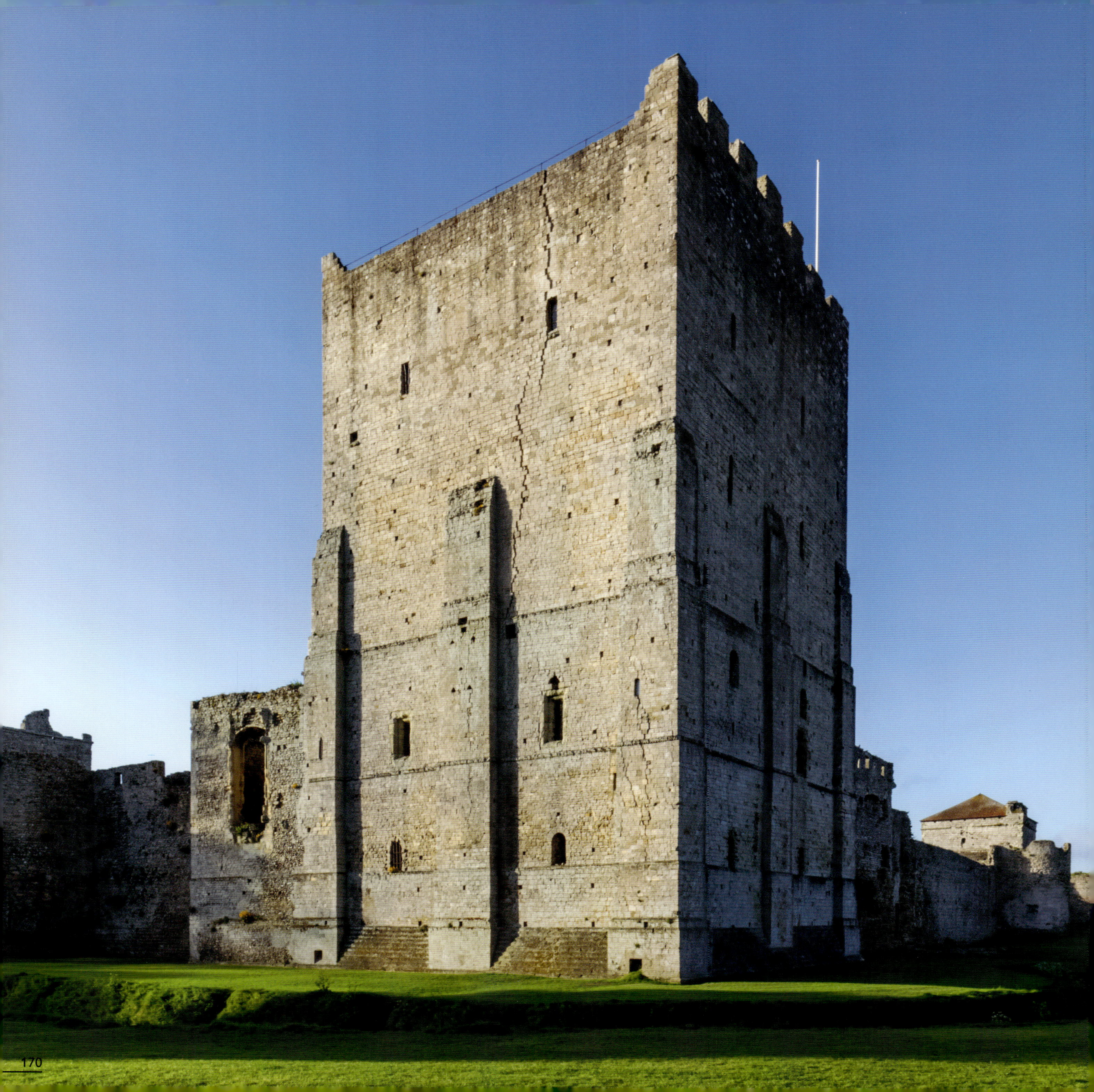

Overlooking Portsmouth Harbour stands Porchester Castle, a Norman fortification that was built within the walls of a vast Roman fort. Dating from the 3rd century, the Roman fort is the only one in northern Europe whose perimeter walls survive virtually unaltered. After the Romans left England, the fort was a Saxon settlement until the Conquest in 1066, when it became a Norman castle. It is not known precisely when the keep was built, but it had been extended to its present height by 1150 *(left)*. Henry II confiscated the castle when he came to the throne in 1154 and it remained in royal hands for nearly five hundred years, before being sold to a local landowner, whose descendants still own it today.

Porchester Castle was used as a prison for captured enemy soldiers from the 1660s, with the last prisoner leaving in 1814. It became a tourist attraction in the 19th century and has been managed by English Heritage since 1984.

Porchester was once a small village, but it sits on the main route linking Portsmouth and Southampton and so has seen rapid expansion and development. Castle Street *(above bottom right)*, which leads down to the castle and is lined with historic houses, was designated a Conservation Area in the late 1960s so that its character and appearance could be protected.

Fort Nelson is a Victorian fort that was built to protect Portsmouth harbour in the 1860s. It is one of five Palmerston forts, which were positioned strategically on Portsdown Hill. Now fully restored, the fort is open to visitors who can discover the history of the building and enjoy the fine views from its ramparts. The Royal Armouries' national collection of artillery and historic cannon is housed here, and the museum has more than 700 examples of artillery from around the world.
Right: 18-inch Howitzer 'Railway Gun', designed to fire on German trenches in WWI but not ready before end of war. *Above from top:* Indian Bronze 24-pounder; Italian Bronze 2-pounder with carriage (1773); Mallet's Mortar (1855-7).

173

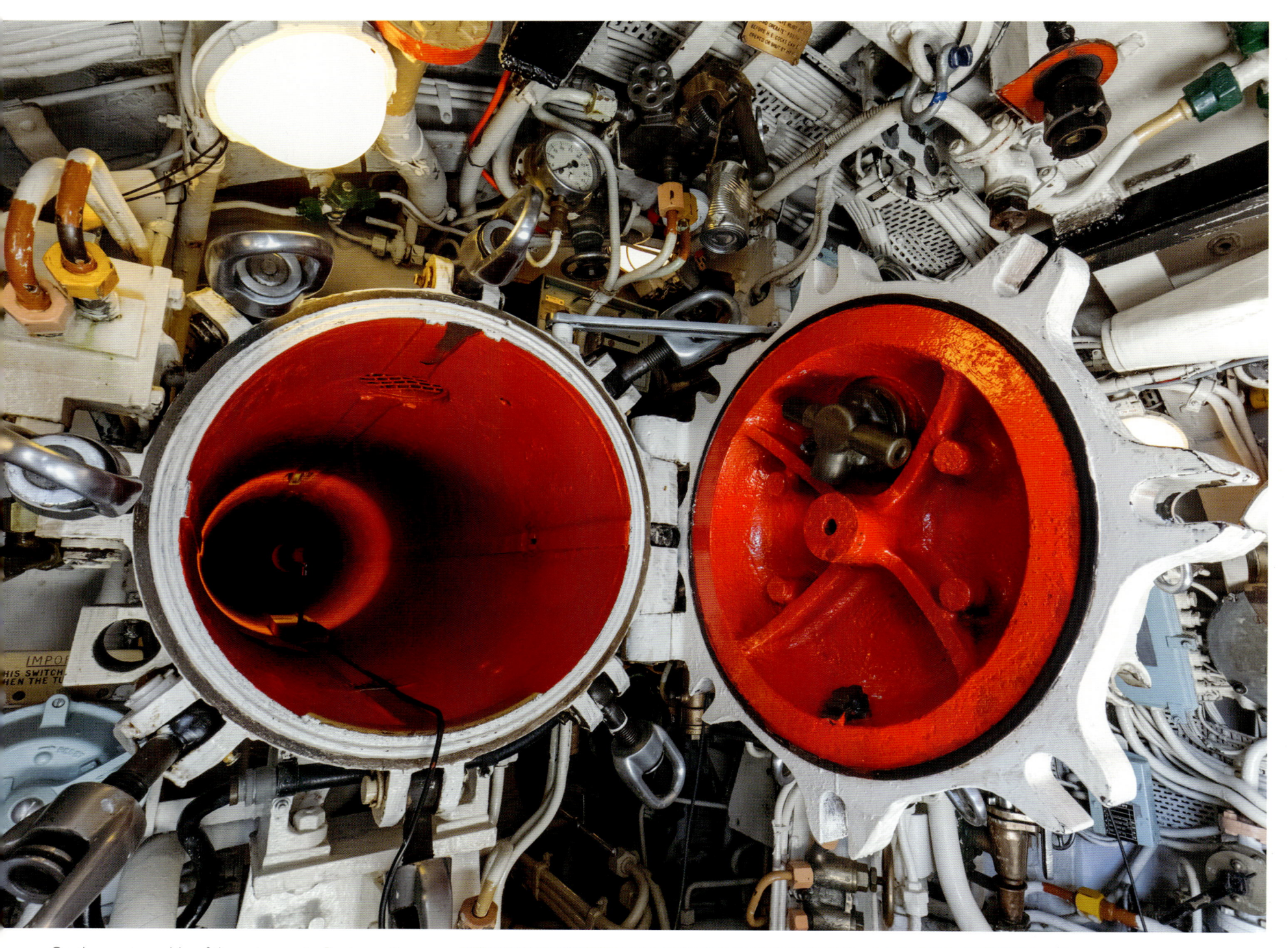

On the western side of the entrance to Portsmouth Harbour is Gosport, home of the Royal Navy Submarine Museum where visitors can discover more about these fascinating vessels and the role they have played in maritime history. Exhibits include Holland 1 *(right & far right)*, the first submarine to be commissioned by the Royal Navy dating from 1900, and X24, a midget submarine built around 1943.

The centrepiece of the museum is HMS Alliance, Britain's only remaining A-class submarine from the World War II era (above & p.174 top). Following a major restoration project, which was completed in 2014, the Alliance stands as a memorial to the 5,300 British submariners who have lost their lives in service since 1904. Visitors can tour the interior (left) to see the cramped conditions in which they lived and worked.

Far left: On Patrol (1918) by George Bradshaw.

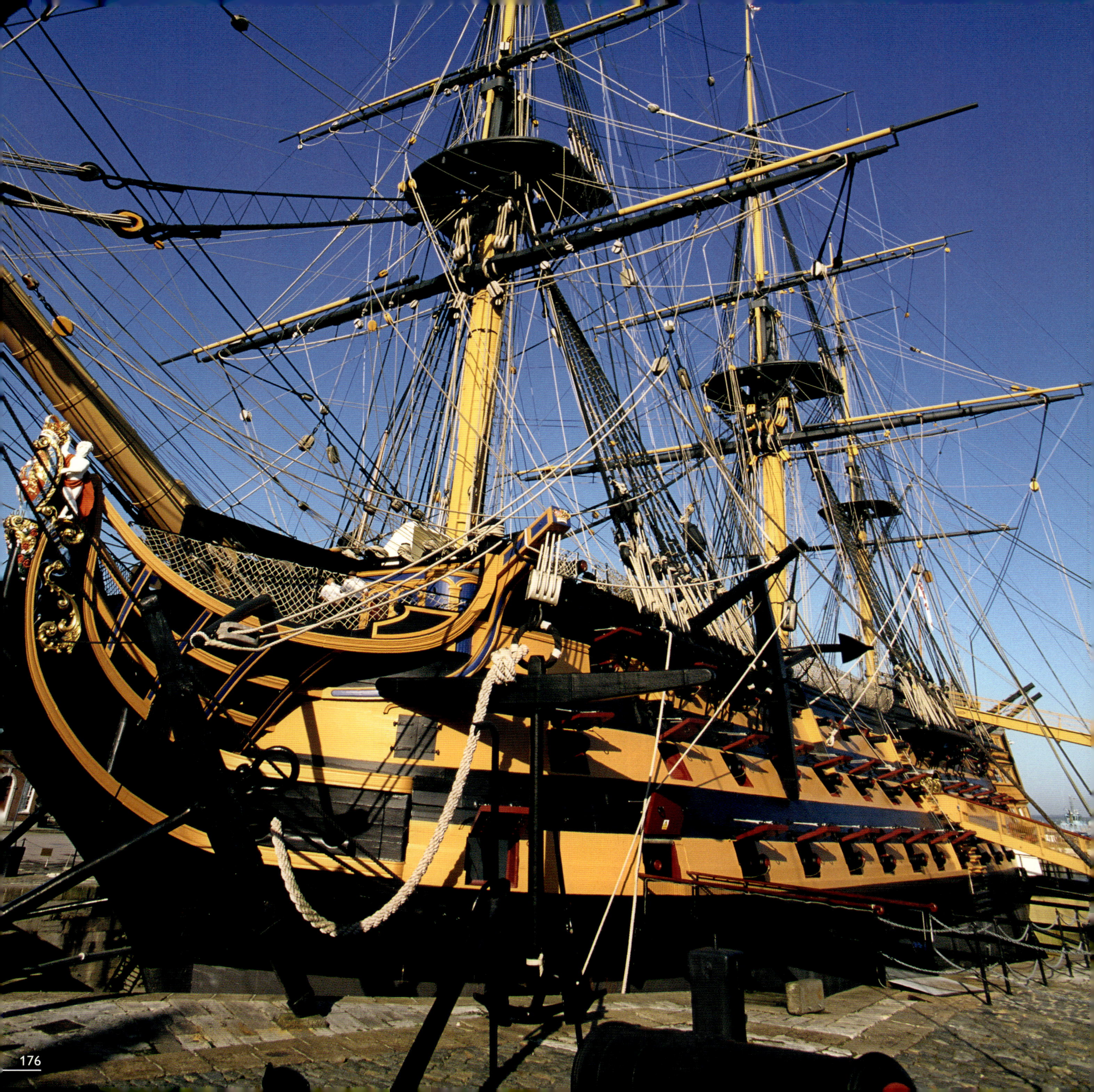

On the opposite side of the harbour to the Submarine Museum is the main site of Portsmouth Historic Dockyard, which has a number of historic buildings and ships that are open to the public. The Royal Navy's most famous warship, HMS Victory, is berthed here. First launched in 1765, she was the flagship of Horatio Nelson *(top left)* in the Battle of Trafalgar and the scene of his death. A plaque on deck marks the spot where he fell.

At the time of the battle, in 1805, there were 104 guns arranged over four decks *(top middle & above right)*. The masts *(left)* were removed from the ship in 2011, as part of an ongoing restoration project. The Victory is currently displayed with temporary masts *(above left)*, but the full rigging will be returned when the ship's structure is stable enough to hold the weight. The Under Hull Walkway enables visitors to walk down into the dry dock to see the ship from below.

HMS Victory is not only a public museum but also the flagship of the First Sea Lord, which makes her the oldest warship still in commission.

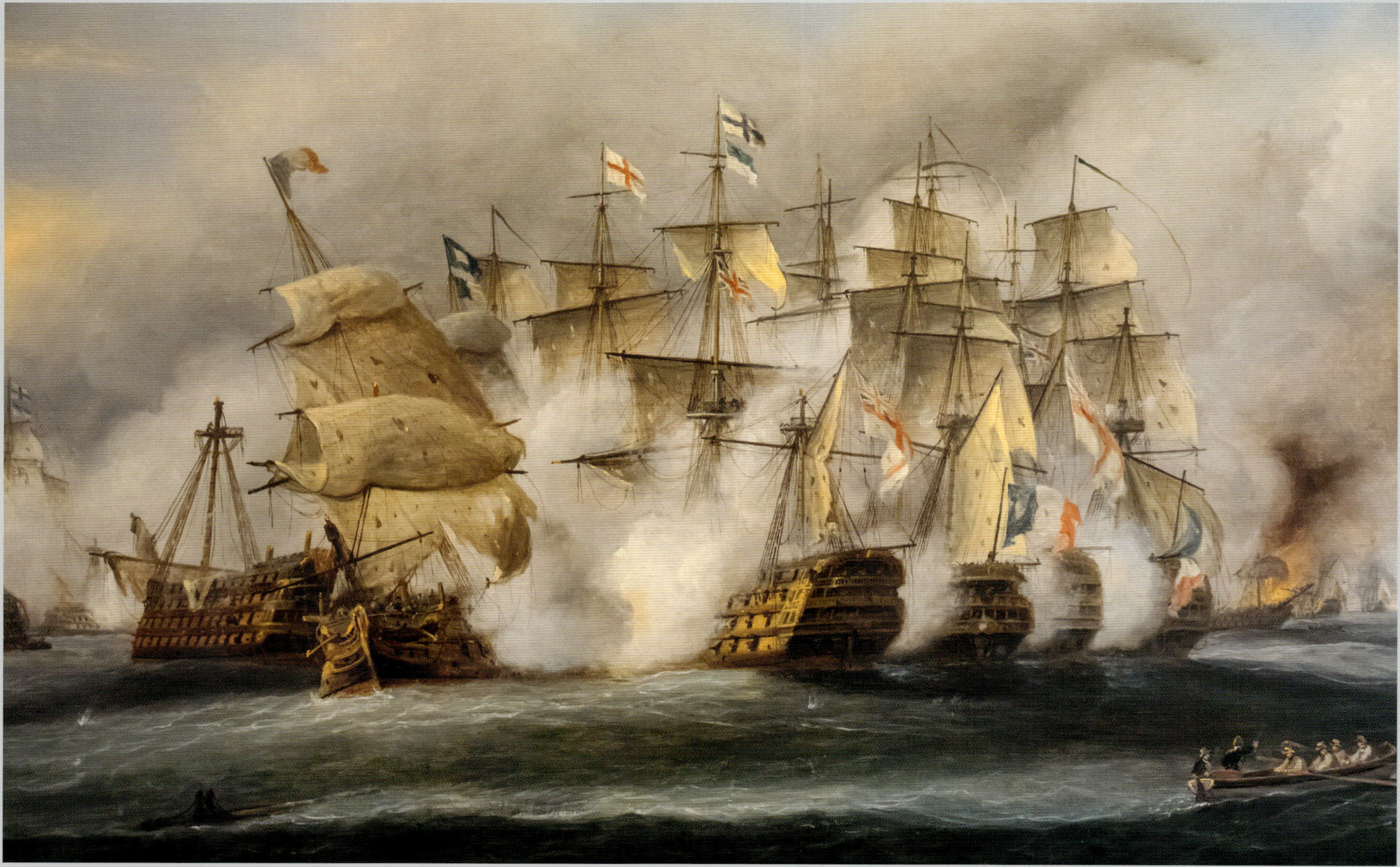

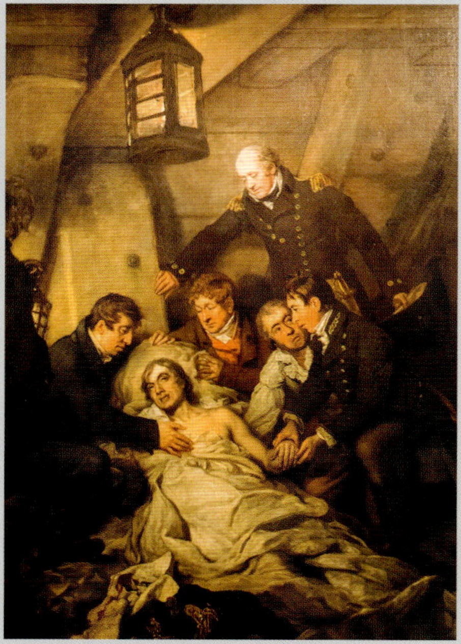

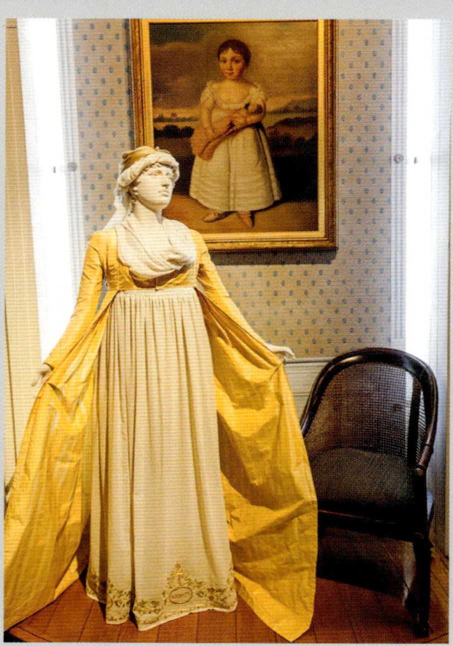

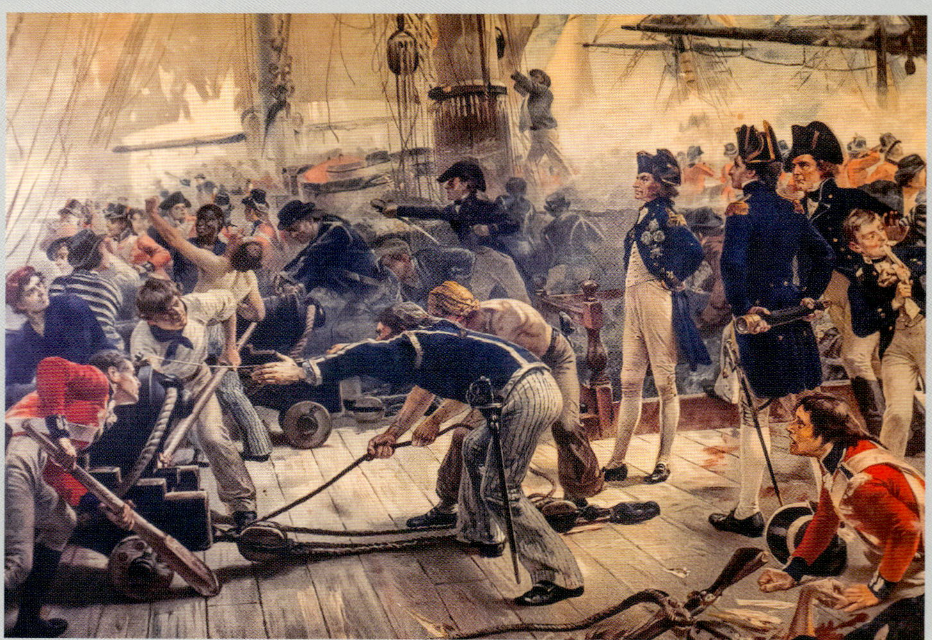

The National Museum of the Royal Navy also sits within Portsmouth Historic Dockyard. Telling the story of the Royal Navy, it contains several galleries, each with a different focus. The Nelson Gallery features not only the heroic achievements of Horatio Nelson, but also gives an idea of the private man and compares the two personas.

Exhibits include a figure of his mistress, Emma Hamilton *(bottom middle)* in a dress that she designed herself and wore to celebrate the Battle of the Nile.

Right: Lord Nelson (Detail) by Lemuel Francis Abbott (1760-1803)

Top left: The Battle of Trafalgar, 21 October 1805 by Thomas Luny (1759-1837)

Bottom left: Detail from *The Death of Nelson* by Arthur William Devis (1762-1822)

Bottom right: The Hero of Trafalgar by William Heysham Overend (1851-1898)

The Victory Gallery, dedicated to the late Vice-Admiral Sir Donald Gosling, is part of the National Museum of the Royal Navy. HMS Victory was built more than 250 years ago, and this gallery has many fascinating exhibits relating to her dramatic history, as well as a multi-media experience that gives some idea what it must have been like to be at the Battle of Trafalgar. Visitors can see a section of the original mainmast with shot-damage, and a ship's wheel *(above)* that replaced the one destroyed during battle.

The gallery is also home to 'Spirit of a Ship', the museum's remarkable collection of warship figureheads *(right)*, which is one of the best in the country.

p.181 bottom left: Figurehead from HMS Illustrious at the entrance to the Sailing Navy Gallery.

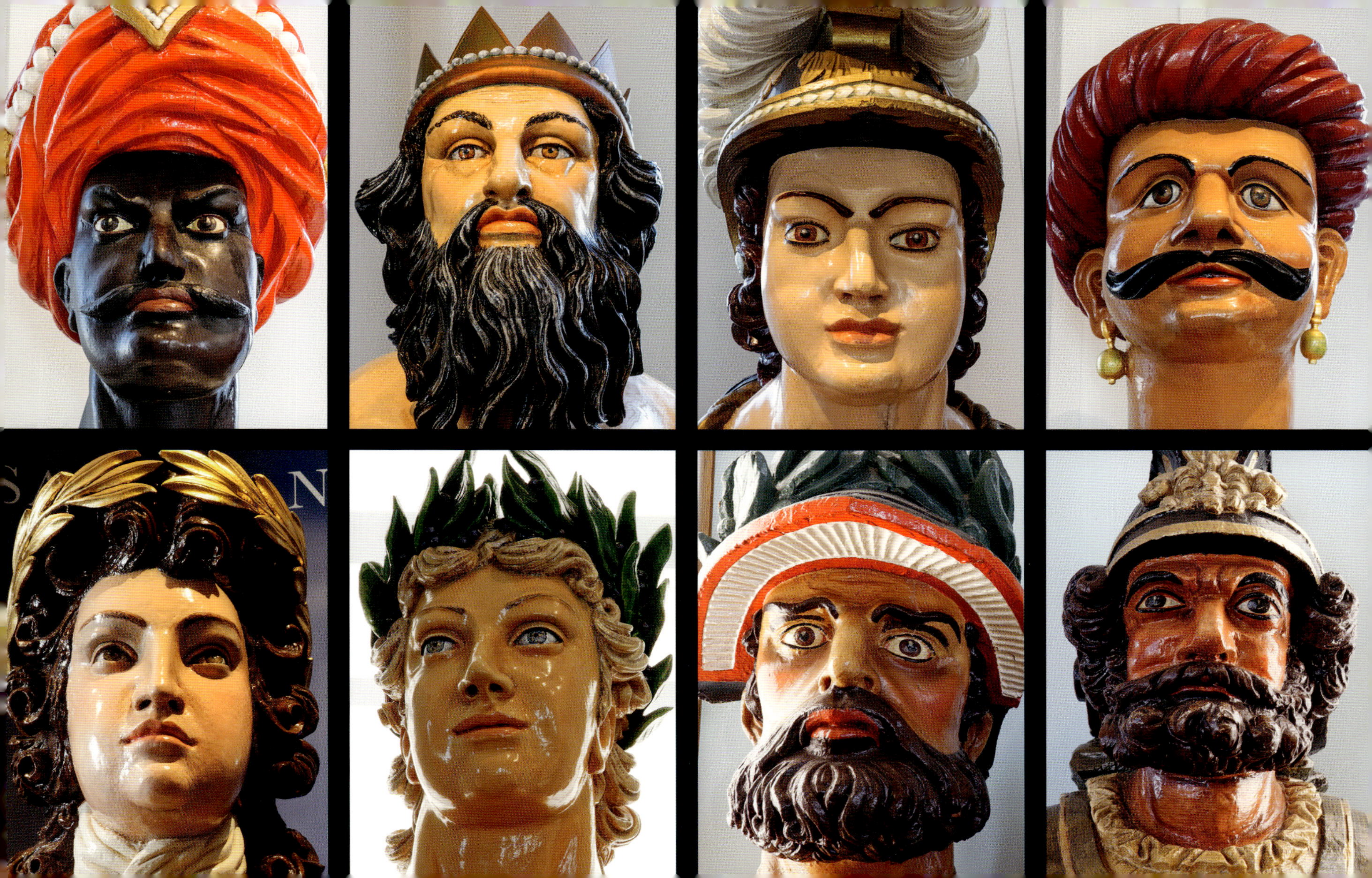

The journey around Portsmouth Historic Dockyard continues with a visit to Boathouse 4 (right). This huge building has its own dock and was originally built in 1939 as part of a rapid rearmament programme that was needed at the start of World War II.

As well as being a family attraction with exhibitions and interactive activities for children, it is now a training centre for boatbuilding skills, ensuring that the techniques required to build and restore wooden boats are not lost. A high-level gallery allows visitors to look down on the work going on below. Also within the boathouse is a restaurant with fine views over the harbour.

Above: Royal Navy Ship's Plaques.

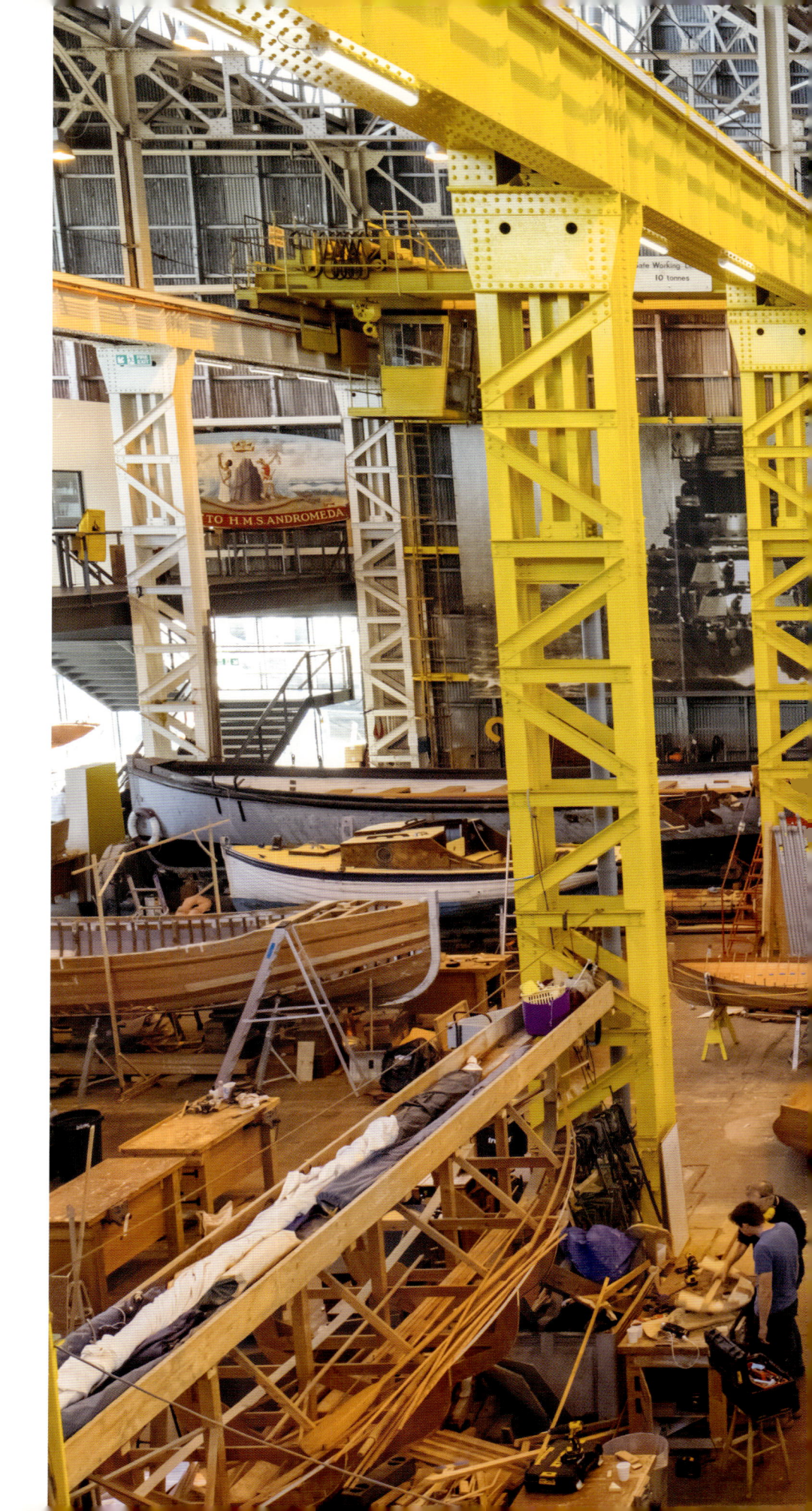

183

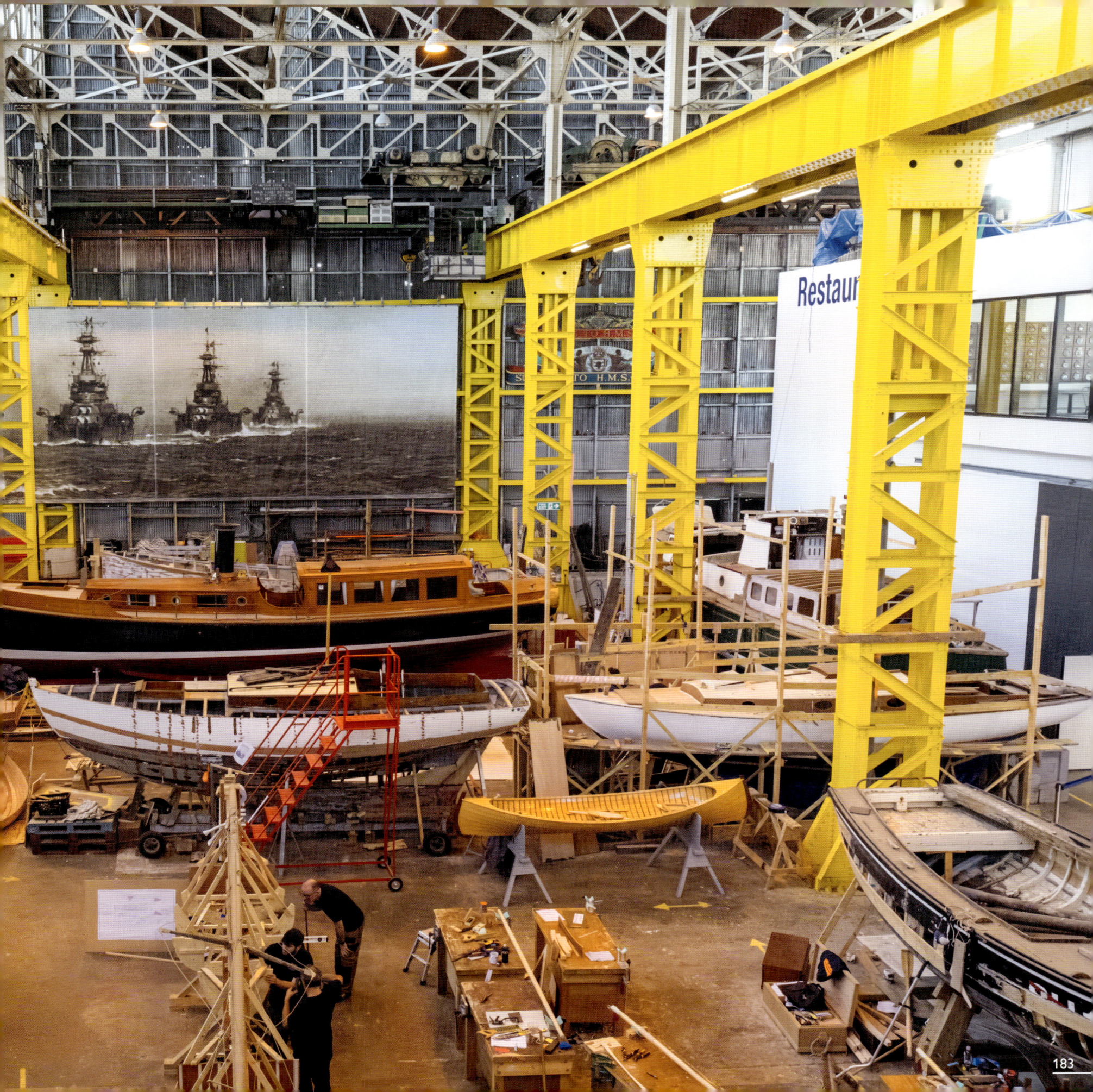

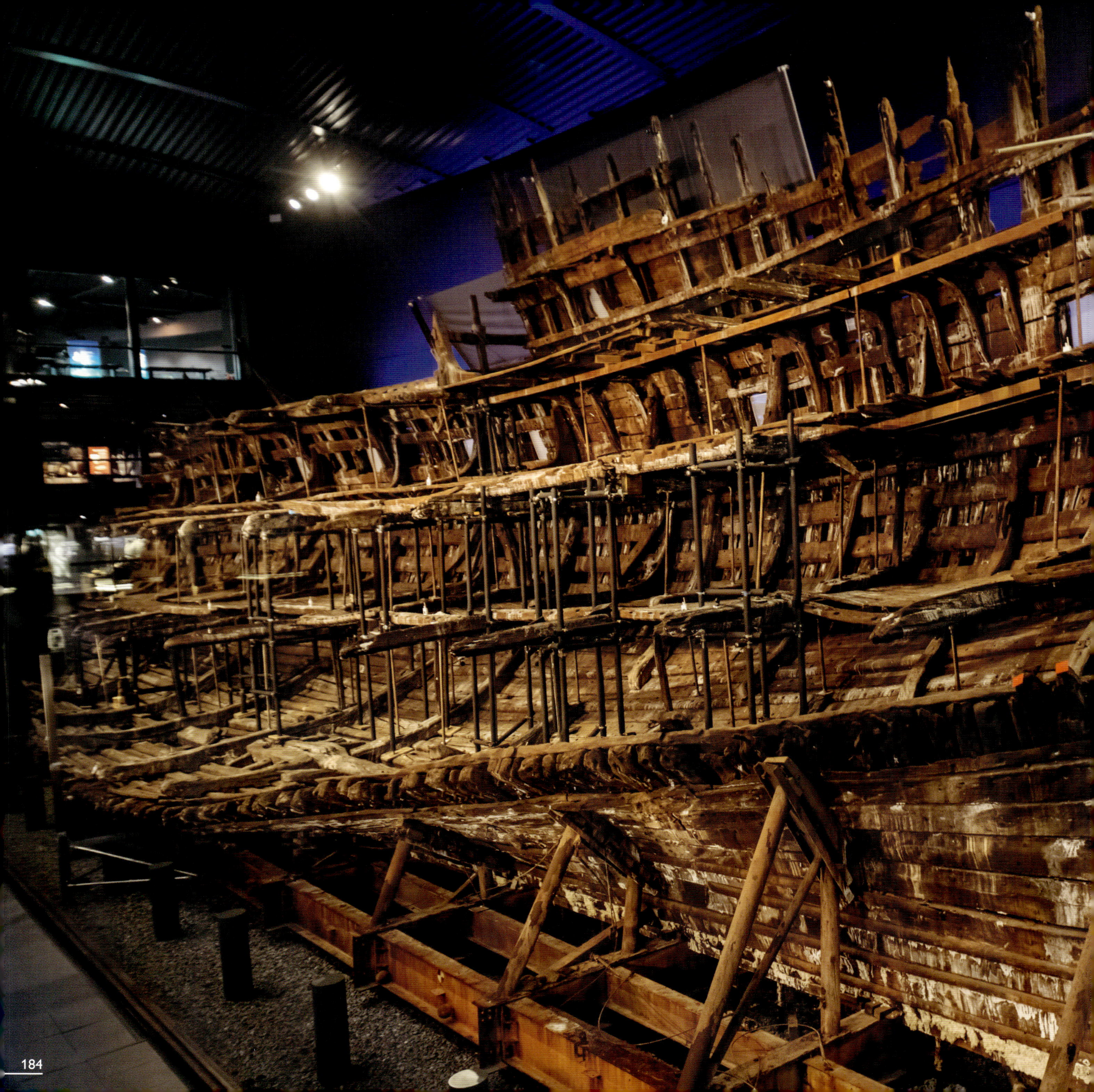

The dramatic oval building of the Mary Rose Museum is an eye-catching addition to the Historic Dockyard. Dedicated to the Tudor navy warship, Mary Rose, the museum had to be constructed around the hull of the ship *(left)*, which was already in dry dock.

Built in 1510 for Henry VIII, the Mary Rose was one of the first English ships to be designed as a warship and was a favourite of the King. She served successfully in his navy for 34 years before being sunk in the Battle of the Solent in 1545, while Henry watched from Southsea Castle. Over 400 men were on board and fewer than 35 survived. The hull was raised from the seabed in 1982 and objects from the wreck are also on display in the museum, including artillery, tableware and the skeleton of the ship's dog *(above)*.

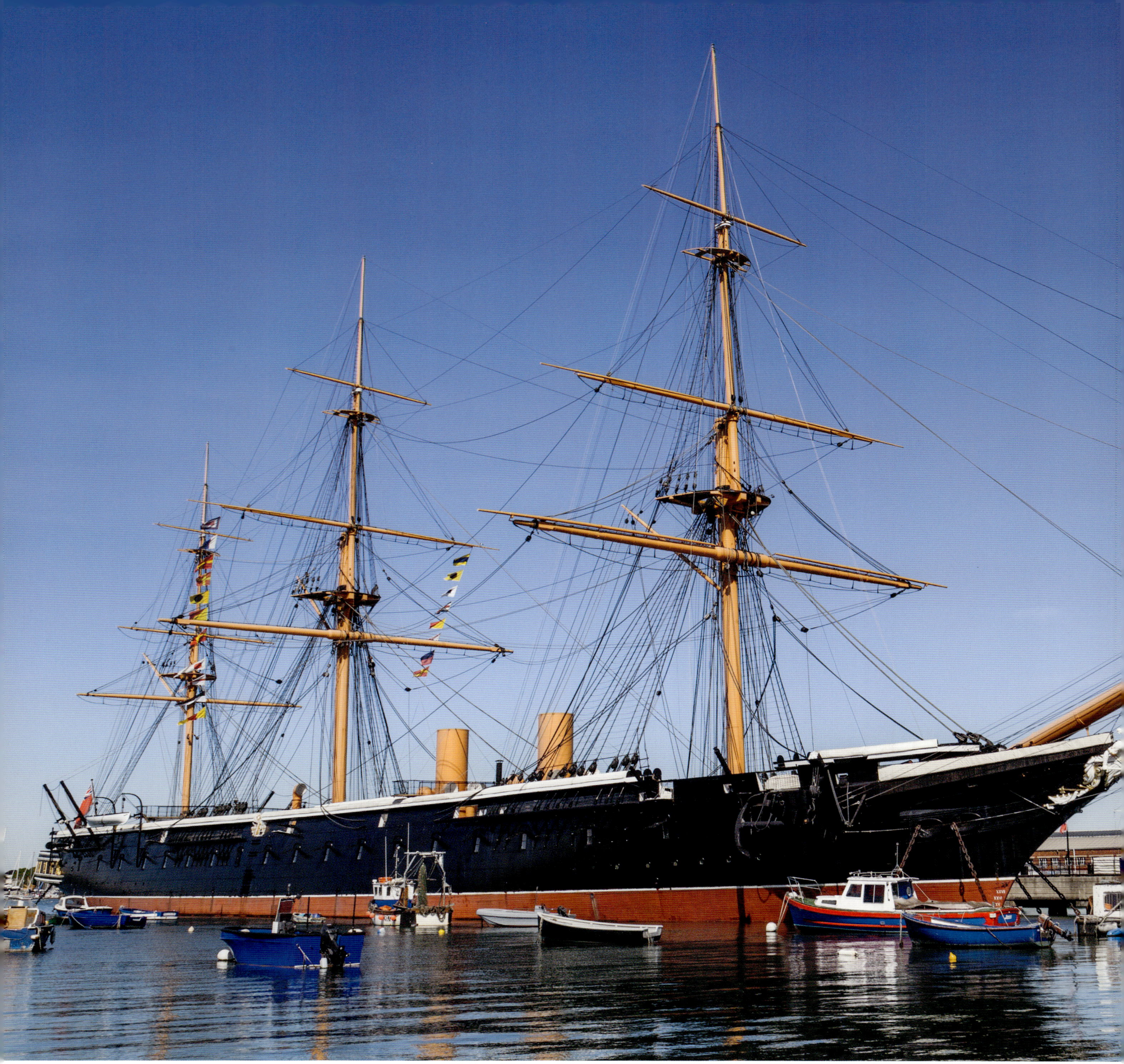

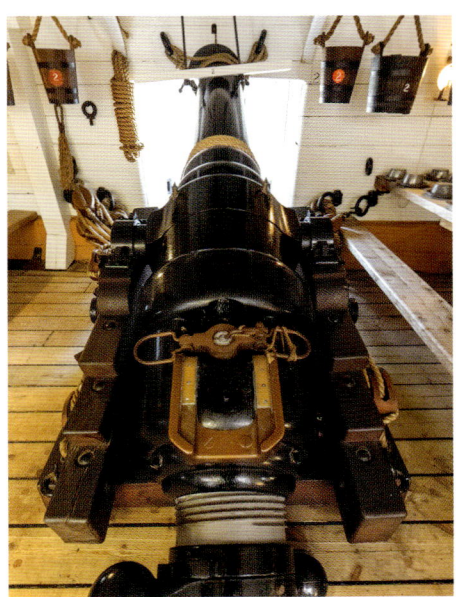

Our final visit within Portsmouth Historic Dockyard is to HMS Warrior *(left & above)*; the largest and fastest warship in the world when she was launched in 1860.

Warrior is a 40-gun steam-powered frigate and the only survivor of the Victorian Black Battlefleet, a name given to the 45 iron-hulled ships built for the Royal Navy in the 1860s and 1870s. Although never used in anger, she was an important and much-feared deterrent and her influence on naval design was significant.

Back in Portsmouth since 1987, Warrior is now a museum ship and popular attraction that can be hired for private events.

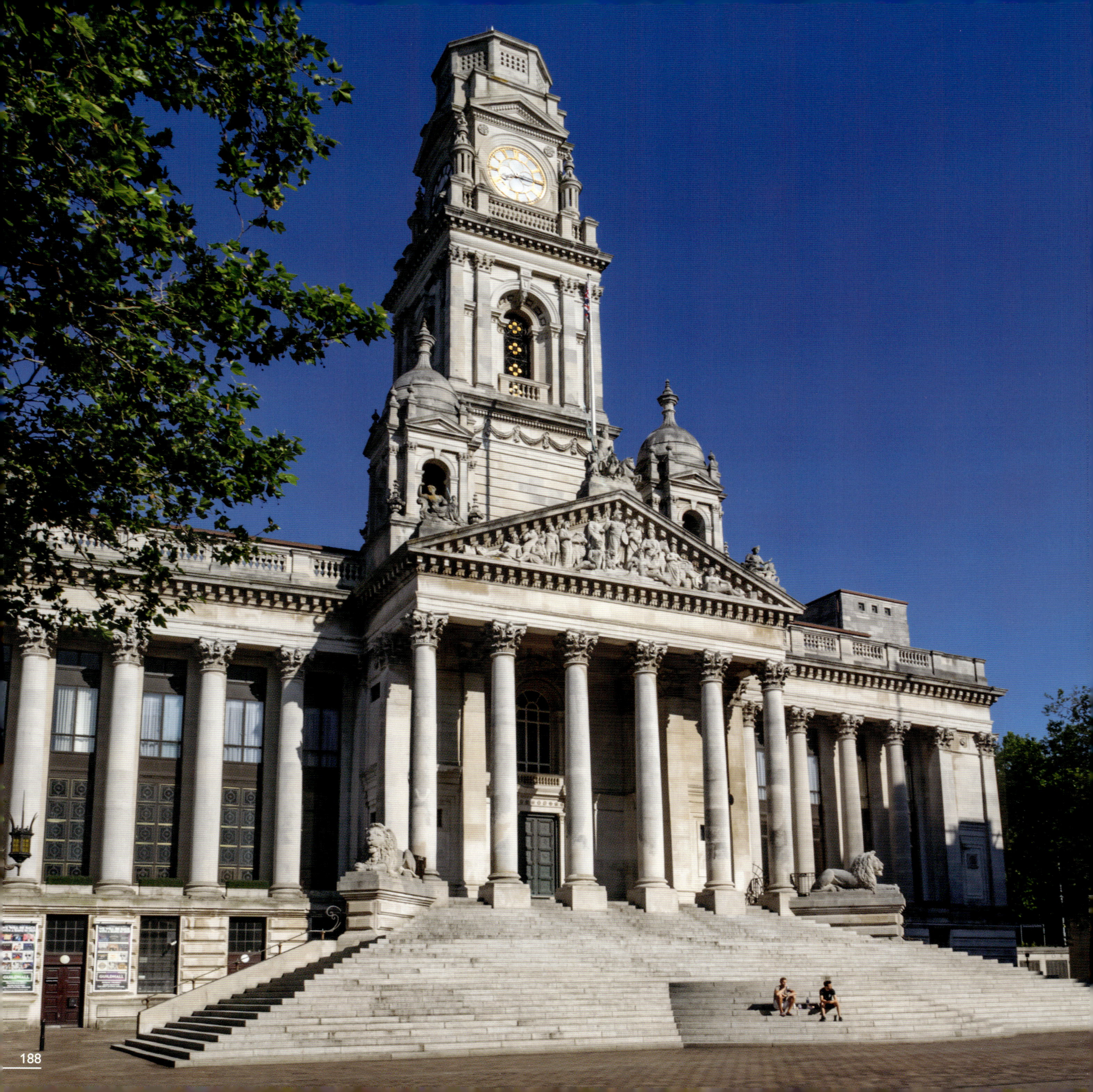

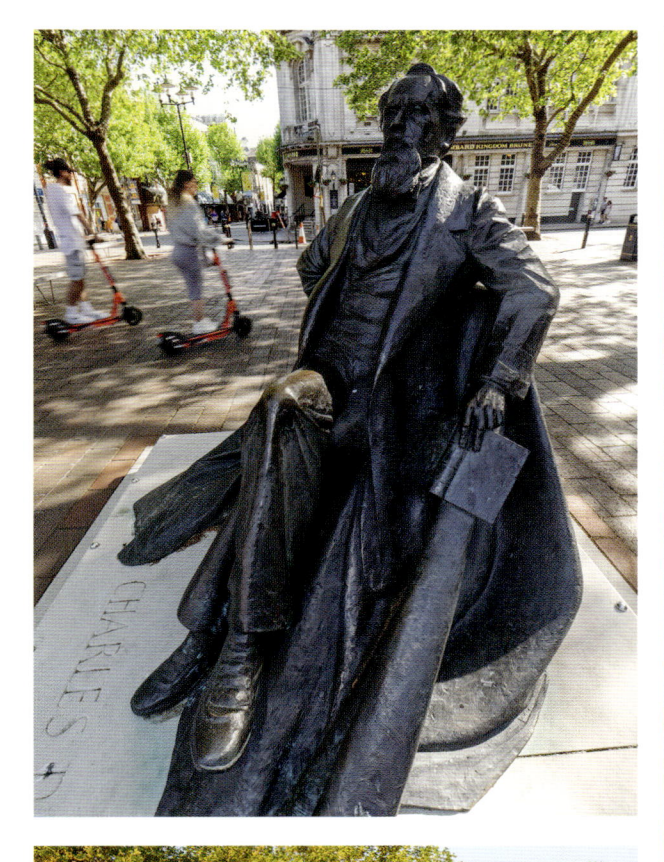

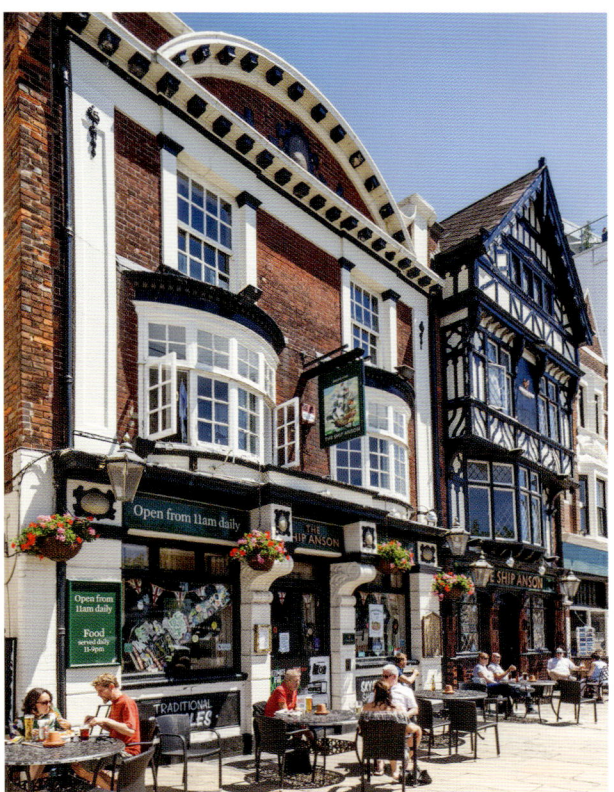

The port and city of Portsmouth is one of the most densely populated areas of Britain, with almost a quarter of a million people living in its environs. Most of the city's attractions and landmarks are linked to its naval history and long association with the armed forces. There are many war memorials, including the City of Portsmouth War Memorial in Guildhall Square *(above left)*, which commemorates those who lost their lives in the Great War.

The Guildhall *(left)* dates from the late 1880s but was heavily damaged in the Second World War and rebuilt in the 1950s. It is now a venue for events including weddings, concerts and exhibitions.

Top left: Statue of Charles Dickens, who was born in Portsmouth. *Top middle:* Portsmouth and Southsea Railway Station. *Top right:* Statue of Queen Victoria in Guildhall Square. *Above middle:* Ship Anson on The Hard. *Above right:* Façade detail, New Theatre Royal.

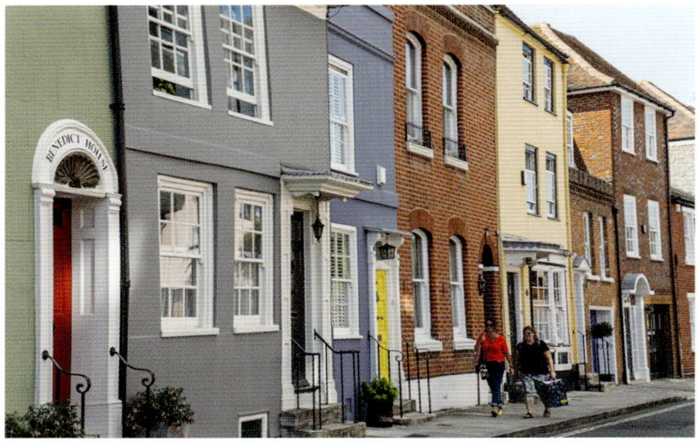

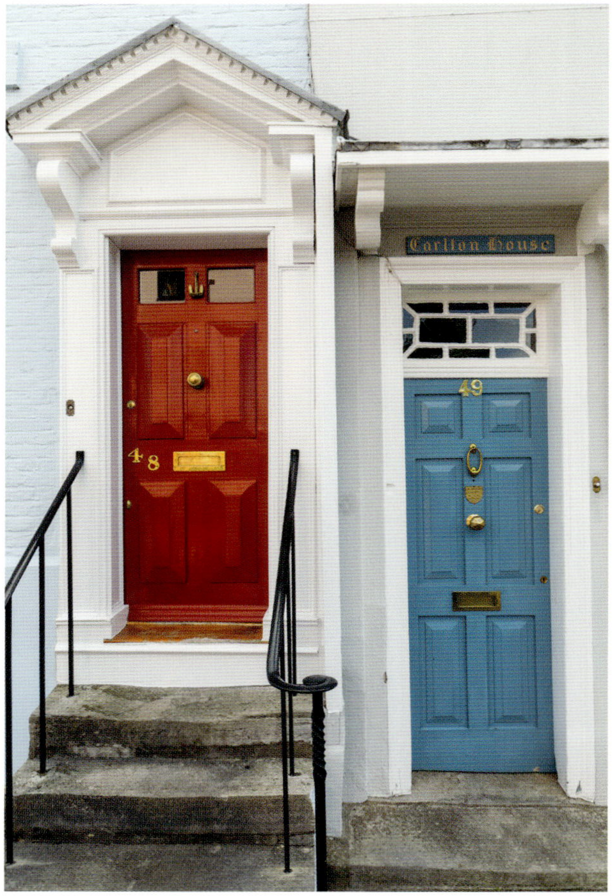
Carlton House
49

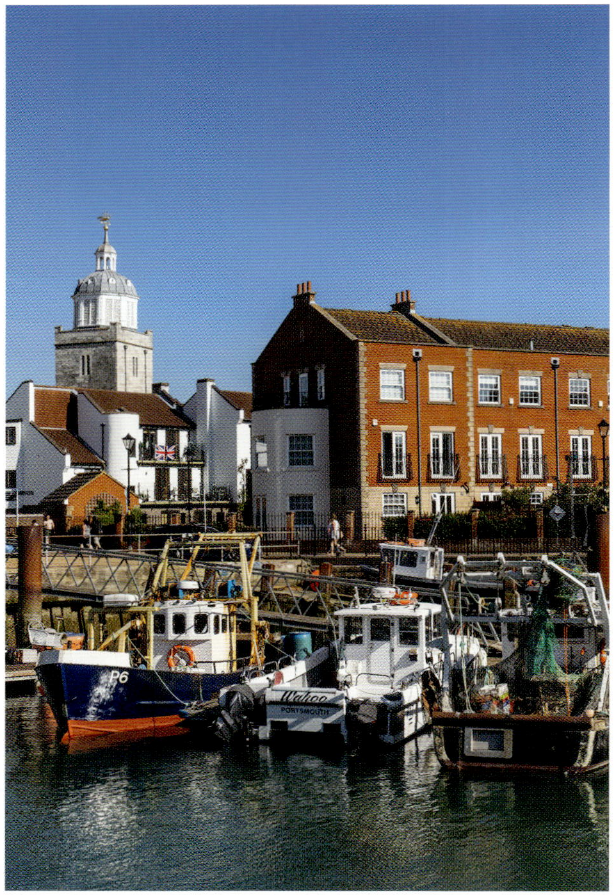
P6

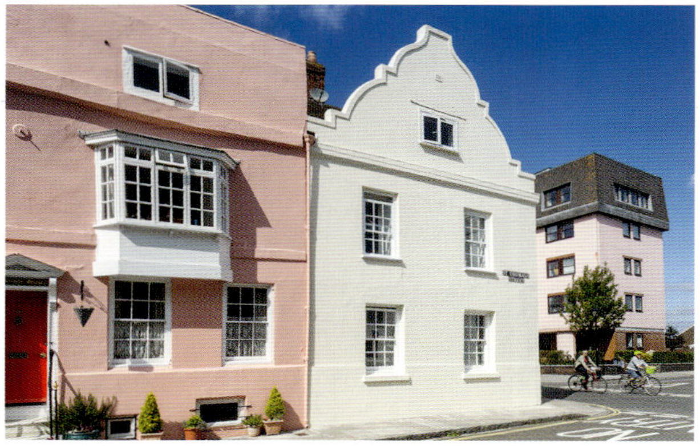

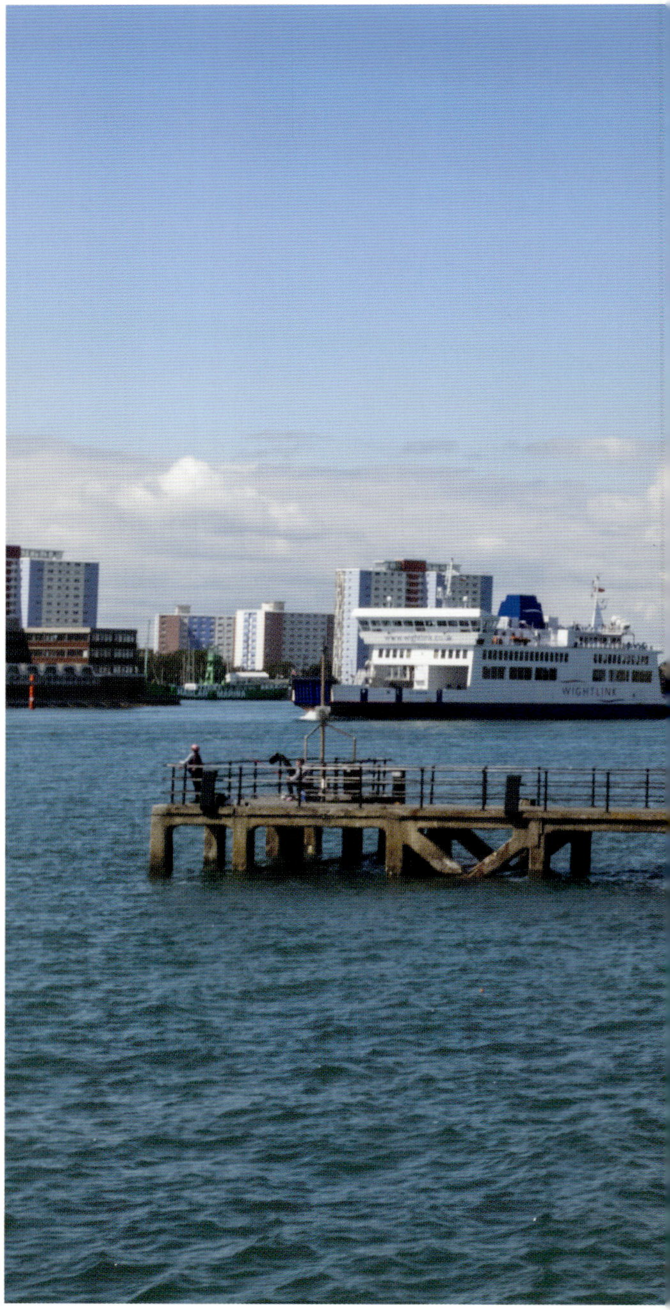

The district of Old Portsmouth has some of the most attractive buildings in the city and covers the same area as the original medieval town. Founded in the 12th century by Jean de Gisors, this town was built using a grid layout, which created a pattern for later development.

Buildings of interest include the Square Tower and Round Tower, which form part of the fortifications and were constructed during the 15th century *(above)*. Camber Docks *(top middle)* are Portsmouth's oldest commercial docks and provide moorings for pleasure craft as well as being home to the local fishing fleet and quayside fish outlets.

The full name of Portsmouth Cathedral *(above)* is the Cathedral Church of St Thomas of Canterbury. Dedicated to Thomas Becket, it sits at the centre of Old Portsmouth and is built in Romanesque style. There has been a religious building on the site since the 12th century, but it was not until the 20th century that the existing church was redeveloped and extended to become the cathedral seen today. The completed building finally opened in 1991, although it had been a cathedral since 1927.

The architectural layout is unusual and forms two separate parts. The quire is used for most services, with the nave being used for concerts and celebrations.
The West Great Organ *(far left)* was added to the nave in 2001 and is one of three organs within the cathedral. The stained glass includes a window honouring those who fought in the Burma Campaign of World War II *(left)*.

Also in Old Portsmouth is Portsmouth Point, where visitors can sit in Bath Square *(below)* and watch the ships go by. Whether it is the sound of car alarms set off by the sharp left turn as the Isle of Wight Ferries set off from the Wightlink Gunwharf Terminal, or the might of a British warship, such as the HMS Prince Charles aircraft carrier *(left)*, returning home, there is always plenty to see and hear.

Now a desirable and attractive area, things were very different in times long past, when Portsmouth Point was known as a place of entertainment for sailors, offering many drinking establishments and other services. Such behaviour was immortalised in Thomas Rowlandson's etching of 1814, which inspired a mural on the wall of the Bridge Tavern on Camber Docks, which has been recently repainted and reimagined by artist, Mark Lewis *(p.152)*.

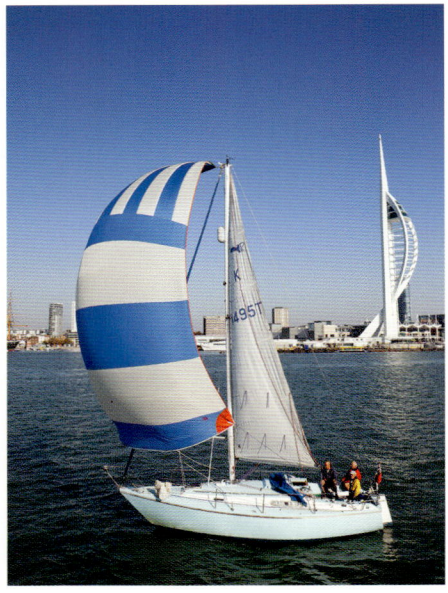

The most distinctive landmark in Portsmouth Harbour is the Spinnaker Tower *(right)*, whose shape resembles the sail of the same name *(above right)* and links to the city's maritime heritage. Opening in 2005, it stands at the head of the Gunwharf Quays development on the east bank of the harbour.

Illuminated by a changing display of colours after dusk *(above left)*, this dramatic tower stands 170 metres high, around the height of thirty-four giraffes arranged end to end, and can be seen for miles around. Far-reaching views await visitors who travel by lift to the observation deck and there is a glass *Sky Walk* for those who dare.

The figurehead from HMS Marlborough *(above top)* was placed at Gunwharf Quays in 2002, having been saved when the ship was scrapped in the 1920s.

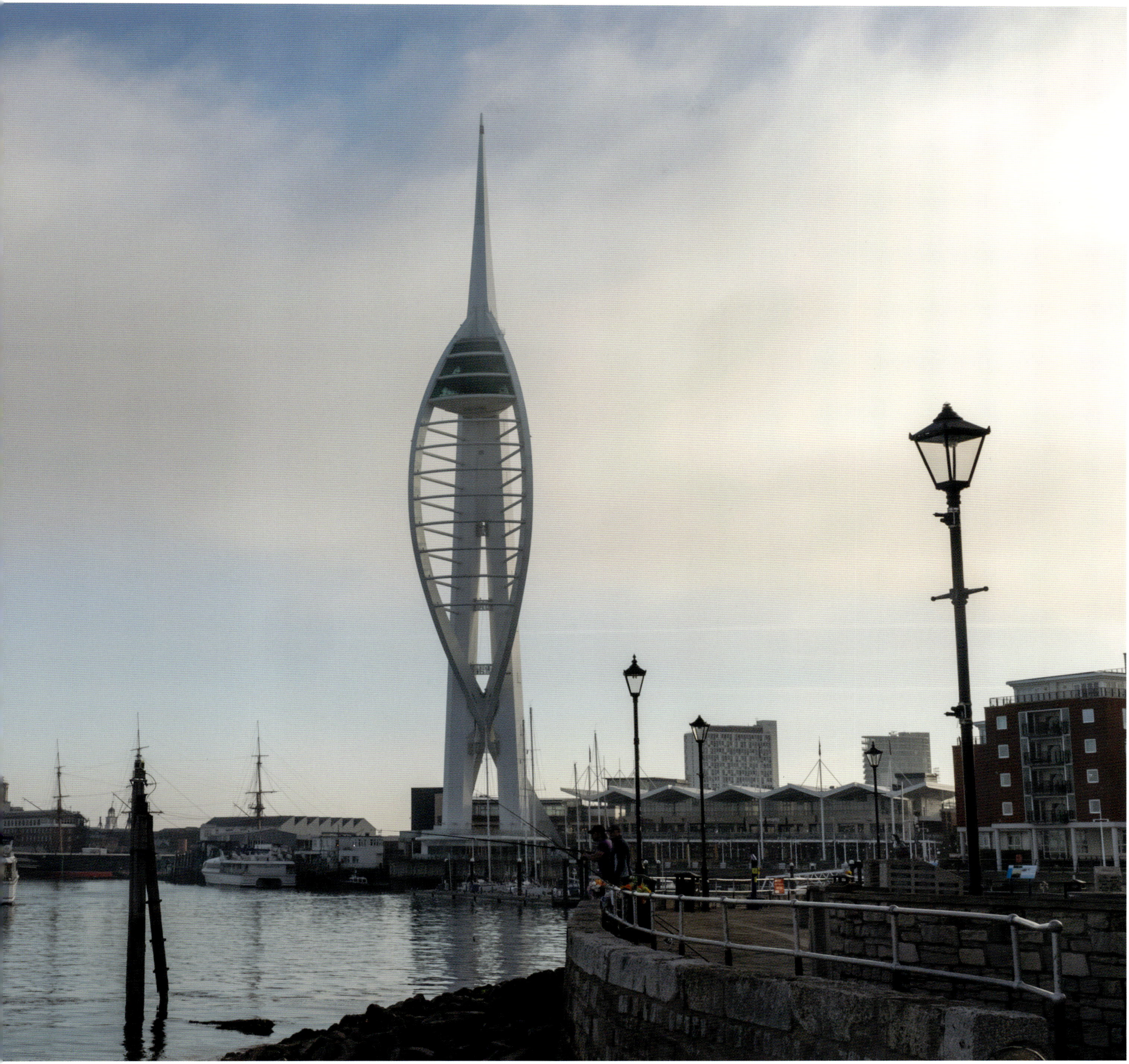

INVASION

This is a COMPLETE Edition

Pittsburgh Sun-Telegraph

FINAL HOME Late News

OUR TROOPS LAND IN NORTH FRANCE

SUPREME HEADQUARTERS, ALLIED EXPEDITIONARY FORCE, June 6.–(AP.)–Allied forces landed in Northern France early today in history's greatest overseas operation, designed to destroy the power of Hitler's Germany and wrest enslaved Europe from the Nazis.

The German radio said the landings were made from Le Havre to Cherbourg, along the north coast of Normandy and the south side of the bay of the Seine.

BULLETINS

Allied Headquarters did not specify the locations, but left no doubt whatever the landings were on a gigantic scale.

Ringing in their ears, the American, British and Canadian forces who made the landings had these words from their supreme commander, Gen. Dwight D. Eisenhower:

INVASION COAST

Announcement Delayed

At the southern point of Portsea Island, is Southsea, home of the D-Day Story. Originally the D-Day Museum, it opened in 1984 but later underwent a comprehensive refurbishment programme before re-opening as the D-Day Story in 2018. It tells of the remarkable events of the 6th June 1944 and the Allied invasion of Normandy in World War II. Listed by the Guinness Book of Records as the largest invasion in military history, this massive logistical operation involved the landing of forces, primarily from America, the United Kingdom and Canada, on five beaches along the Normandy coastline. Known officially as Operation Overlord, it was a pivotal moment in the Second World War.

Visitors to the D-Day Story can discover more about the events leading up to the invasion, as well as the actual battle. The last surviving landing craft tank, LCT 7074 *(p.196 top)*, is on permanent display following restoration. A Sherman Tank and Churchill Tank *(p.196 bottom middle)* have been placed on deck to give an idea of scale; ten tanks would have been carried in 1944.

The Overlord Embroidery *(above)* is on display in the Legacy Gallery. Commissioned by Lord Dulverton in 1968, this artwork is 83 metres long and commemorates those who took part in the action. Designed by British artist, Sandra Lawrence and created by the Royal School of Needlework, it took five years to complete.

P.196 Bottom left: Statue of Field Marshall Viscount Montgomery of Alamein *P.196 Bottom right:* Front page of Pittsburgh Sun-Telegraph.

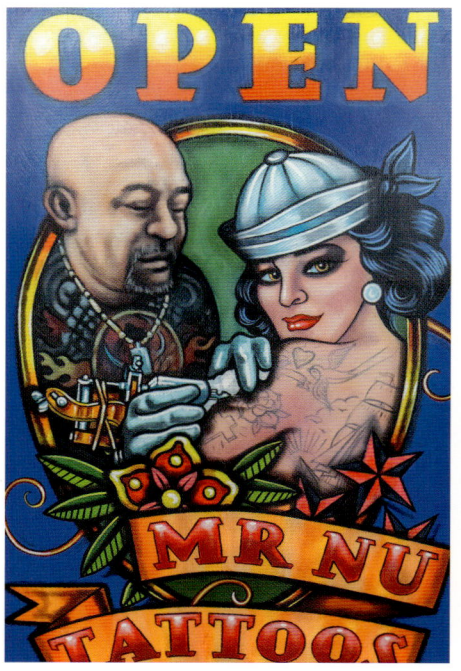

Also in Southsea is South Parade Pier *(above top & middle)*, which sits at the centre of a beautiful stretch of coastline and offers stunning views across to the Isle of Wight. As with many of Britain's piers, its history has been chequered. Originally opened in 1879, it has been destroyed by fire on three occasions; once during the making of Ken Russell's film *Tommy*. It has recently been fully restored and is now a pleasure pier offering attractions for all the family, 364 days a year.

West of the pier is Southsea Castle *(above right)*, another of Henry VIII's artillery forts. Now owned by Portsmouth Council, it was restored in the 1960s with many of the changes that had been made after 1850 being stripped back. Opened as a museum in 1967, there are exhibits and displays in the keep that explain the castle's history, and a walk round the ramparts offers good views. The lighthouse was built in the 1820s and was in continuous use until 2017.

A well-known Southsea landmark is The Strand mural *(right)*, by Mark Lewis, which sits at the junction of Waverley Road and Clarendon Road. Originally painted in 1997 and repainted thirteen years later, it constantly evolves to reflect changes in the local community.

199

Our journey along Hampshire's coast ends at Hayling Island, which is joined to the mainland by a road bridge at its northern end, which links to the village of Langstone.

The island developed as a holiday resort from the 1930s following the increased use of cars, and its excellent beaches *(below & bottom right)* are still popular today. Windsurfing was invented here in 1958 and there is also plenty to attract sports enthusiasts who enjoy walking, swimming and sailing. Funland Hayling Island is an amusement park on the south coast that has a selection of rides, an amusement arcade and a play area for children.

On the other side of the bridge, in Langstone, is a 18th century tower mill *(bottom left)*. Now a private residence, it can seen from the Royal Oak, one of two pubs that overlook the water. The village High Street is a conservation area.

Right: Langstone Harbour at sunrise.

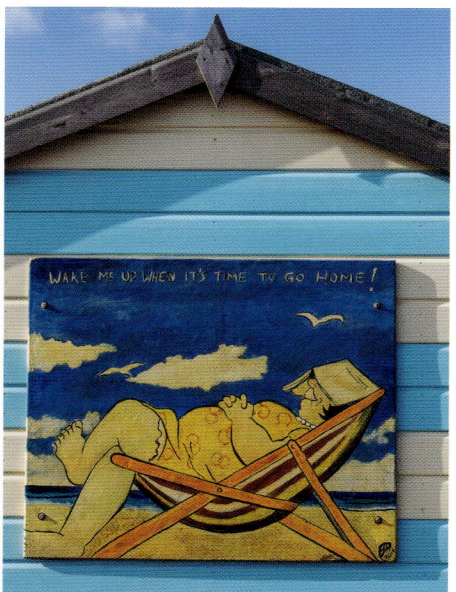

201

The Solent is a major shipping lane with a long history, including the sinking of Henry VIII's warship, the Mary Rose. It also saw the departure of the Titanic on its fateful maiden voyage. For enthusiasts, there is a website showing each day's shipping activity as it happens, as well as sites set up by those who log their sightings and photographs.

The variety of shipping is of particular interest, with not only passenger, freight and military vessels, but also sailing yachts that all have to share the same space safely. Some travel along the twenty-mile channel while others, particularly the frequent ferries to the Isle of Wight, cross it.

Top: Gosport skyline & Wightlink passenger ferry at first light.
Above: Wightlink MV St Clare and Spinnaker Tower, Portsmouth.
Right: Wightlink Wight Ryder I and Victoria of Wight, with P&O Cruises Britannia.

202

203

VICTORIA OF WIGHT

SAIL ACROSS THE SOLENT

Although the Isle of Wight is less than a mile from Hampshire at its nearest point, it is a county in its own right, and has been since 1890. The largest island in England, it covers an area of 380 square kilometres. A commonly repeated belief in the 1970s was that the world's population would fit on to the Isle of Wight if standing shoulder to shoulder. Many have tried to calculate whether this statement was true at that time but, with the rapid increase in population over the last fifty years and a current global total of 7.8 billion people, it certainly wouldn't be now.

The Isle of Wight vies with Rutland for the title of smallest county in England. If you use the list of ceremonial counties as a guide, then it is a close-run thing and it has been suggested that the result may change with the rise and fall of the tide, with the Isle of Wight winning when the tide is in; although there are those that say that the City of London is the outright winner. It is nonetheless irrefutable that the Isle of Wight is one of England's smallest counties.

This diamond shaped island measures only 36 kilometres from west to east and 22 kilometres from north to south and has a residential population of around 140,000. This number is dramatically increased by visitors, with more than two million trips made over the Solent in an average year. Owing to its geographical separation, the local dialect of the island used to be richly diverse but improvements in communications, particularly during the Victorian period, reduced the differences. However, those born on the island are still traditionally known as caulkheads and incomers as overners.

It is said that the ferry crossing from Portsmouth to Fishbourne is the most expensive per mile in the world, so it is lucky that there are less than seven miles to travel. There are no commercial air routes to the island and so most visitors arrive by ferry. The world's only commercial hovercraft route still in operation runs between Ryde and Southsea. The foot passenger service takes about ten minutes and is the fastest route to the island. The first modern hovercraft, invented by Sir Christopher Cockerell, was made in East Cowes by the marine firm Saunders-Roe in the late 1950s.

The mild, sunny climate enjoyed by the Isle of Wight has attracted visitors over the centuries. Queen Victoria's connections to the island are well known and she and her family enjoyed many happy times at their palatial holiday home, Osborne House. Karl Marx visited here on several occasions and described the island as a little paradise when writing to his friend, Friedrich Engels.

For wildlife enthusiasts, the Isle of Wight is particularly rich in native species that have become rare in similar habitats on the mainland. There are fewer introduced species, such as mink and grey squirrels, enabling animals including red squirrels and dormice to survive well. The Glanville Fritillary butterfly, seldom seen in the rest of England, is also found on the island.

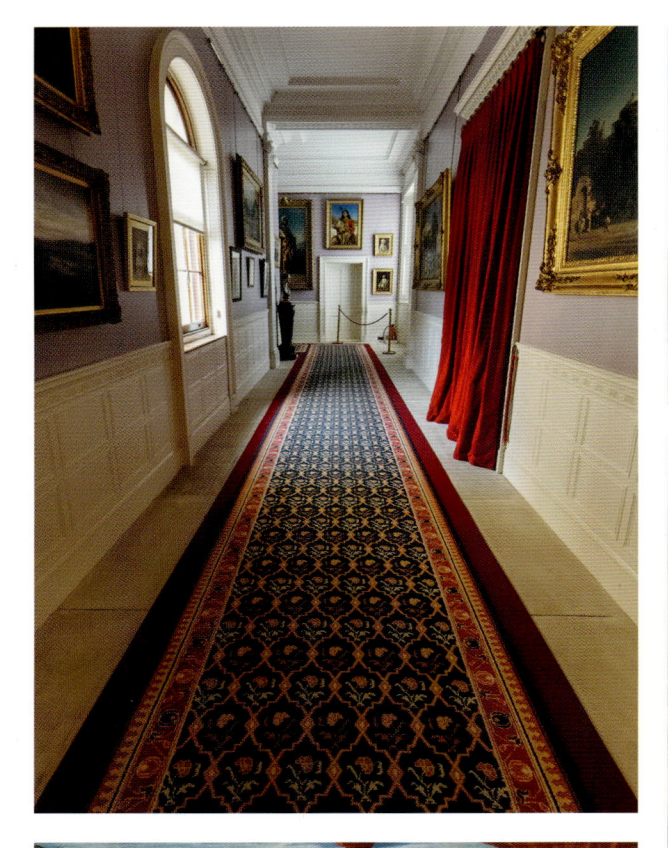

In the mid-1840s, Queen Victoria and Prince Albert were seeking a place where they could escape from the rigours of court life. As a young girl, Victoria had visited the Isle of Wight for holidays and, in 1845, she and Albert bought Osborne House in the north of the island. It was the location that held great appeal, with views across the Solent reminding Albert of an earlier visit to the Bay of Naples. The house soon proved to be too small for their needs and was demolished to make way for a new Royal Palace, which was built between 1845 and 1851.

Prince Albert was a very forward-thinking man and Osborne provided an opportunity for him to explore the latest ideas and to work closely on the design of the new house with architect and builder, Thomas Cubitt, so ensuring that this Royal Palace became a comfortable and much-loved family home. The exterior is styled as an Italianate palazzo, with two towers and terraces linked by steps. The House is filled not only with priceless furniture and artworks but also with many personal items, which provide visitors with a fascinating insight into the Royal couple and their family.

Top right: Bronze statue of Prince Albert's much-love greyhound, *Eos,* by John Francis and Prince Albert. *Above left: The Royal Family in 1846* painted by Enrico Belli in 1851 (after Winterhalter) *Above right:* The Shell Alcove, recently restored to its original colour scheme.

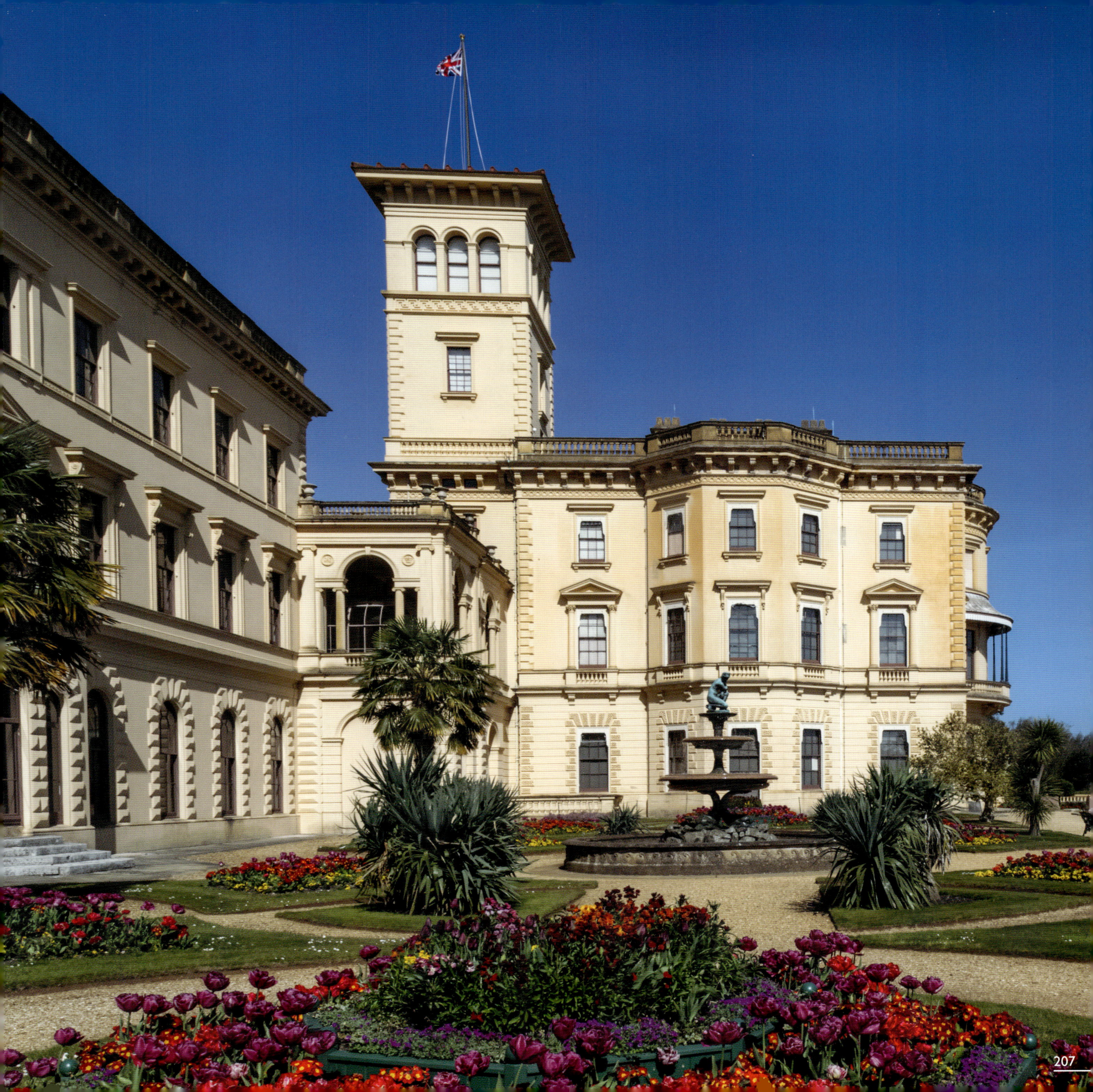

Much of Osborne House was completed before Prince Albert's death in 1861, with three of the four connecting blocks that can be seen today being built in his lifetime. The Royal Family had their principal apartments within the original block called the Pavilion, where the reception rooms on the ground floor were designed with large windows that not only bring in light but provide views out to sea.

Top left: the Drawing Room. *Middle left:* Principal Staircase. *Bottom left & Lower middle right:* the Dining Room.

Following Albert's death, one of the most important additions to the house was the Durbar Room *(right)*. Although the external design of this fits with the rest of the house, its décor is very different. The elaborate Indian interior was designed by Lockwood Kipling, father of Rudyard, and symbolises the importance of Victoria's role as Empress of India. Queen Victoria continued to visit Osborne House for the rest of her life and died here in 1901. Although she wanted the house to remain in the family, her love of Osborne was not shared by her successors and Edward VII gave it to the nation in 1902. English Heritage have managed this former royal residence since 1986 and it is open to the public.

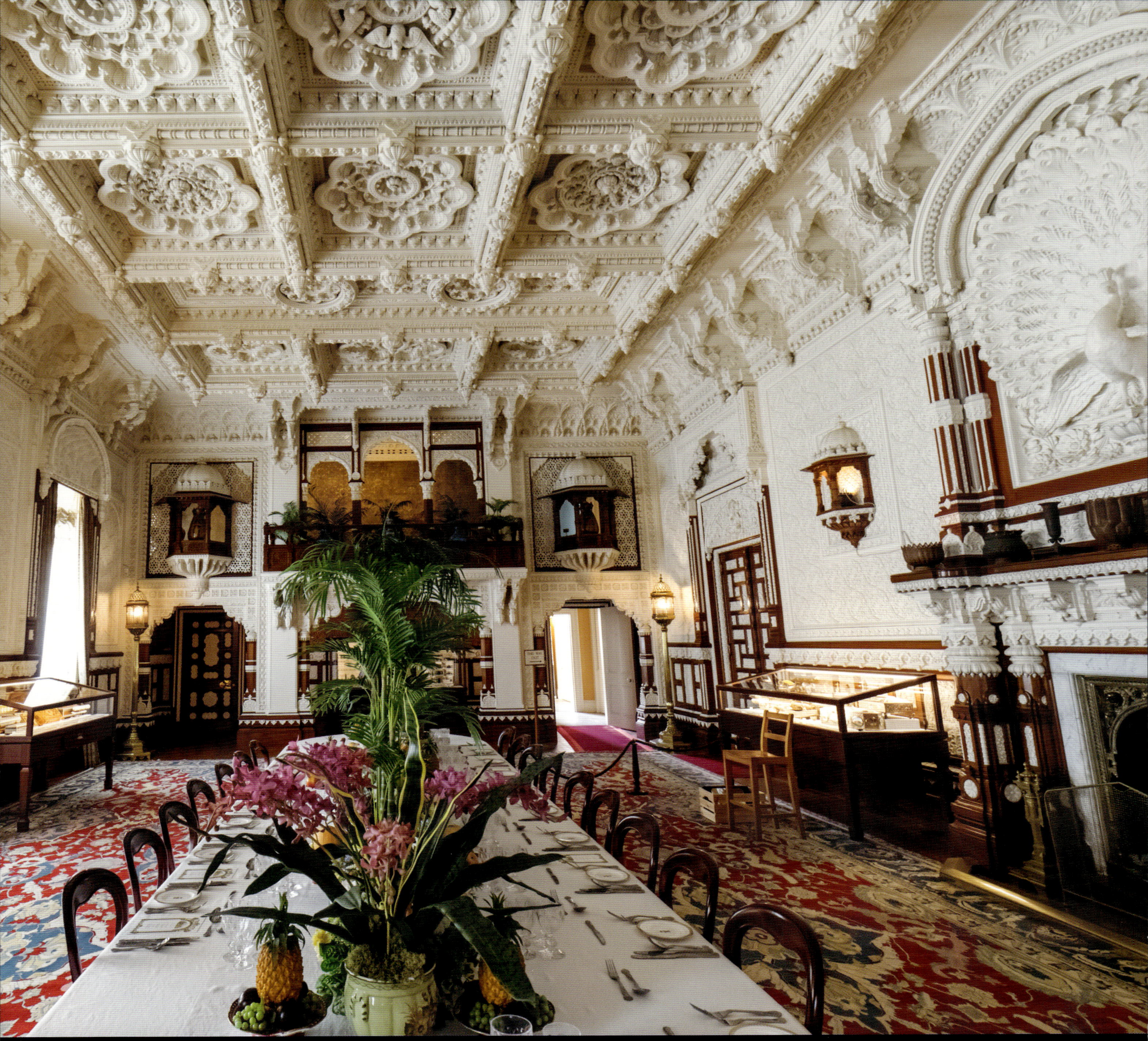

Osborne House enjoys a mild Mediterranean climate that makes the formal gardens and wider grounds a visual spectacle throughout the year. Although very little remains of the 18th century house, the front porch was reused to form the entrance to the walled garden *(above)*. In the 19th century, the grounds eventually exceeded 2000 acres, although the current estate is 354 acres. Prince Albert was very involved in the development of the grounds and planted many of the trees within the park himself, sometimes with the help of his family.

Near to Osborne House is the village of Whippingham and St Mildred's Church *(right & below)*. The church was rebuilt in the mid-19th century, with Prince Albert taking an active role in its design. Visited by Queen Victoria when in residence at Osborne, the church has interesting memorials to members of the Royal Family and their household. On the south side of the Chancel is the Royal Pew, which has its own private entrance. During Queen Victoria's time, they would have sat on chairs, but Edward VII later requested that pews be fitted, although the Queen's original chair has been kept at the centre.

In the churchyard is the grave of Prince Louis of Battenberg and his wife, Princess Victoria of Hesse, who was the grand-daughter of Queen Victoria. They were grandparents of Prince Philip, Duke of Edinburgh.

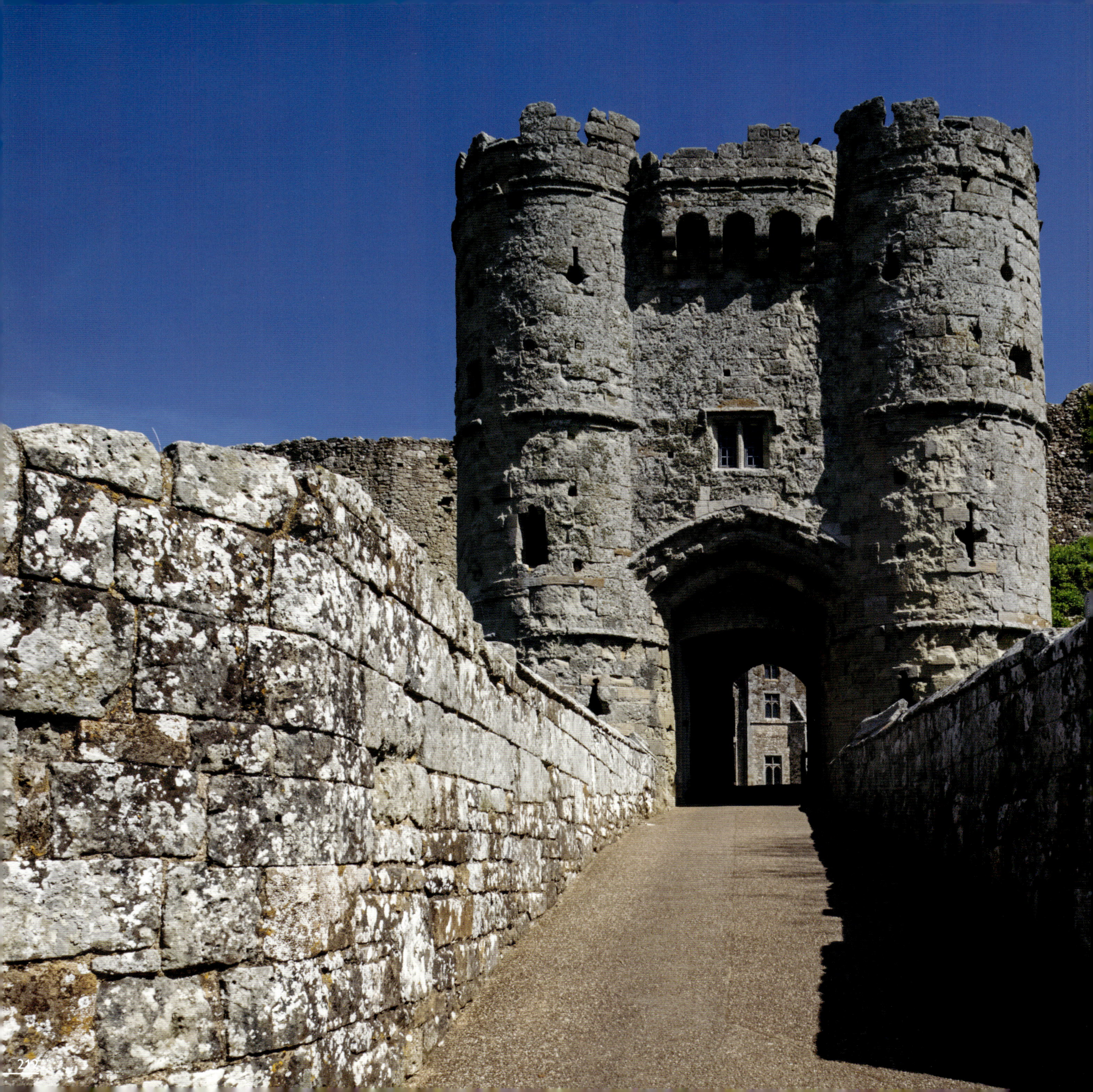

Six miles inland of Osborne House, towards the heart of the island, is Carisbrooke Castle, also managed by English Heritage. The castle has a long history and has been both an artillery fortress and a royal palace; but was also a prison for a king. Following the English Civil War, King Charles I was imprisoned here for fourteen months, before eventually being sent for trial. He was originally shown some leniency. He was attended by members of his own household and a bowling green was built for him. However, he was more closely guarded after failed escape attempts, the first of which ended with him stuck between the bars of his window.

A walk around the castle's battlements provides stunning views over the island and there is also an exhibition in the 16th century guardhouse and a museum *(above top)* with over 30,000 items of local interest. The castle is also known for its resident donkeys, who work the 16th century treadwheel that raises water up 161 feet from the castle well.

Left: Medieval Gatehouse. *Above:* St Nicholas' Chapel.

Within the precincts of Carisbrooke Castle stands St Nicholas' Chapel (above). The current building dates from 1904, although there is evidence of a chapel at the castle since the Middle Ages. It was built to commemorate the 250th Anniversary of the execution of Charles I and was designed by Percy Stone, whose work can be seen in buildings around the island.

The full name of the chapel is St Nicholas-in-Castro and, after World War I, it became a war memorial that commemorates the 2000 men from the island lost in both world wars.

Adjoining the chapel is the Princess Beatrice Garden (right), which was designed by TV gardener, Chris Beardshaw and inspired by the Edwardian walled garden retreat of Queen Victoria's youngest daughter, who lived at the castle when she held the post of Governor of the Isle of Wight between 1896 and 1944.

215

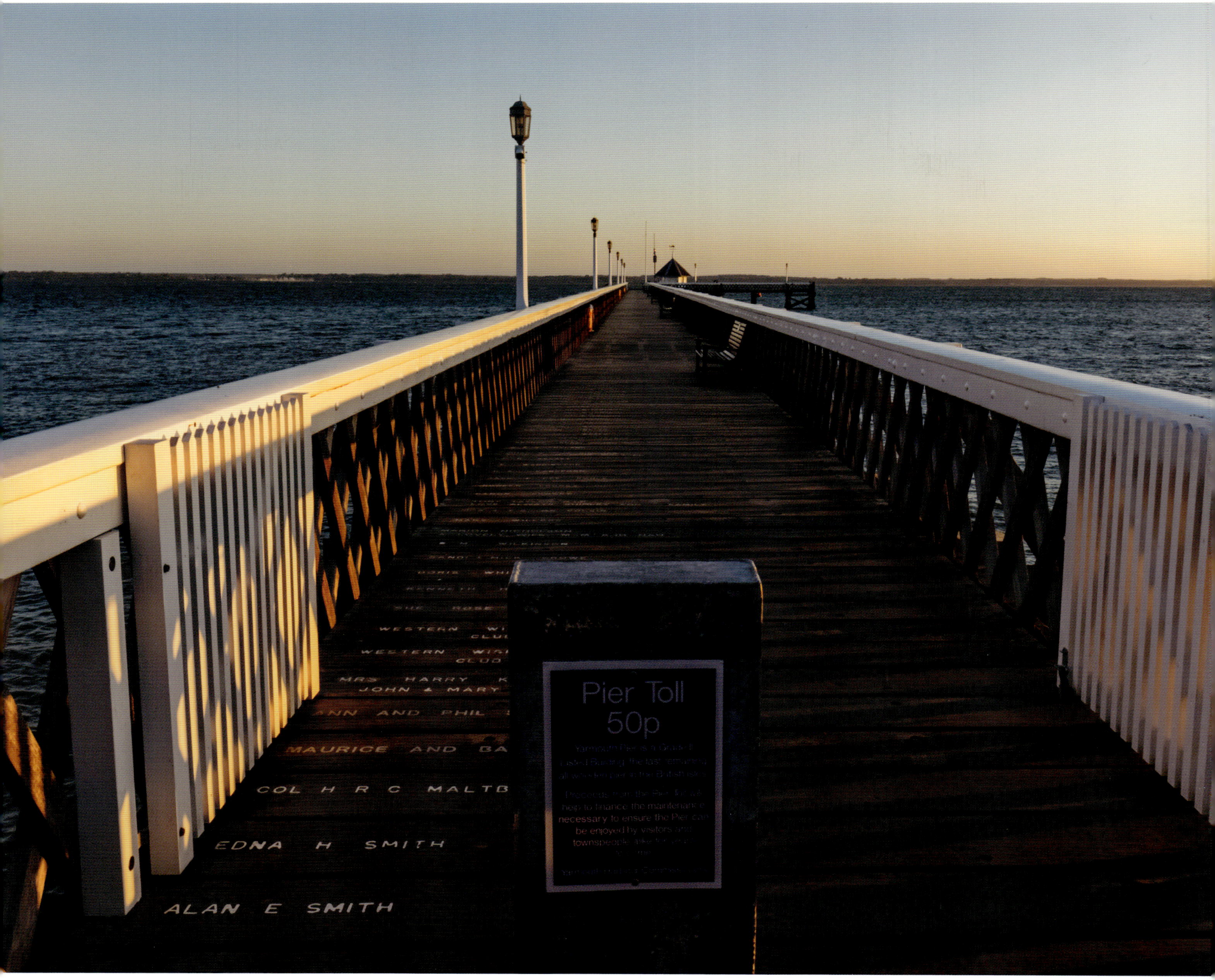
Pier Toll
50p
EDNA H SMITH
ALAN E SMITH

Back on the coast and towards the west of the Isle of Wight is the town and port of Yarmouth. As well as being one of the main access points to the island, the town is home to the longest wooden pier in England that is open to the public *(left)* and its cobbled streets are filled with quaint shops and cafes *(above)*. Notable buildings include Yarmouth Castle, which dates from 1547 and a 17th century church in the main square.

Alum Bay *(above top)* sits at the western tip of the island and is popular with visitors keen to see its famous multi-coloured sand and to enjoy the views across to the chalk sea stacks called The Needles *(right)*. The Alum Bay Glass Company has been producing decorative glassware since 1972 and it is possible to see live demonstrations of the skilled craftsmen at work *(above)*.

Each summer, the Round the Island Race *(pp.220-221)* attracts big crowds who enjoy the spectacle of competing yachts sailing the 93km circuit. The race passes the Needles Headland, a viewpoint that provides a panorama of the yachts, with their brightly coloured spinnakers, jostling for position. Starting and finishing in Cowes, the first race was held in 1931 and had 80 entries. Now, the number exceeds 1000.

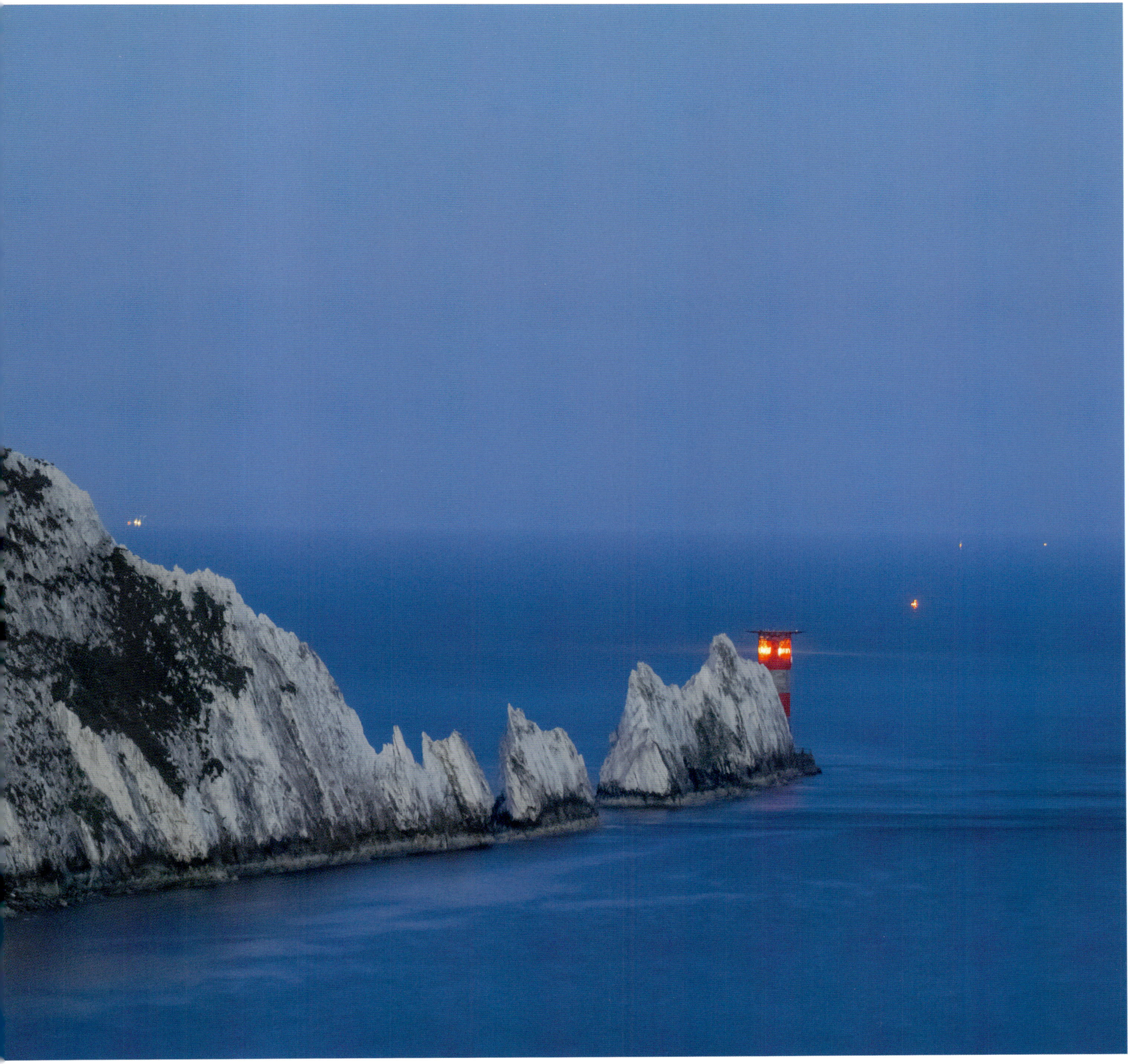

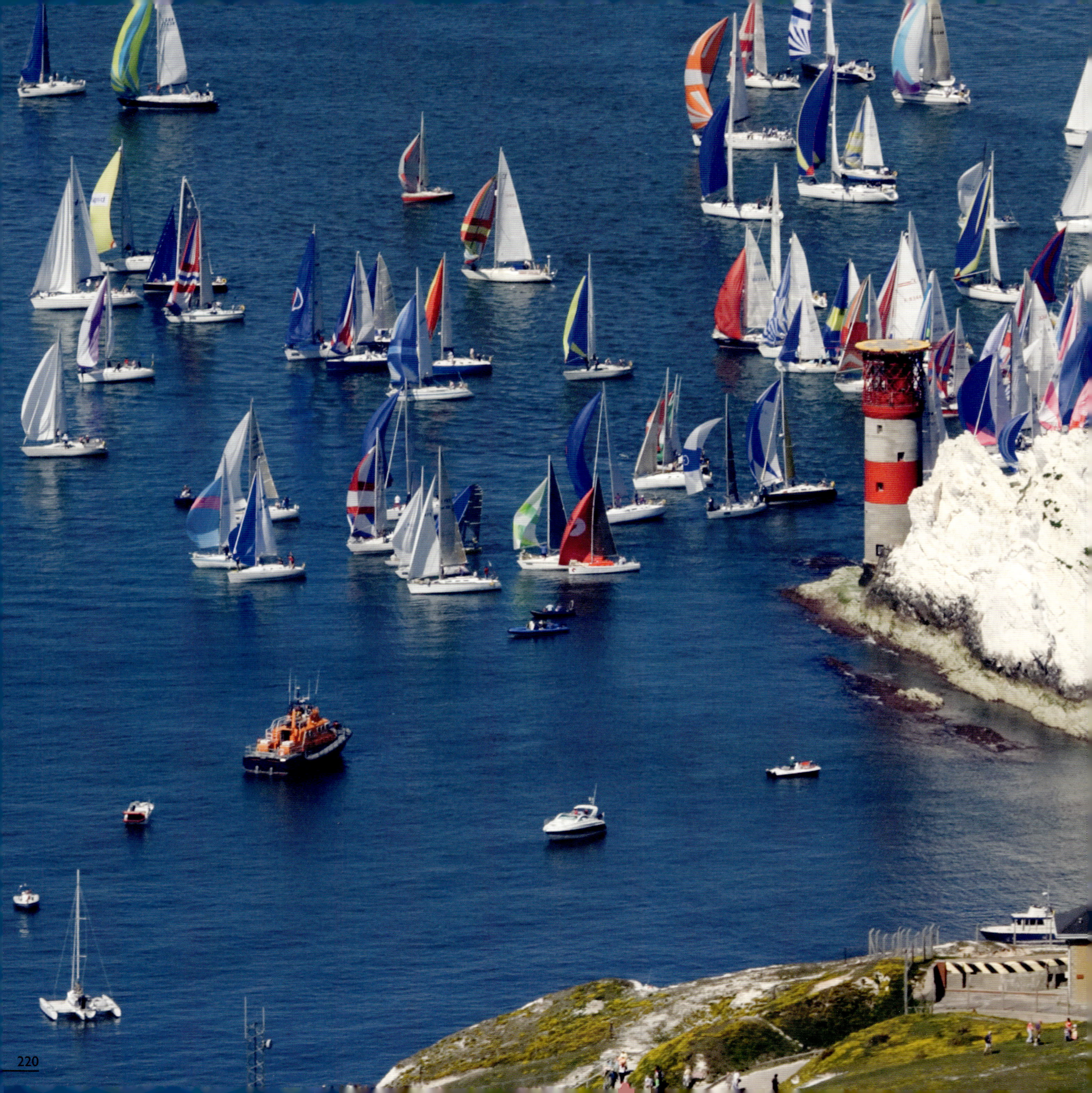

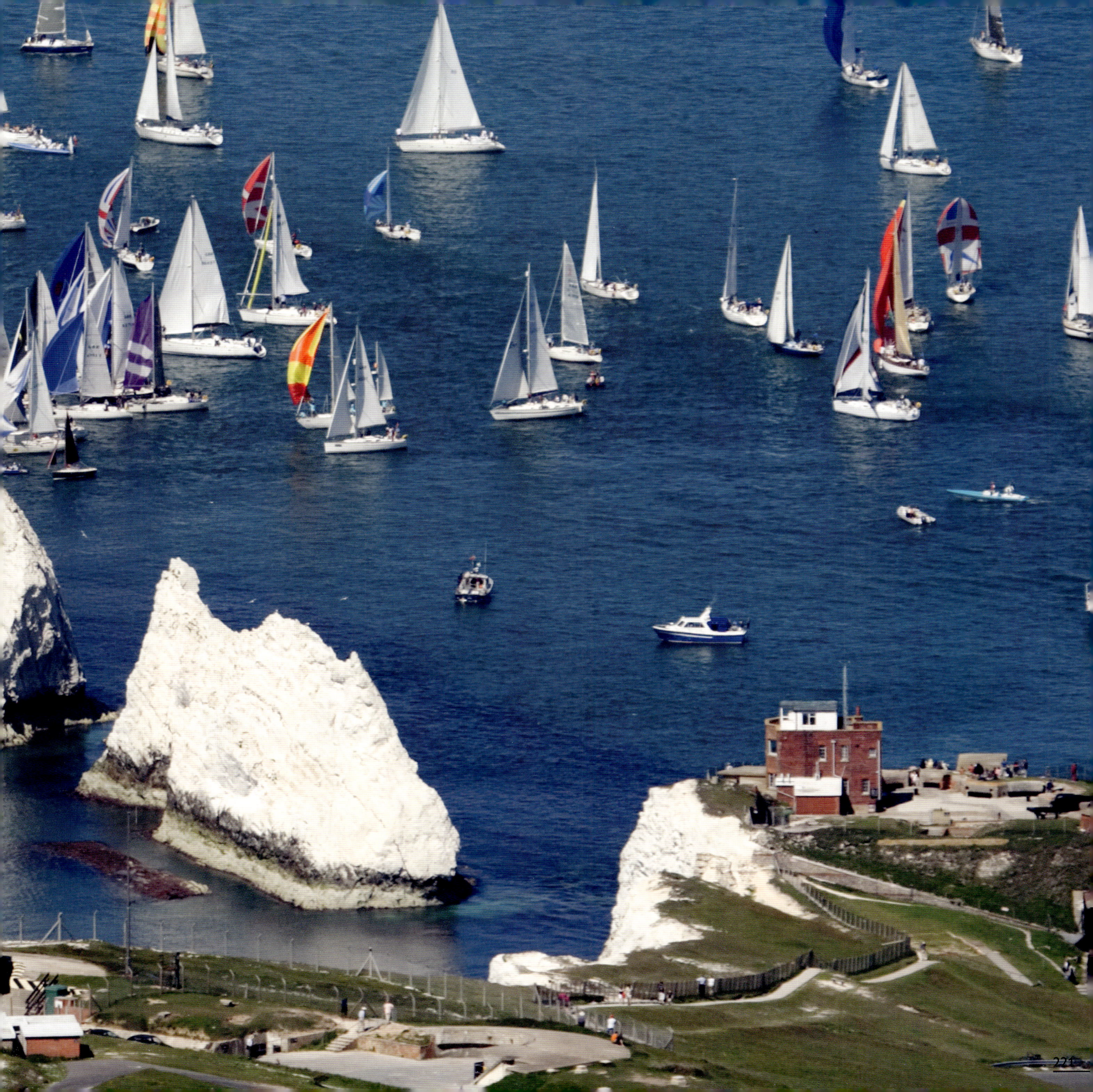

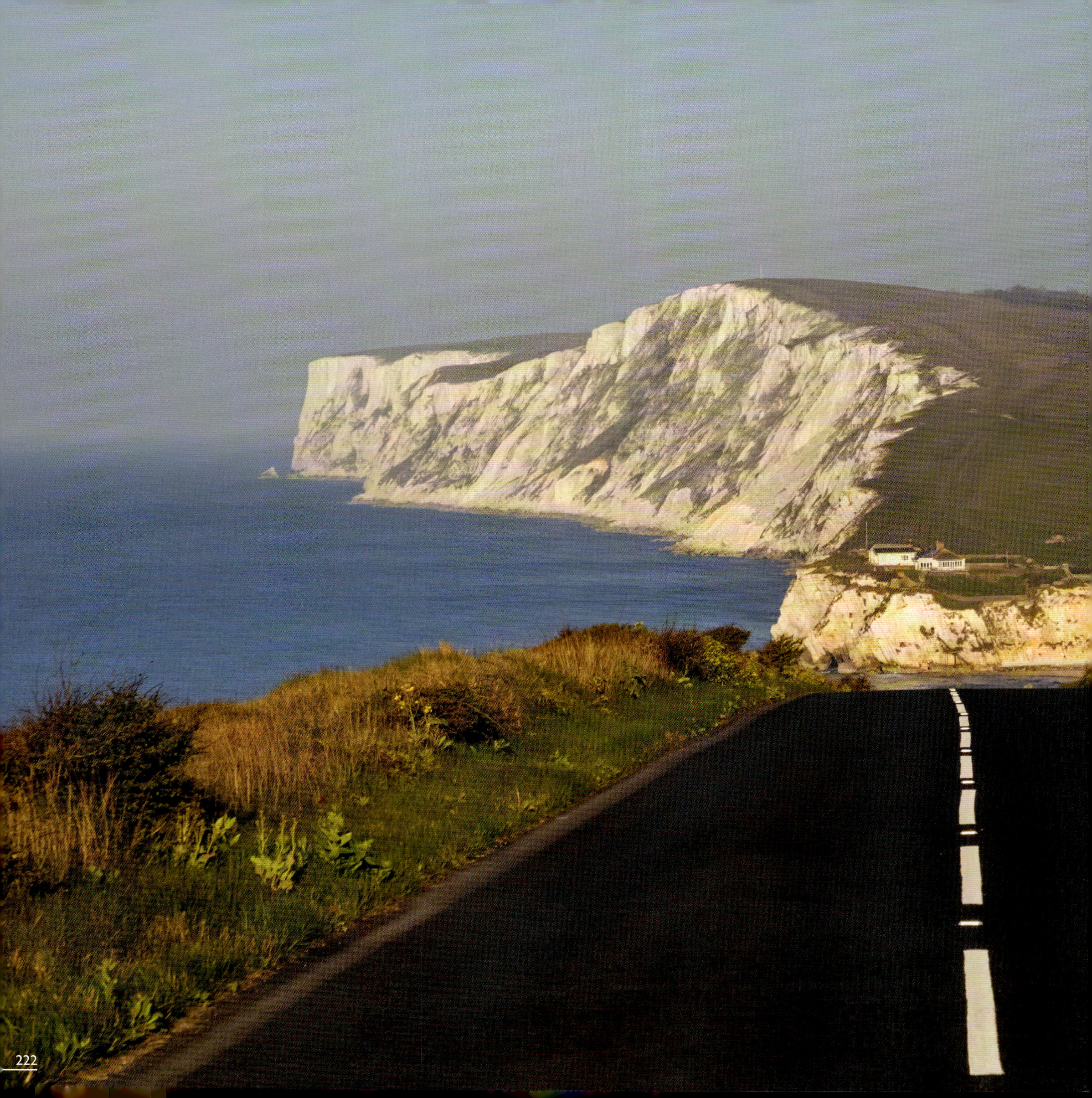

The most westerly point of the island has now been turned, and the coastline heads in a south-easterly direction. There are a number of pretty bays that break the line of the chalk cliffs, the first being Freshwater Bay, with its beach of grey flint and chalk pebbles. At the top of the cliffs is the Freshwater Bay Golf Club *(above)*, which enjoys spectacular sea views.

There are good walking routes in the area, including the Tennyson Down Circular, named after former Poet Laureate, Alfred Lord Tennyson, who walked here when spending winters on the island.

Left: Looking west to Freshwater Bay and the Tennyson Monument. *Above middle:* Surfer at Brighstone Bay.

The A3055 road forms the southern portion of the A-class loop that circles the island and the section from Freshwater Bay along to Chale is called the Military Road. Originally constructed around 1860 as part of a defence network, it was not until the 1930s that it was donated for public use. Coastal erosion, especially in recent years, has caused landslips leading to temporary closures of road sections and emergency repairs.

Above: Looking west from Blackgang Chine with the A3055 in middle distance.

At the most southerly point of the Isle of Wight stands St Catherine's Lighthouse. There has been a lighthouse on St Catherine's Down since 1323, making it one of the oldest lighthouse locations in Britain.

The new lighthouse was built in 1838 by Trinity House and was originally forty metres high but its use was badly affected by fog and so the height of the tower was later reduced by thirteen metres. The revolving optic from 1904 was still in use until 2020, giving the lighthouse a range of 46km but recent changes have reduced this to a still impressive 35km.

Beyond St Catherine's Lighthouse the coastline swings round to the north-east and the seaside resort of Ventnor. The town has a unique micro-climate which made it one of Victorian Britain's best-known health resorts. It became very fashionable and was described as 'The English Mediterranean.'

Above the town is St Boniface Down, the highest point on the Isle of Wight, and Ventnor's streets are built on steep slopes that lead down to the sea, with most amenities found in the lower town.

Ventnor has more sunny days and fewer frosts than the rest of the island and so sub-tropical plants can thrive here, with many examples to be seen at the Ventnor Botanic Garden, founded by Sir Harold Hillier in 1970.

As with many seaside resorts, the increased availability of cheap foreign holidays that began in the 1960s led to a decline in Ventnor's popularity, but its Victorian character and strong cultural scene are once again proving attractive to visitors.

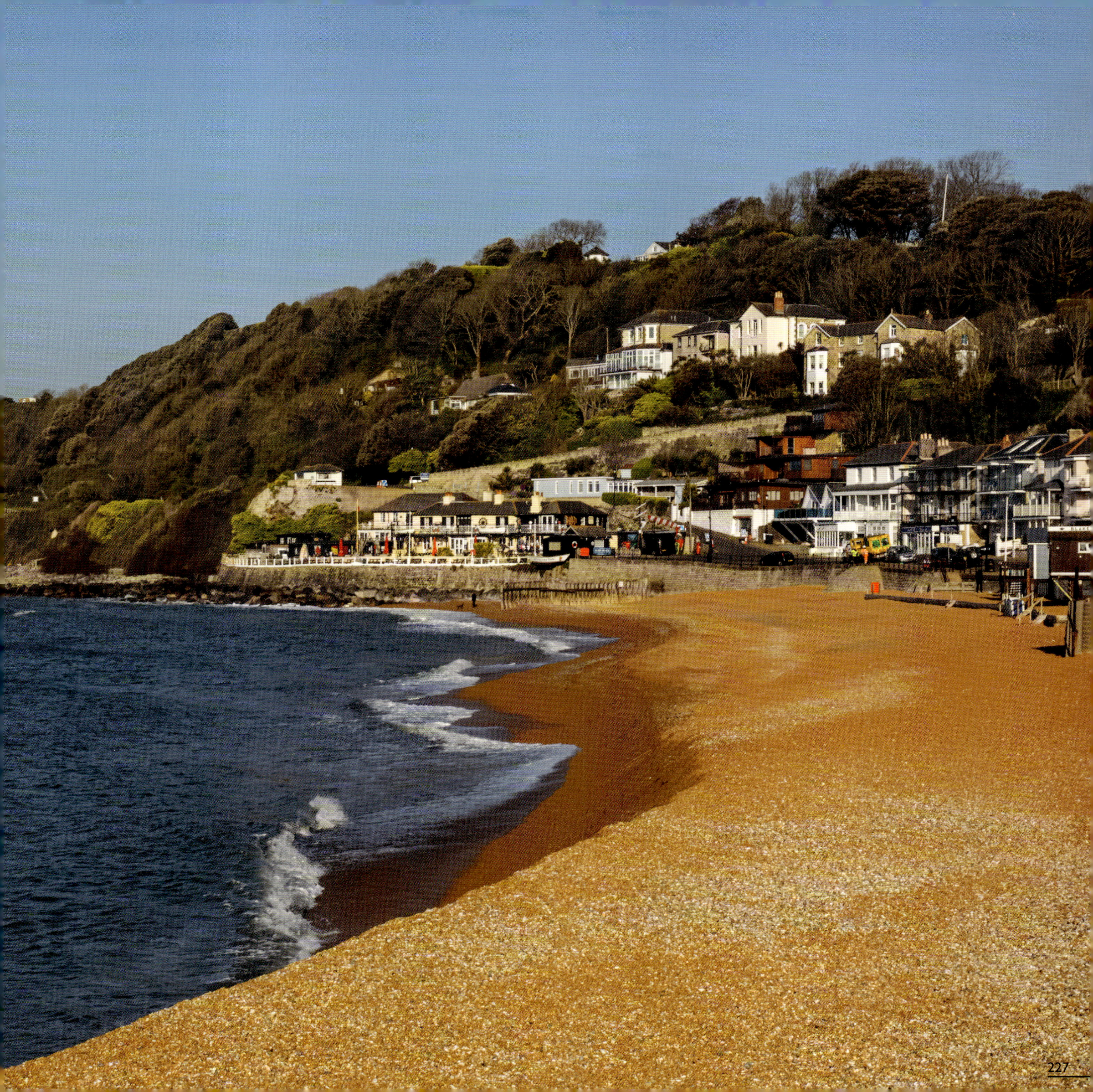

Pencil Cottage
GIFTS · ANTIQUES & TEA GARDEN
Pencil Cottage
GIFTS · ANTIQUES & TEA GARDEN
Old Thatch Teashop
Cream Teas
Homemade Food
OPEN
20
URCH ROAD

Just five miles along the coast from Ventnor is the town of Shanklin, with its near neighbours, Lake and Sandown. All three resorts look over Sandown Bay, a broad bay that extends for over eight miles.

The Old Village of Shanklin is a big draw for visitors with picturesque, thatched cottages that are homes to gift shops, tea rooms and hostelries for those needing a refreshing cup of tea, or something a little stronger.

The award-winning Old Thatch Teashop in the Old Village at Shanklin is highly regarded for its cream teas, and customers can either sit inside the pretty thatched cottage or enjoy the frequently fine weather in the enchanted garden, where a fairy or two may be in attendance.

The building was originally fishermen's cottages and dates back to 1690. It is Grade II listed and has been a tearoom since the 1940s. There is a secret tunnel beneath the Old Thatch, which would have been used by smugglers.

231

Shanklin beach *(top)* is part of a long, sandy sweep that runs from Luccombe up to Yaverland. Sadly, the pier was destroyed in the Great Storm of 1987, but traditional amenities still border the esplanade, with restaurants, hotels, an amusement arcade, crazy golf and various play areas for children. With an average of over 1900 hours of sunshine per year, Shanklin is one of Britain's sunniest villages.

The neighbouring resort of Sandown still has a pier *(right)*, which is 270 metres long and offers a range of indoor entertainments, including ten-pin bowling, as well as a funfair in the summer.

Above: Sandown beach and Culver Cliff.

233

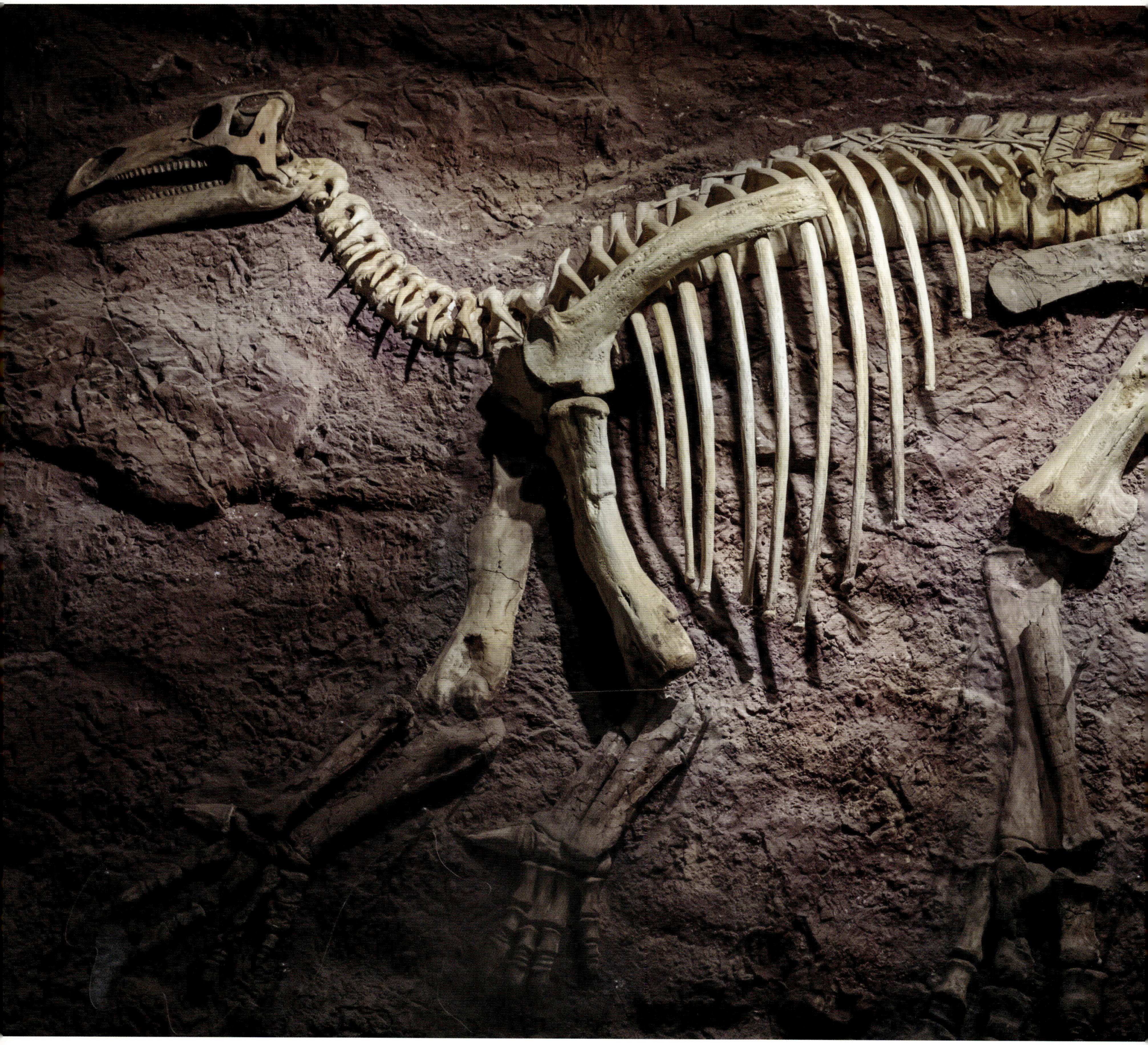

The Isle of Wight provided a perfect habitat for dinosaurs 125 million years ago and is now known as Dinosaur Isle because of the large number of fossils that have been discovered. The Wealden Outcrop, which runs between Compton and Sandown is the best location for finds. It is an area of soft clay that can be eroded by up to ten metres per year by the sea. As the clay recedes, treasures are revealed. Over twenty-five different species of dinosaur are believed to have lived on the island, which was still connected to mainland Europe when they were alive, and new discoveries are still being made. Dinosaur footprints can be seen at low tide on the beaches at Compton and Brook. The island's link with these fascinating creatures has been embraced by the tourist industry, resulting in a number of dinosaur themed attractions.

The Museum of Isle of Wight Geology had been based above Sandown Library for nearly a century but, in 2001, the exhibits were moved a short distance to Britain's first purpose-built dinosaur museum and attraction. Also called Dinosaur Isle *(left & above)*, this includes an impressive animatronic Neovenator and a range of interactive experiences, as well as a display of over 1000 fossils.

Just north of Sandown and enjoying fine views over Sandown Bay are the remains of Brading Roman Villa *(above top)*. The Isle of Wight was conquered by the Romans in 43 CE and the West Range of the villa, which has been preserved by the museum, was built around 300 CE. Items found on-site include jewellery and games that suggest the residents would have been of high-status.

After 400 years of occupation, the villa fell to ruin and was not rediscovered until 1879, when a local farmer called William Munns found part of a mosaic floor when digging holes on his land. Half of the villa was on the neighbouring Oglander estate, and it was Lady Oglander who bought all the land and continued the excavations. The site was soon open to visitors, one of whom was Queen Victoria.

Following a flood in the 1990s, a new visitor centre was built in 2004, to protect the excavations and improve the public displays. Further digs between 2008 and 2010 added to the discoveries.

The fine mosaics are amongst the best in Britain and date from the 3rd and 4th centuries. Designs include Medusa *(above left & right)*, who is believed to protect the home and ward off evil, and one of the Venti *(above right)*, a God of the Winds.

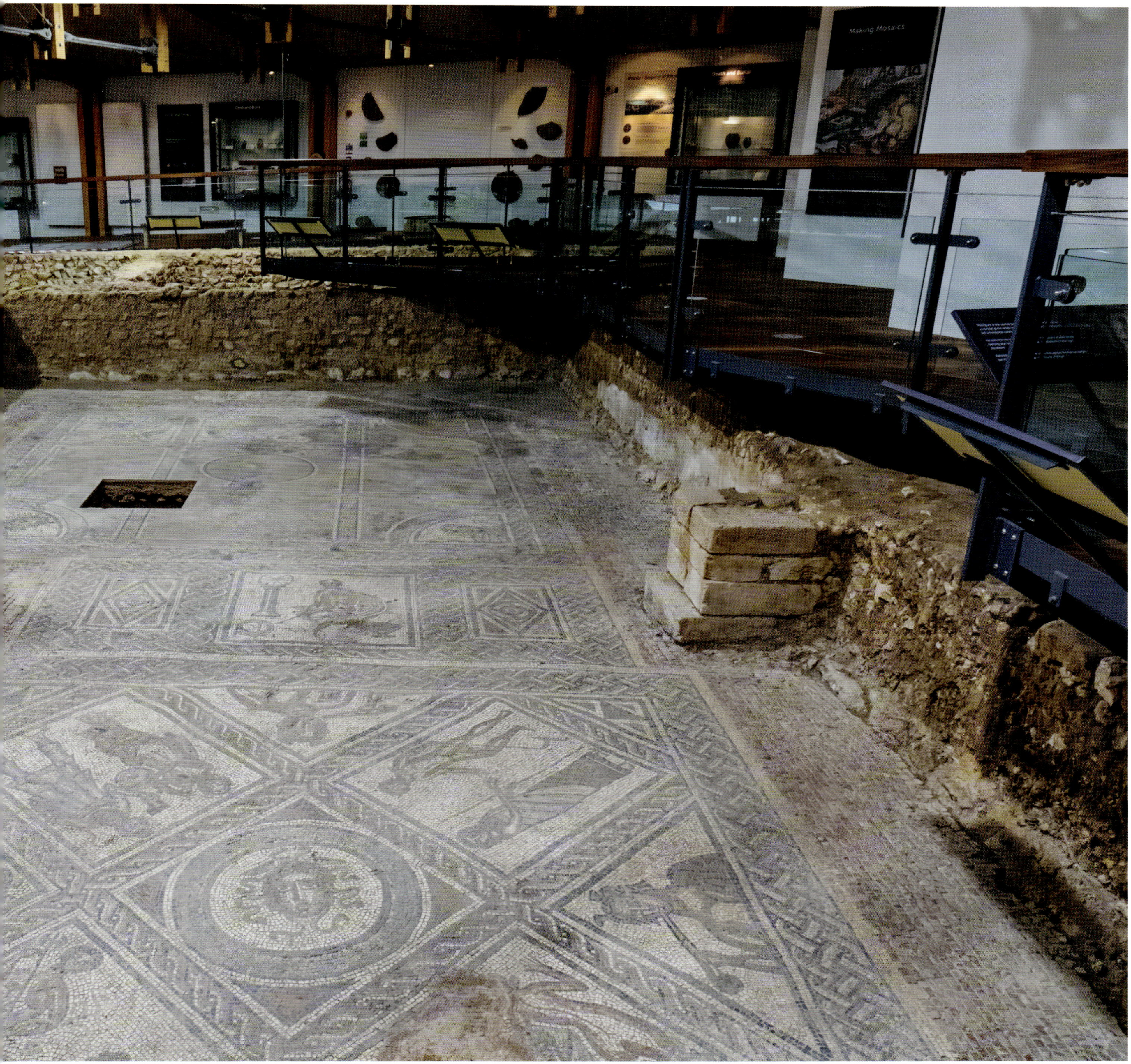
Making Mosaics

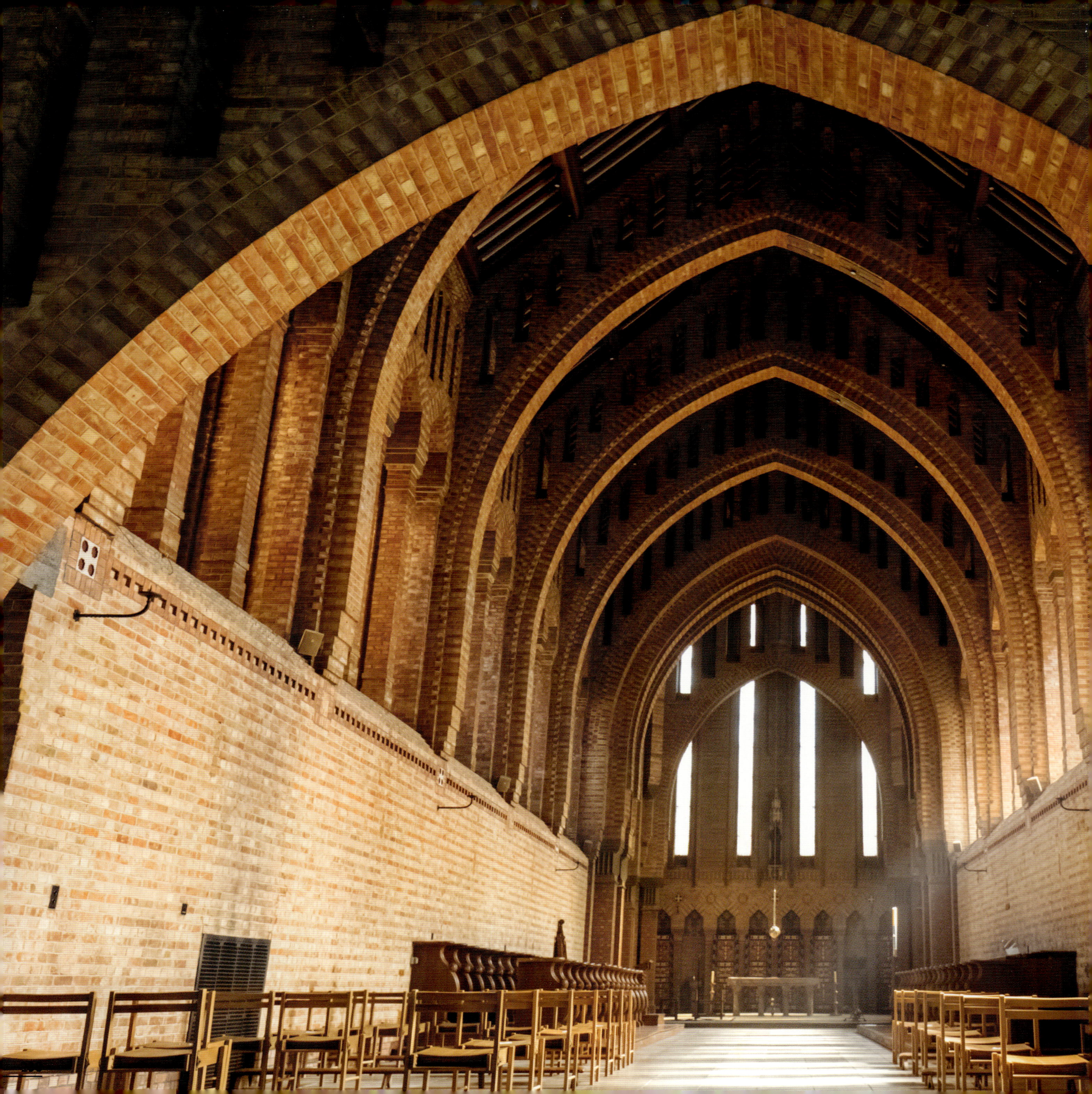

Beyond Ryde and overlooking the Solent is the Grade I listed building, Quarr Abbey, which is owned by the Catholic Order of St Benedict and is a working monastery. The unusual name, Quarr, is thought to come from the word Quarry, as there was one nearby. The original abbey on the site was Cistercian and was founded in 1132. Following the Dissolution of the Monasteries in the 16th century, this abbey was demolished, although some important ruins remain.

It wasn't until the start of the 20th century that a community of Benedictine Monks from Solesmes Abbey in France arrived on the Isle of Wight, seeking a new home following a change in French Law. On their arrival, they took up residence near Wroxall, but one of the monks, Dom Paul Bellot, was an architect and drafted plans for a new monastery, which was built on the front of older Victorian buildings at Quarr Abbey House. Work began in 1907 and the building was consecrated in 1912. It is seen as one of the most important examples of 20th century religious architecture in Britain.
The community now only numbers around ten monks, who also look after the attached farm. It is possible to visit the church and grounds and there is a visitor centre that gives information on the estate and the monastic way of life.